HORACE

FOR ENGLISH READERS

BEING A TRANSLATION OF THE POEMS OF
QUINTUS HORATIUS FLACCUS
INTO ENGLISH PROSE

BY

E. C. WICKHAM, D.D.

DEAN OF LINCOLN; HON. FELLOW OF NEW COLLEGE, OXFORD

OXFORD UNIVERSITY PRESS
LONDON: GEOFFREY CUMBERLEGE

A. O. P.

Animae qualem neque candidiorem
Terra tulit, neque cui me sit devinctior alter.

NOTE

In the present photographic reprint a number of small corrections have been made to bring the translation into correspondence with the revised text in Scriptorum Classicorum Bibliotheca Oxoniensis.

PREFACE

NO Latin poet has been translated into verse, in this country at least, more often than Horace. Perhaps the long list of poets, scholars, and statesmen who from generation to generation have tried their hands at the task may suggest the reflection that part of its fascination must consist in its insuperable difficulties. The humbler part of translating him into prose has been scantily attempted in England, though the example has been set us in France. By translation into prose I understand that which has been done for Virgil by Conington and more lately by Mackail, for Homer by Lang and his coadjutors, or again in part for Dante by Dr. Carlyle—a translation which, while literal in the sense that every thought is exactly represented in its proper order, tone, and emphasis, has also just so much of literary form that it can be read by a modern reader without distress, and understood without perpetual reference to the original; and that (to adapt Horace's own expression) if in the process the author be necessarily dismembered, the fragments can at least be recognized for those of a poet. Conington's prose translation of Virgil, which was published posthumously, but which had been read by him in his Professorial lectures, was perhaps the first attempt of the kind for a Latin poet. Nowadays a translation into English prose is coming to be thought as necessary to a complete edition of a classic as a translation into Latin was to a Greek classic at the beginning of the last century. That

is the true parallel. English translations have come
with full English commentaries. They are their
natural complement; and any mischief which they may
be supposed to cause to classical study—I should prefer
to say, any change that they indicate in its methods—
has come already with the commentaries.

Perhaps in saying so much an old schoolmaster is
betraying a twinge of conscience at seeming to publish
a 'crib.' But in truth if the present translation owed
its origin to an Oxford lecture-room some thirty years
ago, it has been given to the printer now not so much
with any view to schoolboys or Academic students as
to two other classes of readers. Horace was more
read in the generation which is passing away than he is
now; and it has been thought that some who, though
their classical books are not often disturbed, have not
altogether lost the memory of his genial wisdom may
turn over these pages with interest and find in them
some echoes of the past. And there is an increasing
class of persons who, without first-hand knowledge of
the classical languages, are interested to make the great
writers of Greece and Rome something more than mere
names to themselves. Perhaps these will care more to
feel that they have the exact things which Horace said
than to have a distant and questionable imitation of the
poetical form in which he said it. Even in plain prose,
it may be, they will find some charm in his company,
and feel across the centuries the 'touch of nature.'

LINCOLN, *June* 1903.

CONTENTS

	PAGE
INTRODUCTION: HORACE'S LIFE AND WRITINGS	1
TABLE OF PROBABLE DATES OF HORACE'S LIFE AND WORKS	23
ODES :—	
BOOK I	25
II	60
III	79
IV	114
THE SECULAR HYMN	134
EPODES	137
SATIRES :—	
BOOK I	158
II	204
EPISTLES :—	
BOOK I	261
II	316
THE ART OF POETRY	340

INTRODUCTION

HORACE'S LIFE AND WRITINGS

WE have always been more chary than some other peoples in naturalizing the classical writers. Even among the more commonly read Latin classics we make a selection. We write Horace and Virgil (unless we prefer Vergil) and Ovid, but Propertius and Lucretius, Terence but Plautus, Livy but Tacitus.

We indicate in this way our favourites, those who seem most at home among us, perhaps those whose writings have been most continuously used as school-books. Horace has both claims to be treated as an old friend. He and Virgil have shared the place of the universal school-books from the days when Juvenal, not a hundred years after their death, wrote of a class of Roman schoolboys with their 'thumbed Horace and Virgil as black as soot,' to the day when Byron, in a fit of half-humorous spleen against his schoolmasters rather than against the poet, wrote :

> Now farewell, Horace, whom I hated so,
> Not for thy faults, but mine !

And he has been the favourite of as many generations. The poet Persius, some fifty years after his death, describes him as a Satirist : ' Horace has a knack of putting his finger on every flaw, yet leaving the reader smiling and his friend: every heart opens to him, and he plays about its strings.'   One of the most recent of English writers on Latin literature gives a list, not exhaustive but representative, of the great men of letters in different ages and countries to whom he has been a friend and companion: 'He has forged a link of union between intellects and temperaments so diverse as those of Dante, Montaigne, Bossuet, Lafontaine, Voltaire, Hooker, Chesterfield, Gibbon, Wordsworth, Thackeray. Mystic and atheist, preacher and scoffer, recluse and leader of fashion have in Horace one subject in which they are sympathetic with each other.'   Professor Tyrrell's list reminds us of one point about Horace's popularity; though it has been as wide as the world of European civilization, he has found a special home in the hearts of Frenchmen and Englishmen.

What we know of him we know almost entirely from his own writings. A few facts are added by a short memoir written, it seems, originally by Suetonius, the biographer of the twelve Caesars, but which has only reached us in a fragmentary state, and mixed up with passages which evidently refer to a totally different person. But Horace's poems are full of autobiographical matter. Though the opposite of what we call an 'egotist,' he tells us incidentally a great deal about himself, of his parentage and early home, of the events of his life, of his friends, his haunts, his daily occupations in Rome and in the country, and (if we are careful to read between the lines) of his personal tastes and character.

He was born on December 8, sixty-five years before the Christian Era, two years before Augustus Caesar. It was the year of Catiline's first abortive conspiracy. Pompey was in Asia winning military renown and the attachment of the army in the war against king Mithridates. Julius Caesar was in Rome serving the office of Aedile, and ingratiating himself with the populace by his magnificent expenditure on public buildings and shows of games. It was a moment of pause in the civil wars; but everything was preparing, both in respect of conditions and of persons, for the great impending struggle and political resettlement, the issues of which were so largely to affect Horace's life.

Like most of the great Roman writers, he was country-born. His father belonged to Venusia, a town which lay on the Eastern slope of the Apennines, among a network of valleys which run down from Monte Voltore, an extinct volcano, carrying their waters into the Aufidus or Ofanto, the largest of the torrents that cross the Apulian plain to the Adriatic. Horace's poetry has many references to the scenery and associations of his early home. There is the well-known story of his childhood, how (no doubt when he was in *villeggiatura*, perhaps at his nurse's cottage in the hills, for Mount Vultur was ten miles from Venusia) he lost himself in the forest and was found, like the babes in the wood, covered up with leaves by the wood-pigeons. We find in his verses the names which still exist of villages and forests near. In one of the Satires, when describing a journey over the Apennines with Maecenas, he notes with delight the place from which he caught the first sight of the familiar outlines of his Apulian hills. It seems an unconscious and therefore more touching tribute to his fondness, that when he is speaking of the richness of Italian soil, the valour of Italian soldiers, the sturdy industry of Italian peasants, where others would have used the epithet 'Roman' or 'Italian,' he slips frequently into 'Apulian,' or what is its equivalent, 'Daunian.'

Venusia was a 'colony': that is, it was originally a frontier town, an outpost planted in a conquered country, where veteran soldiers were settled and a miniature Rome created. It was founded in B.C. 291, near the end of the last Samnite war. Horace makes in Sat. 1.10 an interesting use of this position of Venusia. He is defending himself for writing Satire, and he says that he is as the Venusian settlers in old days, set on the border, of a fighting stock, ready to do battle with any one who assails the territory which he has undertaken to guard. In other words his Satire is one of defence, not of defiance. He writes not to wound or injure, but to protect the sacred interests of virtue, good sense, and patriotism.

Whether this means that Horace claimed descent in any way from the colonists of Venusia does not appear. If so, his family had come down in the world, for his father had been a slave. He had obtained his freedom in some way before his marriage, for Horace himself was *ingenuus*, born, that is, of parents free at the time of his birth. But still the 'freedman's son' was in a social position which exposed him by-and-by, when he began to rise in the world, to jealousy and taunts which he felt keenly. He lived through them; and when the completion of his volume of lyric poetry (Odes i–iii) had given him full self-confidence, we find him actually making it a boast that like Daunus, the mythical founder of the Apulian race, '*ex humili potens*,' he too had risen from humility to greatness; as he puts it in another place, that 'born of a freedman sire and in a modest home he had spread wings too wide for his nest, so that anything you took from his birth you must add to his merit.' But to be magnanimous when success is assured is easy. What strikes us in Horace is the way in which he met the criticism when he still felt it, at the time that he was writing his first book. I refer of course especially to the passage in Sat. 1. 6, in which, after speaking of the taunts against his birth, which had pursued him from the first, but especially since he became the friend of Maecenas, he first explains the history of their friendship, in order to show that he owed it neither to chance nor to any base arts, but to his own personal qualities, and then turning the tables on his detractors he avows that any merit which may have been found in him was due to the parentage on which they poured scorn. He describes his father's anxious and tender care for him, how though his means were small he had spared nothing to give his son the best possible education, had brought

him to Rome instead of sending him to a country
school, as men richer and grander than he did, had
taken care that his boy should never lack what others
had in the way of dress and attendance, but had dele-
gated to no one the duty of guarding him from the
dangers and temptations of a great city, had gone
himself with him daily to and from school. This is
his conclusion (I give it in Conington's version):

He feared not lest one day
The world should talk of money thrown away,
If after all I plied some trade for hire
Like him, a tax collector or a crier:
Nor had I murmured: as it is, the score
Of gratitude and praise is all the more.
No! while my head's unturned, I ne'er shall need
To blush for that dear father, or to plead,
As men oft plead, 'tis Nature's fault, not mine,
I came not of a better, worthier, line.
Not thus I speak, not thus I feel: the plea
Might serve another, but 'twere base in me.
Should Fate this moment bid me to go back
O'er all my length of years, my life retrack
To its first hour, and pick out such descent
As man might wish for, e'en to pride's content,
I should rest satisfied with mine, nor choose
New parents, decked with senatorial shoes.

A nobler tribute has seldom been paid to a father.

Horace tells us nothing of his mother, nor of any
brother or sister, and this probably means that he was
an only child, left early on his father's hands. The
father had made, it seems, a little money; how, we know
not. Horace speaks of him as having been a '*coactor*,'

and the author of the Suetonian life adds '*exactionum*,' a 'collector' of debts or dues, either in the way of ordinary business or of revenue. The latter authority says further that he dealt in salted goods. He had retired and bought a small farm. He saw no doubt his boy's unusual gifts and carried him off to give him every chance of a refined education at Rome. He had married, probably, as was said, after he obtained his freedom, that is, rather late in life, and it would seem likely that he died before his son attained eminence.

Besides the account to which reference has been made we have a few scattered hints as to Horace's education. We know the name of his schoolmaster, and Horace adds an epithet which will stick to him to the end of time—'*Orbilius plagosus*,' fond of the rod. But as we know from other sources, he was a scholar and schoolmaster of note; and since he came from Beneventum, on the road from Venusia to Rome, Horace's father would probably have heard of his reputation. We cannot but sympathize with him, poor Orbilius! His great pupil called him '*plagosus*,' and a short biography of him which exists tells us that he 'taught with more reputation than remuneration,' and that he wrote a book on 'the wrongs which schoolmasters suffer at the hands of parents.' Horace tells us that one of his earliest school-books was a Latin translation by Livius Andronicus of Homer's Odyssey. When school was over, a young Roman who was to finish his education went, much as we go to a university, to Athens, with the view chiefly of listening to the

lectures of the philosophers who still made that city
their head quarters.   Horace's 'university life' made
its mark on him in two ways.   The interest in
philosophy as it was then chiefly understood—moral
philosophy, that is—the ends of moral action and the
practical conduct of life—he never lost.   It is the subject to which in all his writings he returns.   He could
never bind himself to any single school : he was, as he
describes himself, a wanderer on the sea, putting in
now to one haven and now another, as wind and
wave carried him ; fingering the philosophers' problems
always with some interest, though playfully, pointing out
their paradoxes, pressing home their serious lessons.
But his sojourn had another result.   He was at Athens
in the fatal year of Caesar's assassination, and Brutus,
soon after the 'Ides of March,' came there also, and
for the moment was keeping quiet, professing to study
philosophy and frequenting the lectures of Theomnestus
the Academic.   It was a moment to stir a young
poet's blood.   We think of our own Coleridge and
Southey and Wordsworth in the first fervour of the
French Revolution.   And Brutus, the student and
idealist, was the man to attract his sympathy and
dominate his imagination.   The two came together,
and when in a few weeks Brutus departed to his
Province, he took Horace with him on his staff, and
eventually (it suggests that the Republican army was
not very well officered) gave him the command of
a 'cohort' or battalion.   And so Horace came to
fight on the side of Brutus and Cassius against his

future patron and friend in the disastrous battle of
Philippi. Every one knows the story of his throwing
away his shield in the rout, but it is not always remembered on what authority the story rests. It is on a
few words of his own, and these, as evidently as anything
that was ever written, not to be taken with prosaic literal-
ness. When he is writing seriously at the end of the first
book of the Epistles he claims that it should be remembered of him that both at home and in the field he
had found favour in the eyes of the first men of Rome.
We may be quite sure that if he had misbehaved at
Philippi he would not have touched the question. It
was the confidence that his readers knew better that
enabled him in this way to impute cowardice to himself.
On the one hand it is said playfully. Alcaeus, the Greek
lyric poet (and he is always desiring to be thought the
Roman Alcaeus), had sung (also, probably, in irony) of
himself that in a famous battle he had flung away his
shield. Horace says in effect 'I played the poet's
part—you know what that has always been.' On the
other hand it is part (if we read the whole Ode and try
to estimate its core of meaning) of a generous tribute to
a lost cause. Horace is addressing a friend who in
that campaign had been his close companion, and who,
when Horace gave up the contest and came home, had
gone on fighting, but who now to his friend's surprise
and delight has appeared in Rome safe and unmolested
by the new government. 'What, Pompeius,' he says,
' at home again safe in limb and rights? Pompeius who
shared with me the dangers and snatched pleasures of

the campaign under Brutus!' Then comes the
stanza in question: 'We were together when I felt
the shock of Philippi and the headlong rout, my
poor little shield ingloriously left behind me, what time
Virtue broke and those who threatened high bit the
dust in defeat.' His own part is purposely made little
of. It was a fit part for a poet—and who was he
when Virtue herself was broken? The words are few,
but the more weighty for that. There is reference to
the story that Brutus when the battle was over fell,
broken-hearted, on his own sword, expressing his despair in a quotation from a Greek poet, 'Poor Virtue!
so thou art a name: but I took thee for a reality
and set my life to follow thee.' It has been worth
while to dwell on this point at length, for two con-
clusions may be drawn from the review: (1) It is an
illustration of the independence and dignity which
Horace maintained in his great change of political
position. Having fought by the side of the murderers
of the first Caesar, he became the apologist and eventually the court-poet and the intimate friend of the
second. It was a difficult transition to make without
the sacrifice of principle or self-respect, but he so made
it. He was not a politician, but a poet. He felt
deeply the horror of civil wars, with their aimless
bloodshed and the impotence abroad which they entailed.
He felt also the moral defects of the Roman people, the
luxury, the loss of discipline, the decline of patriotism,
which were at the root of their political troubles. In
a moment of enthusiasm he had thought that in the

enterprise of Brutus and Cassius he saw the way back to the better social and political ideals of the past. Events destroyed the illusion, and he came, not at once, but by stages which we can trace, to see that the best hope of the reforms which he desired lay in the acceptance of the rule of Octavianus. He gave his adhesion to him and put his muse at his service, but he was not expected to bespatter his old friends. He was not a prophet, but his enthusiasm was for what was great and promising in the imperial government. It was not for power or splendour of the court, but for the social and moral reforms promised and sought, for the return of peace and stability, the restoration of religion, the rule of moderation, culture, and refinement. (2) Secondly, it is an illustration of the necessity, when we would understand Horace from his writings, of making full allowance for the playfulness and irony with which he always speaks of himself. He never makes the best of himself. He never would have us think him too much in earnest. It is always 'Who am I to preach? I am no saint. I am as bad as my neighbours.'

It is the same spirit in which he so often begins or ends his great political and patriotic Odes with apology for meddling in such high matters, with profession, obviously untrue, that his real interest and poetic gift lie in concerns of love and wine. It is the explanation of several things in his writings which we should gladly miss in them.

The immediate results of Philippi were disastrous to him. He came home, as he says, ' humbled and with his wings clipped.' He found his Venusian estate forfeited in the proscription which followed the defeat. His father, it would seem, was dead. But he had made friends, and he was pardoned, and what we should call a clerkship in the Treasury was procured for him; and so we find him started on life in Rome. At some time, probably during his schooldays, he had made the acquaintance of the poet Virgil, who was five years older than himself, and they became warm friends. Through him he was introduced to Maecenas, the powerful minister and munificent patron of literature; and then, in the modest sense in which he sought fortune, his fortune was made. We hear no more of the clerkship, save that we find his fellow clerks once or twice claiming the help of their former colleague. Maecenas gave him a small country house and farm among the Sabine hills, some twenty-eight miles from Rome and ten from Tivoli. The exact position of the house is still doubtful, but the valley and all the points on which he dwells so fondly, the spring, the stream, the hills, the site of a temple then in ruins, the village high on the opposite hill, the market-town three miles down the valley at its junction with the valley of the Anio, can all be identified and are the objects of frequent pilgrimage. This was his delightful and beloved home for much of his time henceforth. He spent part of the year, but a diminishing part, in Rome (he says that he came with the first swallow and left before the first fig), and as he got older, the winter months at some warm seaside place. At one time his

favourite place was Tarentum, at another time he frequently went to Baiae, on the coast a few miles north of
Naples.   One year his physician, the famous Antonius
Musa, who was the inventor and a great upholder of
the cold water cure, forbade him Baiae where the
treatment was sulphur vapour baths; and he writes
a poetical letter to a friend to ask him about the
watering places further down on the gulf of Paestum.

We have many glimpses of Horace's mode of life
in his Sabine retreat.   The estate was a small one, but
there was room on it for a small home farm, managed
and tilled by a bailiff and eight other slaves, and also
for five small holdings let to tenants.   We see Horace
walking about his little property, talking to his bailiff
about the possibility of growing vines in one warm corner
(the bailiff says they may as well try to grow pepper or
frankincense) or as to the necessity of banking the
stream.   We see him plying a mattock or moving
stones with his own hands to the amusement of
his neighbours.   We see him strolling in the forest,
his mind full of some stanza of an Ode which he
is composing, and forgetting how far he is from home
till suddenly a huge wolf confronts him, yet such is
a good conscience that the poet is less frightened
than the wolf.   He tells us of his building plans.
He tells us of the books he brought with him when
he came out for a short holiday from Rome.   He
tells us of his happy evenings with chosen friends
and some honest neighbours, of their simple suppers
which the home-bred slaves share after them, of their

freedom from the foolish rules of deep drinking which made town banquets odious to him, of their talk, not as in town on frivolous topics, about their neighbours' affairs or the merits of a popular actor, but of that 'which comes nearer home to us and on which it is a misfortune to be ignorant,' whether happiness is to be found in wealth or in virtue, what is the true ground of friendship, what is the highest good.

In the same way he tells us how he spent a day in Rome. He was awake by daybreak, but moved to his sofa and read or wrote undisturbed for three hours ; then he took a stroll in the town (one such stroll and all its incidents he has preserved for us), or else he went to the Campus Martius and played with Maecenas what he calls the 'game of three,' apparently a game of ball. When the sun grew hot, perhaps between ten and eleven, he went in and took his first meal, a light luncheon, 'just enough,' he says, 'to save him from going all day without food.' As the afternoon came on he went out again, looked into shops and asked how prices were, strolled about the Circus and the Forum, stopped to listen to the fortune-tellers who haunted them, amused himself, in fact, with the humours of the town, and so came home again to his frugal supper of vegetables and maccaroni. This was a quiet day ; but the picture is given from his earlier years in Rome as a man of letters, when he had less position and fewer acquaintances than he had later. There were many distractions also, which he disliked increasingly, and of course he did not always sup at home. He was frequently at Maecenas's great house on the Esquiline; and Maecenas's friendship and the company of literary men whom he met there were his great attraction to Rome. But as soon as he had his country house he called it his '*arx*,' his stronghold of refuge, and fled to it as often and as early as he could.

Through Maecenas he became known to Augustus, and the Emperor made an effort to persuade him to live with him and act as his private secretary. He had the courage and good sense to refuse, and it is to Augustus's credit that he did not resent it but treated him as a friend to the end of his life. Some fragments are preserved of letters from Augustus to him, both playful and affectionate.

Horace was a man of delicate health. He had always, as we say, to 'take care of himself.' In spite of the bacchanalian tone of a few of his Odes it is clear that he was temperate in the use of wine. His first two questions about a place proposed for his sojourn are 'what is the bread like?' and 'what is the water like?' He seems ordinarily to have eaten sparingly. He was unmarried, although he was an ardent upholder of Augustus's legislation to encourage marriage.

People who look at the headings of his Odes run away with the idea that he was always in love with some fresh young lady and that he treated some of them very badly. Some ingenious critics have gone the length of writing a life of him from this point of view; but it all means a misunderstanding of his poetry and its relation to his life. Horace's love poetry is not like that of some other Latin poets, Catullus for instance, the outpouring of the stress and passion of youth. It is the conscious and artistic work of a man between thirty-five and forty-two. These are pretty certainly the limits of the commencement and conclusion of his chief volume of lyric poetry. It may be true that, even with a lyric poet of this type, each poem had some starting-point, but the occasion may be the slightest. He versifies not his own experience only, but that of others. A remark made at a supper-party, an incident narrated to him, a casual image in conversation or in a book, are enough to set his fancy working, and the result is a dramatic sketch of the situation or feeling suggested. This may be held to deduct from the interest of his poetry, but at least it must be remembered before he is supposed to plead guilty to crimes against love and good feeling.

In the year 17 B.C., when Horace was forty-seven, an event happened which made a certain change in his position. He became, to use a modern phrase, 'poet-laureate.' Amongst many antiquarian and religious revivals, Augustus determined, on the renewal to himself, in that year, of the imperial power (which at first he had only accepted for ten years), to celebrate with great magnificence the so-called Secular games, of which though there is little actual record there was a tradition linking them with the fortunes of the Roman State, and suggesting that they should be performed once in a *saeculum*, a period variously estimated at 100 and 110 years. By way of giving *éclat* to them and of drawing attention to the distinction of his reign as the greatest literary epoch in Roman history, he wished a special Ode to be written for the occasion and sung at the performance, and he chose Horace to do this. This selection gave the poet a public and, as it were, official position which he had not before, and it was followed a few years later by a pressing invitation to write (as a poet-laureate might be expected to write) two Odes to celebrate the victories of the two imperial princes, the stepsons of the Emperor, Tiberius and Drusus. This led to the preparation of a fourth book of Odes, although he had then for ten years laid aside lyric composition. We are now in the year 13, and his life was drawing to a close. Some years before he had addressed an Ode to Maecenas, who was himself an invalid and nervous about himself, in which, partly in playful remonstrance and partly in seriousness of feeling, he protested that if Maecenas died he should die also. So in effect it happened. They died in the year B.C. 8 within a few weeks of one another, Maecenas first, Horace on November 27, when he was within a few days of his fifty-seventh birthday. His ashes were laid close to those of his friend on the Esquiline hill.

Horace's writings follow two streams. There are his lyrical poems, and there are what he himself calls his 'talks' or prose poems, the Satires and Epistles. Though the form of the two is so different, the man is the same behind both, and to a very great extent the subjects that interest him and call for expression are the same, and in both cases there is a process of development to be traced of the same kind and in the same direction. He describes in one place[1], making an anecdote serve as a parable, with some irony and exaggeration, no doubt, but with some substantial truth, the motives and temper of his earliest writings. It must be true that, when he came home from Philippi to find himself homeless and without an income, he felt out of temper with himself and the world; and it is true that his first literary efforts were of the nature of invective. But if he wrote in the first instance coarsely and bitterly, and two or three very disagreeable poems which remain look as if he did, his good taste and feeling made him destroy nearly all of such work. The little collection of poems which we call Epodes, though in their original idea personality and sting belong to their essence, yet soften and generalize till they are hard to distinguish from the later Lyrics which we call Odes. And Satire in the same way softens and humanizes in his hands, so that when we pass from the so-called 'Satires' to the mellow and beautiful 'Epistles' we hardly feel that the character of the poetry is changed.

The Epodes (17) represent all that he left to posterity of his lyrical work between the years 41, when he returned to Rome, and 31, the year of Actium. One of the poems is of great historical interest, for if the interpretation now generally given to it is right, it is the only contemporaneous record of that great battle. It was written, it is suggested with high probability, on board Maecenas's galley at

[1] See Epist. 2. 2.

some time on the day of the engagement. It ends with a humorous picture of Horace's own division of mind between the battle and his own personal feelings of sea-sickness. No picture so vivid has survived of the terror, scorn, and loathing which had been excited in the minds of patriotic Romans by the dread of Mark Antony's success in this battle, meaning, as it would have meant, the appearance in Rome of the barbarian queen, Cleopatra, the introduction of feminine rule, and of the degrading accessories of an Oriental court. This feeling went far with Horace, and doubtless with many others, as it became clear that Rome had only a choice of masters, to determine him to the warm support of Octavianus.

It was in writing the Epodes that Horace learned that he had a lyrical gift. As they occupied the years from 41 to 31, so the first three books of the Odes, which form a unity, occupied the years from 30 to 23. It is easy to feel the charm of the Odes, and yet the difficulty of assigning them their proper place in poetry. They are lyrical, yet there is not in them what has been called the 'lyrical cry'; there is not passion nor profundity of thought or of feeling. They 'rise sometimes,' as a Latin critic said of them, to considerable force and dignity, especially in dealing with themes of patriotism; but on the whole they are playful, ironical, commonplace in topics, exquisite in form rather than in substance. Yet they are no mere 'verses of society.' They travel from land to land and from age to age, and are always at home. There is no collection

of poems which has been so frequently quoted: and
this is because there is none which has given such
perfect expression to the elementary experiences and
universal sentiments of the general readers of literature.
The shortness of life, the mutability of fortune, the
delights of friendship, the pleasures of ease, mirth,
jollity, and wine, the lighter and superficial aspect of
love, its caprices, jealousies, quarrels, and reconciliations,
the rudimentary lessons of practical philosophy, patience,
contentment, moderation; these are all touched again
and again in phrases which catch the sense with their
music and dwell in the memory from their terseness,
simplicity, and happiness.   If the poetry of the Odes is
the poetry of art rather than of nature, it is art that has
proved inimitable.   When Horace ceased to write, 'the
mould was broken [1],'

To turn to the other class of his poetry.   The first
collection of poems that he published is the First Book
of the Satires, which he gave to the world some four
years before the Epodes.   The term Satire has had
a curious history.   By its derivation and in its first use it
meant a hotchpot—a dish of many ingredients; and was
applied in literature to a medley, a collection of essays
in verse on various subjects.   In the hands of Lucilius
it acquired from the special use he made of it the sense
which we now give to it, viz. the censorious criticism
of men and manners.   In this sense Horace inherited
it, and his first essays were in this vein: but for Satire
of this kind (the Satire of Juvenal or of Pope, though

[1] H. A. J. Munro.

Pope calls his Satires 'Imitations of Horace') Horace
had too much good nature and too little self-confidence.
Satire softens in his hands. It returns to something
more like its original meaning. Of the fact that this
had happened he showed his consciousness by dropping
the word and giving his writing another name which we
have never adopted in his sense. He calls these poems
(and indeed apparently the Epistles also) '*Sermones,*'
a word which had several colours on it. It meant that
they were something between poetry and prose. He
calls the Muse that inspired them '*Musa pedestris,*'
she went 'afoot,' without the wings of poetic flight.
But it had the more definite sense of 'talks,' '*causeries.*'
They were imitations of conversation, on men and
things, on the art of living, on conduct and character,
on the weaknesses of mankind, but also on other things,
on literary topics, on himself, incidents of his life, his
relations to Maecenas. When we pass to the Epistles
little has been altered. There is the form of an Epistle;
even that sometimes is nominal; but the subjects are
the same, the folly of avarice, the wisdom of enjoying
instead of wishing, the charms of country life and
modest tastes, the paradoxes of philosophers. The
style is the same, the free and unrhetorical style of the
best conversation, playful and serious by turns. In some
ways they are an advance on the Satires. Horace is
older; his position is more recognized; his views of
life are wider and more mature. One point we cannot
but notice with pleasure: there is not a line in them
which we would wish to blot.

The Epistles fall into two divisions. The first Book occupies the space from the publication of the three Books of the Odes to the year B.C. 19, his own forty-sixth year. There are three more Epistles of greater length and later date; these last are all on literary subjects, the Epistle to Augustus and the Epistle to the Pisos (often called the Art of Poetry) being in substance expositions of Horace's views on poetry. These views fall mainly under two principles. First he defends the Classical School of Roman poetry, of which Virgil and he himself are to us the great representatives, against those who unduly cried up the rougher poets of earlier time, and also against the more affected poetry (of which no specimens have come down to us) which in his own day was becoming popular. And secondly he insists upon the doctrine, not unconnected with that estimate, that poetry is a serious art, requiring like other arts not merely natural gift but also long preparation and practice. One of the most often quoted of his lines tells us that though there are some things in which the moderate and the tolerable are rightly allowed their place, poetry is not one of them.

TABLE OF PROBABLE DATES

B. C.

65   Birth of Horace.

44   Horace at Athens.

43, 42   Campaign with Brutus.

41   Return to Rome.

38   Introduction to Maecenas.

To 35   Composition of Satires, Book I.

To 30   Satires, Book II, and the Epodes.

To 23   Odes, Books I–III.

To 20 or 19   Epistles, Book I.

19   Epistles, Book II. 2 (to Florus).

17   The Secular Hymn.

17–13   Odes, Book IV.

13   Epistles, Book II. 1 (to Augustus).

8   Death of Horace.

The Art of Poetry is of less certain date. It is placed either within the same period as Epistles, Book I, viz. B.C. 23–19, or more probably in the last years of Horace's life, B. C. 10–8.

ODES

BOOK I

I   *Maecenas atavis*

*An apology for the composition of Lyric poetry as one of
the very many tastes and ambitions of mankind, and
not the least happy and honourable of them. It is
written as a prologue to the first three Books of the
Odes, and (like the first of the Epodes, of the Satires, and
of the Epistles) it is addressed to Maecenas, and so
serves as a dedication.*

MAECENAS, in lineage the child of kings, but
oh! to me my protector, pride, and joy, there
are whose pleasure it is to have raised a cloud of dust
in the racecourse at Olympia, whom the pillar just
cleared by the glowing wheels and the palm-branch of
glory lift to the gods, the lords of earth. One is happy
if the fickle crowd of Roman citizens rush to the poll
to raise him through the triple grade of honours[1]:
another if he have housed in his own granary all that is
swept from Libyan threshing-floors[2]. The man whose
joy it is to dig the stiff soil of his paternal farm, never
with the offers of an Attalus[3] would you tempt away from
it to plough the sea round Myrto in a bark of Cyprus,
a frightened sailor. The trader with the fear before his
eyes of the wind of Africa wrestling with rough Icarian
waters, praises a quiet homestead near his native town:

[1] Aedile, praetor, consul.
[2] A hyperbolical expression for having a large property in the
corn-growing districts of North Africa.
[3] The Attali were kings of Pergamus, of fabulous wealth.

full soon he is repairing his shattered bark; for to be content without wealth he finds too hard a lesson. There is who scorns not cups of old Massic and to filch a part from the unbroken day, stretched at length now beneath a leafy arbutus, now near the lullaby of some haunted spring. Many there are who love the camp and the trumpet-tones mingling with the clarion, and the wars which mothers abhor. The hunter bivouacs under Jove's cold sky without a thought of his young wife, if either his trusty hounds have sighted a deer, or a Marsian boar has broken through the meshes of close-twisted cord. For me, the ivy crown which rewards the poet's brow admits me to the company of gods; cool grove and light dances of Nymphs and Satyrs draw me aside from the throng of men, provided that neither Euterpe forbids the pipe nor Polyhymnia refuses to string the lute of Lesbos. But if you will give me a place among the bards of the lyre, I shall lift my head till it strikes the stars.

II   *Iam satis terris*

Horace has thought over the portents which followed the death of Julius Caesar, and the fruitless horrors of the civil war; and he welcomes Octavianus (the ' Caesar' of the last line) as the restorer both of peace and the arts of civil life, and also of military prestige abroad.

ENOUGH now of snow and direful hail hath the Father showered upon earth, and smiting with the bolt from his red right hand temple and tower hath struck panic into Rome, hath struck panic into the

nations, lest there were coming again the grievous age of
Pyrrha [1], who complained [2] of portents never seen before,
what time Proteus [3] drove all his herd to visit the mountain summits and the kind of fishes [4] was entangled in the
elm-tops where had been the haunt and home of wood-
pigeons, and frightened deer swam on the flooding waters.
We have seen yellow Tiber, his stream flung forcibly
back at the coast of the Tuscan sea [5], go forth to lay
low the king's monument [6] and Vesta's shrine, while he
boasts himself the avenger of Ilia's [7] importunate complaints, and over his left bank sweeps far and wide, beyond
Jove's will, the uxorious river. How for civil strife
men sharpened swords by which the hateful Persian
might more fitly die—how they fought—shall be told to
a young generation scant in number for their parents'
crimes. Whom of the gods shall our people invoke to
save a toppling empire? With what prayers shall the
consecrated maidens importune Vesta, who turns a deaf
ear to their litanies? To whom will Jove assign the
part of atoning for our guilt? Come now, at last, we
pray thee, thy sun-bright shoulders veiled in clouds,
Apollo, god of augury. Or thou, if thou wilt rather,

[1] With her husband Deucalion, survivor in the Greek legend of
the deluge.　　　[2] It implies 'just as we are now doing.'

[3] The sea-god with his seals.

[4] 'The total kind of birds.'　Milton.

[5] Or 'from his Tuscan [right] bank.'

[6] The 'Regia' connected in story with King Numa, and in
use the residence of the 'Pontifex maximus,' and so of Julius Caesar.

[7] Horace, following one form of the legend, identifies her with
Rhea Silvia, the mother of Romulus, and also connects her name
with the Julian house.

laughing Queen of Eryx, round whom hover Mirth and Love. Or if thou hast aught of care for thy neglected race, thy son's sons, thou our Sire, sated by the sport— ah! too long—thou who joyest in the war-cry and the polished helms and the fierce glare of the Moorish footman on his bleeding foe. Or thou, sweet Maia's winged child [1], if it be thou that wearest upon earth the disguise of human youth, submitting to be called the avenger of a Caesar; long be it before thou returnest to heaven: and many a year mayst thou linger well pleased among the people of Quirinus; nor ever, impatient of our crimes, may any air waft thee from us all too soon! Here rather mayst thou learn to love glorious triumphs, here to be called our father and first citizen; nor let the Mede ride the foray unpunished, while thou art our leader, Caesar [2]!

III   *Sic te diva potens*

Addressed to a ship in which Virgil is crossing to Greece. It is a playful tirade against sea-travelling, the point of which is the poet's hope that Virgil's voyage may be safely performed. Compare Epod. 10 on the voyage of a bad poet.

SO guide thee the goddess queen of Cyprus; so Helen's brethren, stars of light, and the sire of the winds, keeping in the prison all save Iapyx [3], O ship, that hast in

[1] Octavianus is identified finally with Mercury, the god of persuasion and of civil arts.

[2] Notice the art which keeps the name of the saviour of society to be the last word.

[3] The wind which blowing from the Iapygian promontory would carry the ship across from Brundisium to Dyrrhachium.

charge Virgil entrusted to thy faith, restore him un-
harmed, I pray, to the Attic shore, and save the half of
my own life.   His heart was mailed in oak and triple
brass who was the first to commit a frail bark to the
rough seas, and to brave a squall from Africa when it
was battling to the death with north winds, and the
weeping rain-stars, and the south wind's ire, than whom
none more lords it over Hadria, whether it be his
pleasure to lift the waves or to lay them.   In what
degree did he fear death, who saw with dry eyes the
monsters of the deep and the troubled sea and those
rocks of evil name, the Thunder Cape [1]?   In vain hath
God in his wisdom severed land from land by the
estranging [2] ocean, if yet in impious defiance ships bound
across the forbidden waters.   In its boldness to bear
and to dare all things, the race of man rushes headlong
into sin, despite of law.   In his boldness Iapetus' son [3]
brought fire, a theft of woe, into the world.   In the
train of fire, filched from its heavenly home, wasting
sickness and a strange horde of fevers swooped down
on all lands, and the doom, slow though sure, of death,
remote before, quickened its pace.   Daedalus essayed the
void air on wings which nature gave not to man.   The
barrier of Acheron was broken through: 'twas a labour of
Hercules.   No height is too arduous for mortal men.   To
Heaven's own gate we would climb in our folly, nor by
our crimes allow Jove to lay aside the bolts of his wrath.

[1] 'Thunder Cape,' Macaulay. Acroceraunia is a headland on the
coast of Epirus.

[2] 'The unplumbed, salt, estranging sea.' M. Arnold.

[3] Prometheus.

IV *Solvitur acris hiems*

Lessons of Epicureanism drawn from the spring-time. Addressed to Sestius, consul in B.C. 23, an old comrade of Horace in the army of Brutus.

WINTER'S sharp chain is loosening before the pleasant succession of spring-time and the west wind, and the rollers are drawing to the sea the keels long high and dry. No longer do cattle find pleasure in their stalls or ploughman in his fireside: no longer do meadows glisten white with hoar-frost. Now Venus, Cythera's queen, leads the dances when the moon is high overhead, and the fair Graces hand in hand with Nymphs shake the ground with rhythmic feet, while Vulcan glowing in the blaze visits his ponderous Cyclops' forges[1]. Now it beseems us to make our brows shine and bind them with myrtle or with the flowers which the loosened earth offers. Now too in shady grove it beseems to do sacrifice to Faunus with a lamb, if so he wills it, or a kid. Pale death with impartial foot knocks at the doors of poor men's hovels and of king's palaces. O Sestius, Fortune's favourite, life's short span forbids us to enter on far-reaching hopes. In a moment night will be upon you, and the shadow-world that men talk of, and the unsubstantial house of Pluto. From the day that you come thither, you shall never again throw dice for the royalty of the banquet, nor cast eyes on fair young Lycidas.

---

[1] This is a mythological way of saying that the amusements and the work of life begin again.

V   *Quis multa gracilis*

Pyrrha's inconstancy.

WHAT delicate stripling is it, Pyrrha, that now,
steeped in liquid perfumes, is wooing thee on
the heaped rose-leaves in some pleasant grot? For
whose eyes dost thou braid those flaxen locks, so trim,
so simple? Ah! how often shall he weep for changed
faith and changed gods, and stare in wonder at the
waters roughening beneath black squalls, all new to the
sight—he that now enjoys thee all golden, the credulous boy! who dreams of thee as ever free, ever amiable,
little thinking how soon the wind may shift. Poor
souls, to whom thy charms are an untried sea! For me,
the temple's wall with its votive picture shows that
I have hung up ere this my dripping garments an offering to the god who rules the waters.

VI   *Scriberis Vario*

*An answer to a request of M. Vipsanius Agrippa that
Horace would write of his exploits. 'Heroic deeds
need a Homer to sing of them,' says Horace, and so in
refusing gives the panegyric asked for.*

THEY shall be told—for Varius is a bird of
Maeonian [1] song—your bravery and your victories,
every exploit which your bold soldiery achieved on
shipboard or on horseback with you to lead them. I,
Agrippa, and such as I, essay no more to tell such tales
than to tell of the deadly wrath of Peleus' son, who

[1] Homeric.

knew not how to yield, or the wandering over seas of
Ulysses, the man of wiles, or the bloody house of Pelops,
themes too great for our humility, whilst modesty and
the Muse that owns an unwarlike lyre forbid us by the
failings of our own wit to spoil the edge of great Caesar's
fame and of yours.   Who shall write worthily of Mars
in his coat of adamantine mail, or of Meriones black
with the dust of Troy, or of Tydeus' son by Pallas'
help the match for gods of heaven?   It is for us to
sing of banquets, of battles of maids flying in their
lovers' faces with nails close-cut [1], heart-whole, may be,
as we sing, or if feeling the fire, triflers still much after
our wont.

VII   *Laudabunt alii*

*To Plancus, who has had to leave his beloved Tibur and
go campaigning.*

I LEAVE others to praise famous Rhodes or Mity-
lene, or Ephesus, or the walls of Corinth on its two
seas, or, if they will, Thebes renowned for Bacchus or
Delphi for Apollo or Thessalian Tempe.   There are
who make it their whole business to chant in an unending
song the praises of spotless Pallas' city and to wreathe
their brow with the olive plucked on every hand.
There are many enough who to Juno's glory will tell of
Argos and its breed of horses, and of Mycenae with its
wealth.   For me neither patient Lacedaemon [2] nor the

[1] So as not to hurt.   'The only battles we sing of are battles
in play.'

[2] The land of discipline.

plain of rich Larissa has such charms as the abode of echoing Albunea [1], and rushing Anio, and the grove of Ti-
burnus, and the apple orchards wet with streamlets never
still.   As the south-wind often sweeps the clouds away
from the darkened sky and does not breed showers un-
ceasingly, so do you too, Plancus, be wise and always
remember to let the sadness and the toils of life find
ending in mellow wine, whether your home be, as now,
in the camp gleaming with its standards, or by-and-by
under the thick shade of your own Tibur.   Teucer,
they tell us, when he had to fly from Salamis and from
his father's house, yet put a poplar [2] garland on his temples moist with the dews of the Enfranchiser [3], and spoke
thus to his downcast friends: 'Where Fortune shall
lead us, kinder than a father, there will we go, partners
and comrades.   No lot is desperate under Teucer's conduct and Teucer's star.   For sure is Apollo's promise
that in a new land there should be a Salamis to dispute
the old name.   Brave hearts, heroes who have weathered
with me worse storms than this, to-day chase your
cares with wine: to-morrow we set out once more
upon the boundless sea.'

[1] The Tiburtine Sibyl, 'echoing' because her temple was above
the waterfall.

[2] The poplar was sacred to Hercules, the patron of wanderers.

[3] *Lyaeo* (λύειν).   Horace always uses this name for Bacchus
when the thought is of him as a deliverer from care.

VIII   *Lydia, dic per omnis*

Lydia is bidden not to spoil young Sybaris by keeping him at her apron-strings. The name Sybaris is evidently taken from the historic city on the gulf of Tarentum, which had become a proverb for effeminate luxury.

BY all the gods, Lydia, tell me truly this: why you make such haste to ruin Sybaris by your love; why he hates the sunny Campus, though he has learnt to face sun and dust. Why does he not ride among his compeers in martial exercises, nor tame the mouth of Gaulish colt with wolf-tooth bit? Why does he shrink from the touch of the yellow Tiber stream? Why does he shun the wrestler's oil more cautiously than if it were viper's blood; nor carry any more on his arms the blue marks of manly weapons, though he had so often won fame for throwing the *discus*[1] or the javelin clean beyond the mark? Why does he hide himself, as they say did the sea-nymph Thetis' son before the sad death-day of Troy, lest a man's garb should snatch him away to face carnage and the Lycian squadrons?

---

[1] The *discus* was not a quoit but a solid disk of stone, about a foot in diameter, held between the fingers and the arm, and the object was to fling it as far as possible. It would naturally mark the arm.

IX *Vides ut alta*

*Lessons of Epicureanism drawn from a winter scene.
Compare Epod. 13. The person addressed is called by an
imaginary name to suit the purpose, 'Thaliarchus,' 'master
of the merriment' or 'prince of good cheer.'*

YOU see how Soracte [1] stands out white with deep
snow, and the straining woods bend beneath their
burden, and the keen frost has stayed the running streams.
Pile the logs plentifully on the hearth and thaw the
cold, and draw out with more generous hand the four-
year wine from its Sabine two-eared jar, O prince of
good cheer. All else leave to the gods. When they
have laid the winds that now battle so fiercely on the
yeasty waters, the cypresses are vexed no more, nor
the old mountain-ashes. What shall be to-morrow,
think not of asking. Each day that Fortune gives you,
be it what it may, set down for gain; nor refuse
sweet loves while boyhood is yours, nor (I pray you)
the dance, so long as youth is green and testy old
age is far off. Now again and again seek you the
Campus and the public squares, and the soft whispering
at nightfall at the hour of tryst; now too the sweet
tell-tale laughter from the secret corner which betrays
the hiding girl, and the pledge snatched from arm or
finger that only feigns resistance.

[1] The conical mountain that attracts the eye in all views to the
northward from Rome.

X   *Mercuri facunde*

To Mercury.
An imitation of a Greek Hymn.

MERCURY, Atlas' grandchild eloquent, who by thy wit didst mould the rough manners of new-created man through the gift of speech and the rule of the grace-giving *palaestra*, thee I would sing, the messenger of mighty Jove and the gods, the parent of the curved lyre, of ready skill to hide whatever it hath pleased thee in freakish theft. Thou wast but a boy when, as he tried to frighten thee with threatening words into restoring the kine which thy craft had spirited away, even as he spoke Apollo laughed to miss his quiver. 'Twas by thy guidance that Priam with his wealth left Ilium and passed unseen through the proud sons of Atreus and the watch-fires of the Thessalians and the camp of Troy's foes. 'Tis thou that takest to their rest in homes of joy the spirits of the good, and with thy golden wand drivest the shadowy throng, favourite alike of gods in the height and in the depth.

XI   *Tu ne quaesieris*

Against resorting to Astrologers.

PRAY, ask not, Leuconoe—such knowledge is not for us—what end for me, for you, the gods ordain, nor tamper with the Chaldaeans' tables. How much better, whatever it is to be, to bear it! Whether Jove grants us many more winters, or this the last which is now breaking the force of the Tyrrhenian sea against the wave-worn cliffs, learn wisdom, clear the wine, and by the thought of life's little span cut short long day-dreams. Even while we speak, Time, the churl, will have been running. Snatch the sleeve of to-day, and trust as little as you may to to-morrow.

XII   *Quem virum aut heroa*

Octavianus is hailed as the crown of Roman history and the hope of the human race.

WHAT man or demi-god dost thou choose to glorify with the lyre or treble flute, what god, O Clio? Whose is the name which freakish Echo shall make ring again either on the shady sides of Helicon or on the heights of Pindus or on cold Haemus, whence the woods followed pellmell behind Orpheus, the master of sound, who by the art his mother taught him stayed the rapid rivers' flow and the swift winds, and knew the spell to give ears to oaks and draw them to listen to the music of his strings? Of what can I tell before the wonted praise of the Sire, who rules the life of men and gods, who rules the sea and land and sky with its changing seasons? From him springs none mightier than himself, nor lives there anything in power like or second to him; yet the place nearest in honour belongs to Pallas. Nor shall I have nought to say of thee, Liber, bold in fights, and thee, the maiden foe of savage beasts, and thee, Apollo, terrible with the unerring arrow. Of Alcides too shall I tell, and the

boys of Leda, one famous for victory in the horse-race,
the other in the boxing-match. Soon as their white
star has shone upon sailors, the wind-driven spray
streams down from the rocks, the winds fall, and the
clouds scud away, and on the sea the threatening wave,
for that they have so willed it, sinks to rest. Next
after them I doubt me whether I should tell the tale of
Romulus, or of Pompilius' quiet sway, or of the proud
rods of Tarquin, or of Cato's glorious death. Regulus
and the two Scauri and Paulus, lavish of his great life
when the Carthaginian was conquering, will I gratefully
name with the Muse's peculiar tribute, aye and Fabricius.
He and Curius, of hair unkempt, were bred to do good
service in war, and Camillus too, by stern poverty, and
the ancestral farm with its cottage home to match. As
a tree grows by the unmarked lapse of time, so grows
the glory of a Marcellus. As shines the moon among
the lesser fires, so amongst all others shines the star of
a Julius. Father and guardian of human kind, O son
of Saturn, to thee is given, so fate wills it, the care of
mighty Caesar. Reign thou, with Caesar for thy vice-
gerent. For him—be it the Parthians who threaten
Latium that he shall lead tamed in a well-earned triumph,
or the Seres and Indians who border the land of the
rising sun—he shall rule in justice the wide world while
he bows to thee. Thou with thy ponderous wheels
shalt shake Olympus: thou on the groves which are
haunts of wickedness shalt hurl the bolts of thy displeasure.

XIII   *Cum tu, Lydia, Telephi*

Jealousy and Constancy.

LYDIA, while you praise Telephus' 'neck like a rose,' Telephus' 'arms of wax,' faugh! my liver swells with the hot and angry bile. And then my head reels and my colour comes and goes, and the moisture steals down my cheeks, telling how deep go the slow fires that consume me. It is torture to me if his tipsy brawl has bruised your white shoulders[1] or if the frenzied boy has left tell-tale marks on your lips. If you listened to me as you should, you would never hope that one would prove constant who hurts so barbarously the pretty lips which Venus has touched with the fifth part of her own nectar. Thrice happy they, and more than thrice, whom an unbroken bond holds fast, and whom love, never torn asunder by foolish quarrellings, will not loose till life's last day!

XIV   *O navis, referent*

The ship of the State, at the harbour's mouth, is warned not to drift out again into the sea of civil war.

O SHIP, fresh waves are rising and will bear thee out to sea again. O what art thou about? One bold push more and make the harbour! Seest thou not that broadside is bare of oars, and mast crippled by the rushing south-west wind, and yardarms are groaning, and

---

[1] For the unseemly violence which attended drinking-bouts see the end of Ode 17.

without ropes the hull can scarcely weather the too peremptory sea? Thou hast no whole sails, no gods left to call on next time when trouble is heavy. Whatever thy idle boasts of race and name, that thou art a pine of Pontus, the daughter of a lordly forest, the sailor in his fear trusts not in painted sterns. Have care, I pray thee, unless thou art doomed to make sport for the winds. A moment ago to me a weary sickening of heart, still a fond yearning and no light anxiety, see thou avoid the waters which wash between those bright Cyclades.

XV   *Pastor cum traheret*

The prophecy of Nereus.

WHENAS the shepherd was carrying off Helen, his host's wife, the traitor, across the sea in ships of Ida, Nereus cast on the swift winds an unwelcome calm that he might utter the burden of cruel destiny: 'Under evil omens thou art leading to thy home one whom Greece will come with a host of warriors to reclaim, bound by a common vow to break at one blow thy marriage bond and Priam's ancient realm. Woe is me! How the war-horses, how the heroes will soon be sweating! What a tale of death dost thou open for the Dardan race! Even now Pallas is making ready her helm and her aegis, her chariot and her fury. To no purpose, defiant under the protection of Venus, shalt thou comb out thy head of hair, and with unwarlike cithern give the time to songs such as please women's ears.

To no purpose in lady's chamber shalt thou seek to avoid the heavy spears and arrows of Cretan reed and the battle-din and Ajax swift in pursuit. For all this, ah me! thou shalt one day besmirch in the dust those adulterous locks. Seest thou not behind thee Laertes' son, the ruin of thy race, or Pylian Nestor? Close at thy heels are those who know not fear, Teucer of Salamis and Sthenelus skilled in fight, or if need be to rule the team, no dull charioteer. Meriones too thou shalt come to know. See, Tydeus' relentless son, a better man than his father, is hot to find thee, from whom as from a wolf, seen on the other side of the valley, flies the deer nor stays to think of the grass, so shalt thou fly panting with head in air, like a coward, though thou hadst promised thy mistress a different sight. The angered host of Achilles shall postpone the day of doom for Ilium and the Phrygian mothers. When a fixed tale of winters is told the fire of the Achaeans shall burn the homes of Ilium.'

XVI   *O matre pulchra*

A palinode to a lady who has been libelled in verse. It is very probable that the Ode refers to the quarrel, difficult to read, which gives their occasion to Epodes 5 and 17 and Sat. 1. 8.

O FAIRER daughter of a fair mother, what bound soever you will you shall set to my scurrilous iambics [1], by fire, if so it please you, or by the Adrian

---

[1] 'Iambics' is, from their metre, Horace's own name for his Epodes.

sea. Not the goddess [1] of Dindymus, not the god of Pytho [2] when his full presence is in his shrine, not Liber, so shake their priests' reason ; the Corybantes clashing again their shrill brass show not such empty fury—as fell anger. Neither iron of Noricum can awe it from its purpose, nor wreck-strewn sea, nor fierce fire, nor Jove himself crashing down in tumult terrible. Prometheus, they tell us, when compelled to add to the primal clay an atom taken from every animal, among the rest placed near our heart the force of the lion's fury. 'Twas anger laid Thyestes low in dread ruin. Anger has been to cities built on high the cause far-traced that each was levelled to the ground, and that the host of proud foemen marked with the ploughshare the line of their walls. Keep a firm rein on your feelings. I too in the sweet season of youth suffered from my heart's hot blood, and in my frenzy was driven into impetuous iambics. Now I would exchange harsh thoughts for mellow ones, provided you would become my friend and give me back your heart.

XVII   *Velox amoenum*

To Tyndaris.   An invitation to the Sabine Farm.

FLEET Faunus often exchanges Lycaeus [3] for lovely Lucretilis [4], and protects my she-goats from fiery summer sun and from rainy wind. Without harm through safe woods wander those dames of an unfragrant

---

[1] Cybele.   [2] Delphi.   [3] In Arcadia.

[4] Mte. Gennaro, the mountain-mass overhanging the Sabine valley in which Horace's farm lay.

squire, seeking the lurking arbute-bushes and thyme with no terror of green snake or of Haedilia's wolves that Mars loves, when once, Tyndaris, through the vale of low-lying Ustica with its smooth rocks has run the sound of his sweet pipe.   Yes, the gods watch over me—the gods value my piety and my Muse.   Here Plenty, rich in all the pride of the country, shall stream into your lap till it is full.   Here in my deep-drawn valley you shall avoid the dog-star's heat, and shall tell on the strings of Teos[1] the tale of Penelope and glass-green Circe sick with one and the same passion[2]. Here in the shade you shall quaff cups of harmless Lesbian, nor shall the son of Semele[3]—Semele who is Thyone—wage aimless quarrels with Mars, nor shall you fear Cyrus' rough play if in jealousy he lay tipsy hands on you, a poor little match for him, and tear the garland that clings to your hair and your unoffending robe.

XVIII   *Nullam, Vare, sacra*

The use and the dangers of wine.

NOT one tree, Varus, must you plant before the god-given vine all about the mellow soil of Tibur and the walls of Catilus[4].   To those who drink not, all

---

[1] Teos was the home of Anacreon.   [2] i.e. for Ulysses.

[3] The mother of Bacchus.   Her name Thyone was from the same root as that of the Thyiads—the frenzied votaries of the god.   It is a mythological way of describing the aimless brawls into which a drinking-bout degenerated.

[4] One of three brothers who were the legendary founders of Tibur.

that heaven ever sets before them is hard; and in no way but in this one do carking cares scatter and fly. Who harps on the toils of campaigning or of poverty after his wine? Who speaks not rather of thee, father Bacchus, and thee, fair Venus? And that none lightly overpass the bounty of Liber who loves moderation there is warning in the strife of Centaurs and Lapithae fought to the death over wine: there is warning in the heavy hand of Evius [1] on the Sithonii when in their greedy haste they divide right from wrong by the slender line of their own appetite. For me I will never disturb thee against thy will, bright and beautiful Bassareus [1], nor snatch into the light what is hidden under those many-tinted leaves. Silence the fierce drums and the horn of Berecyntus [2], in whose train follows blind Self-love and Vainglory, lifting far too high her empty head, and Faith that blabs out her secret, more transparent than glass.

XIX   *Mater saeva Cupidinum*
The relapse.

THE imperious mother of Loves and the son of Semele and wanton Idlesse bid me give my heart back to a passion which I had ended. I feel the fire at sight of Glycera's bright beauty, of purer lustre than Parian marble. I feel the fire at her pretty sauciness and that face, to look on which is to slip from your

---

[1] Names of Bacchus.
[2] A mountain on which Cybele was worshipped.

resolve. To descend on me with all her force, Venus
has left Cyprus empty, nor will she suffer me to say
a word of Scythian or Parthian, brave on his flying
steed, or aught that is irrelevant. Here place for me the
fresh turf, here place sacred boughs and frankincense
and a goblet of last year's wine. When I have offered
a victim she will come in gentler sort.

XX   *Vile potabis*

An invitation addressed to Maecenas.

IT will be cheap Sabine that you will have to drink
from my modest cups—wine which I stored my-
self and sealed in a Greek crock at that time, dear knight
Maecenas, when you were greeted in the theatre [1] with
rounds of applause till the banks of your ancestral river [2]
and the freakish echo of the Vatican hill repeated to you
your praises. I must leave you [3] to drink Caecuban
and the grape crushed in the presses of Cales. My
cups are not mellowed by the vines of Falernum or the
produce of the Formian hills.

XXI   *Dianam tenerae*

A hymn in honour of Diana and Apollo.

TELL of Diana, gentle maidens; of unshorn
Cynthius tell, my boys, and of Latona dear to
the inmost heart of supreme Jove. Do you [maidens]

---

[1] On recovery from a serious illness, see Od. 2. 17.
[2] The 'Tuscan' Tiber, Maecenas being Etruscan.
[3] i.e. at home.

praise her that rejoices in the streams, and in every leafy head of the forest that rises high on cold Algidus, or in the black woods of Erymanthus or of green Cragus. Do you, the male chorus, with praise for praise, extol Tempe and Delos, Apollo's birthplace, and him whose shoulder is decked with the quiver and his brother's lyre. Moved by your prayers he will drive away tearful war, drive away the woes of famine and plague from our people and Caesar our prince on to the Persians and the Britons.

XXII   *Integer vitae*

The secret of safety and happiness.

Addressed to Aristius Fuscus.   (*See Epist.* i. 10.)

HE that is unstained in life and pure from guilt needs not, Fuscus, the Moor's javelin or bow or quiver laden with poisoned arrows, whether he be going to make his way through the surf of the Syrtes, or the unharboured [1] Caucasus or the lands which storied Hydaspes washes. For even at sight of me once in a Sabine wood, as I was singing the praise of my Lalage and straying beyond bounds in careless mood, unarmed though I was, a wolf turned and fled, a monster such as Apulia, the home of warriors, does not rear in its broad oak-forests nor the land of Juba breed in her deserts, the nursing-mother of lions. Place me where on the dull plain there is no tree to be wakened to new life by the breeze of summer, the side of the

[1]   ' unharboured heaths,
Infamous hills.' *Comus.*

world on which clouds and inclement Jove press heavily, place me beneath the chariot of the too neighbouring sun in a land forbidden to human dwelling, still shall I love Lalage and her sweet laughter, Lalage and her sweet prattle.

XXIII   *Vitas inuleo*
The shy maiden.

YOU fly me, Chloe, like a fawn looking for its timid dam on the pathless mountain-side not without empty terrors of wind and wood. For if through the light-hung leaves has run the shiver of Spring's approach, or if a green lizard has moved aside a bramble, it trembles in heart and knees. Yet I am not pursuing you as an angry tigress or lion of Gaetulia to crush you in my teeth. 'Tis time to leave off running after your mother now that you are ripe for a husband.

XXIV   *Quis desiderio*

Addressed to Virgil on the death of Quintilius, a man of letters, the honest critic described in the Art of Poetry.

What is offered is a hint of self-restraint rather than a consolation; but we must feel the delicacy and the genuine sympathy with which it is offered. A further insight into the purport of the Ode is given by the statement in the 'Life of Virgil' by Donatus the grammarian, that Virgil had frequently on his tongue the saying that 'there was no virtue more adapted to man's estate than patience, and

*that by wise exercise of it a brave man could overcome
every assault of fortune.'*

WHAT shame or measure should there be in
grief for one so dear? Lead the mournful
strain, Melpomene, to whom the Sire gave with the
cithern the voice of clear tone. So then the sleep which
knows no waking lies heavy on Quintilius! When shall
Modesty find again his peer, and stainless Faith, own
sister to Justice, and naked Truth? Many a good man
may weep for his death: none may weep with more right
than thou, Virgil. Thou askest Quintilius of the gods:
but ah! thy piety has been misplaced [1]—thou didst not
trust him to them for this! What if, with a charm
beyond that of Orpheus, thou wieldedst a lyre which the
trees would listen to? Not even then might the blood
return to the hollow shade which once with his abhorred
wand Mercury, who relents not, nor opens the door of
fate for prayers, has gathered to the black fold. 'Tis
hard. But what may not be altered is made lighter by
patience.

XXVI   *Musis amicus*

Lamia and the Muses.

THE Muses' friend, sadness and fears I will
commit to the wild winds to take with them to
the Cretan sea. Who is the dreaded king of the frozen

---

[1] *Frustra pius.* This is the expression of Horace's impulsive
sympathy. The attitude of Virgil himself, the gentle and reverent
poet, towards unintelligible 'dispensations' is expressed in his
phrase *dis aliter visum,* 'the gods judged otherwise.'

coast near the North Pole, what are the fears of Tiridates [1], I care not, though all the world may care. O
thou who joyest in fresh wellsprings, twine sunny
flowers, twine a chaplet, sweet Muse, for my Lamia.
Without thee honours that I can give avail nothing.
He is one whom it well beseems thee and thy sisters
to immortalize with a new lyre and the quill of Lesbos [2].

XXVII   *Natis in usum*

The drinking-bout and the secret.

WITH cups which Nature meant for uses of joy
'tis for Thracians to fight. No such bar-
barous custom here! Defend from bloodstained brawls
Bacchus the shamefaced. Vast indeed is the interval
that divides the Mede's dagger from wine and lamps.
Quiet the impious clamour, comrades, and lie still with
elbow in the cushion. What, you wish me too to take
my share of the rough Falernian? Well, then Locrian
Megilla's brother must tell us what the wound, whose
the arrow, by which he dies a happy death. Falters
your will? On no other terms will I drink. Whoever
the love-queen that sways you, the passion need raise no
blush: your fancy is sure to be for a freeborn beauty.

---

[1] The two phrases together stand for the foreign politics of the
moment—the 'king' is Cotiso, king of the Dacians, named in
Ode 3. 8; Tiridates was the brother and rival of Phraates for the
Parthian throne.

[2] i.e. a Roman lyric poem after the model of Alcaeus.
Plectrum, translated here and elsewhere 'quill,' was, as the word
implies, an instrument used for striking the strings of the lyre.

Whatever the secret, come, trust it to my safe ear.
Ah! unhappy boy! In what a Charybdis, all the
while, you are struggling—you that deserve a better
flame! What witch, what wizard with Thessalian
enchantments, what god shall be able to set you
loose? Scarce Pegasus [1] will free you from the folds
of that three-formed Chimaera.

XXVIII   *Te maris et terrae*

Archytas, or the claims of our common humanity.

*The view adopted of this difficult Ode is that which puts
the whole of it into the mouth of the corpse of a ship-
wrecked sailor which some one has found lying on the
shore. In the first part of the Ode the dead man is
supposed to address Archytas, the Pythagorean philosopher,
whose tomb is in sight: 'You too are dead: no one
escapes—not even your great master, Pythagoras, in
spite of his belief in the transmigration of souls.' In the
second he appeals to the passer-by, taking him for a sailor
like himself, for the sake of their common humanity, to
cast on his body the three handfuls of sand that would
suffice to enable his shade to pass the Styx, which the
unburied could not do.*

THE measurer of sea and land and of the sands that
are without number [2], the tribute of a handful of
dust holds thee fast, Archytas, by the Matine shore;

---

[1] The winged horse from the back of which Bellerophon shot
at and killed the Chimaera.

[2] Archytas is addressed as the great mathematician, and there is
reference to a treatise by him called 'Psammites,' 'the book about
sand,' the point of which was the possibility of finding expression
for very large numbers.

nor aught avails it thee to have climbed in thought the
homes of the sky and ranged from end to end of the
round heaven; for thou hadst still to die.   Died Pelops'
sire too, the guest of gods, and Tithonus though he was
rapt into the sky, and Minos though he was admitted to
the secrets of Jove.   And the son of Panthus [1] is safe
in Tartarus since he descended a second time to the
lower world, for all that before (for he took down the
shield and proved his knowledge of the days of Troy)
he had yielded to black death no spoils beyond mere
sinews and skin—by thy witness no mean master he
of nature and of truth.   But one and the same night
awaits us all, and the path of death must once be trodden.
Some the Furies give to make shows for grim Mars.
The greedy sea is the destruction of those who go in
ships.   Of young and old without difference the
funerals crowd along.   There is no head that imperious
Proserpine ever feared to touch [2].   Me too the south
wind, boisterous comrade of Orion at his setting,
whelmed in Illyrian waters.   But thou, sailor, grudge
not churlishly a handful of the drifting sand to my
unburied bones and skull: so what promise soever of

[1] The 'son of Panthus' is Euphorbus, a Trojan in the Iliad.
Pythagoras is said, as a proof of his assertion that in a previous
incarnation he had been Euphorbus, to have identified the shield
of Euphorbus in an Argive temple.

[2] Cf. Virgil, Aen. 4. 698 sq., of Dido's death (Conington's
translation):

> Not yet Proserpina had shred
> The yellow ringlet from her head,
> Nor stamped upon that pallid brow
> The token of the powers below.

ill the east wind has in store for the western waves,
may Venusia's woods feel his vengeance and thou be
safe, and a stream of rich reward, whence only it can,
pour into thy lap from kindly Jove and Neptune,
guardian of sacred Tarentum! Art thou careless of
committing a crime that shall bring punishment presently
on thy innocent children? Who knows but that in
thine own person the debt of justice and a return of
contumely may be in store for thee? If I am deserted,
my prayers shall not be unavenged: and for thee, no
expiations shall release thee. Whatever be thy haste,
the delay is not long: sprinkle the dust thrice, and
thou mayst go on thy way.

XXIX   *Icci, beatis*

The scholar turning soldier. For Iccius see Epist. 1. 12.

WHAT now, Iccius! hankering after the
treasures of Araby the blest, and planning
fierce campaigns against the never-conquered chiefs of
Sabaea, and linking chains for the terrible Mede! Have
you chosen the barbarian maiden who is to wait on you
when you have slain her lover, or the court-page with
perfumed locks who is to stand as your cupbearer,
though he was trained to draw the arrows of the far East
on his father's bow? Who can say that the down-
ward streams may not flow back up the mountain side
and Tiber run the other way, when you, despite better
promises, make haste to exchange for Spanish corslets
the costly library you had gathered from far and near,

the rolls of noble Panaetius, and the whole household of Socrates[1] ?

XXX   *O Venus, regina*

Venus is bidden to the shrine which Glycera has prepared for her.

O VENUS, queen of Cnidus and of Paphos, desert Cyprus of thy choice, and transfer thy presence to the comely shrine to which Glycera bids thee with her clouds of frankincense. With thee haste too thy glowing boy, and Graces and Nymphs with kirtles free, and Youth that without thee can scarcely please, and Mercurius !

XXXI   *Quid dedicatum*

The poet's modest prayer. Written for the dedication of the great temple of Apollo on the Palatine.

WHAT prayer to Apollo on his dedication day does his poet offer ? What asks he as he pours from the bowl the libation of new wine ? Not rich Sardinia's fertile cornland ; not the well-favoured herds of hot Calabria ; not gold nor India's ivory ; not champaign through which the quiet waters of Liris' noiseless stream wear their way. Let those to whom it is fortune's gift prune luxuriant vines at Cales, and let the trader drain from goblet of gold wines for which

---

[1] Panaetius was a Stoic philosopher. The 'household of Socrates' will be the schools of philosophy which owed their impulse to his questioning.

he bartered his Syrian wares—the favourite surely he
of the gods themselves, seeing that thrice and four times
in a year he visits the Atlantic sea and comes back safe!
As for me, my fare is olives, endive, and the light mallows.
Be thy boon to me, son of Latona, both in full strength
to enjoy the goods the gods provide me (only, I pray
thee, be a sound mind among them!) and to spend an
old age neither unhonoured nor unsolaced by the cithern.

XXXII   *Poscimur: si quid*

*To his lute, when he has been asked for some poem of a
    graver cast than usual.*

THEY call for us. If ever in hour of leisure
    beneath the shade you and I have carolled together
what may live for this and many another year, come
give voice to a Latin strain[1], my lute, tuned first by
Lesbos' citizen, who though so keen in battle yet even
amid the clash of arms, or if he had moored on the
oozy shore his wave-tossed bark, would sing of Liber
and the Muses and Venus and the boy who clings to
her side, and Lycus with beauty of black eyes and black
hair. O shell, the pride of Phoebus, and welcome at
the feasts of highest Jove, sweet balm of toils, hail, and
help me whenever I duly call thee.

[1] A strain which shall be for Rome what those of Alcaeus were
for Lesbos and Greece. 'Alcaeus too,' he says, 'had his light
themes as well as his serious ones.'

XXXIII   *Albi, ne doleas*

The freaks of fancy.

Addressed (like Epist. 1. 4) *to Albius Tibullus, the poet.*

LEST you grieve, Albius, too much over thoughts of bitter-sweet Glycera[1], or drone for ever those piteous elegies, asking why a younger lover eclipses you in her faithless heart, think how Lycoris with the beautiful low forehead is in despair for love of Cyrus; Cyrus turns aside after prudish Pholoe: but sooner will she-goats pair with Apulian wolves than Pholoe stoop to an ugly lover. So Venus will have it. Her delight is to bind in malicious sport ill-matched faces and souls beneath a yoke of brass. So it happened to myself. Just when a nobler love was offering itself to me, I was fast held in sweet fetters by slave-born Myrtale, of sharper temper than the water of Hadria that breaks into bays the Calabrian shore.

XXXIV   *Parcus deorum*

An Epicurean converted by thunder in a clear sky.

A GRUDGING and infrequent worshipper of the gods, whilst I strayed, the professor of a wisdom that is folly, I have been forced now to turn my sails backward and steer again in the course which I had abandoned. For the Father of day, who commonly flashes his lightning fire through rent clouds, this time has driven through a clear sky the horses of thunder and

[1] A play on the name of Glycera, which means ‘sweet.’

winged car, whereat brute earth and wandering streams,
whereat Styx and the abhorred abode of hateful Taena-
rus and the bound of Atlas rock to their foundations.
God has power to change the place of highest and
lowest. He humbles the famous and brings forward
those that are in the shade. One sharp whistle of her
wings, and Fortune has snatched and lifted the tiara
from one head and is rejoicing to have placed it on
another.

XXXV   *O diva, gratum*

To Fortune.

*Fortune, the mistress of all human life, is invoked to bless
Caesar in his patriotic enterprises.*

O GODDESS, queen of thy loved Antium, a present Power either to lift from the dust frail mortal
man or to change to a funeral train the proud triumphal
procession, thee the poor countryman courts with
anxious prayer, thee, queen of the ocean, whoever tempts
in Bithynian bark the Carpathian sea. Thee the Dacian
fears, who stands at bay, the Scythians who fly,
and towns and peoples, and Latium that fronts the
world [1], and mothers of barbarian kings, and despots in
their purple, lest with contumelious foot thou thrust
before thee the upright pillar [2], lest the crowding popu-

[1] *Ferox* here exactly corresponds to Goldsmith's 'Pride in their
port, defiance in their eye.'

[2] The picture, a metaphorical one, is of Fortune, like Samson,
breaking down the pillar on which the whole edifice of their
estate rests.

lace arouse ' to arms ' the loiterers, ' to arms,' and break in
pieces their power. Before thee goes ever thy handmaid
Destiny, bearing in her brazen hand huge beam-nails and
wedges : nor lack there the inexorable clamp and
molten lead. Thee Hope waits on and Faith so
rare, clad in white garments, nor does she leave thee
companionless whensoever with changed garb thou
desertest in displeasure the homes of the great. But
the faithless crowd, the harlot forsworn, draw away.
When casks are drained to the dregs, friends scatter
who have no mind to take their share of the yoke.
O guard thou Caesar on his coming journey to the Britons
at the world's end ! Guard thou the new swarm of our
young warriors, the terror of Eastern quarters and of the
Indian sea ! Ah me ! the shame of guilty scars from
brothers' hands ! From what has our cruel age shrunk ?
What wickedness have we left unessayed ? From what
has this generation held its hand for fear of heaven ?
What altars has it spared ? O that thou wouldst forge
on some new anvil the blunted sword, to be drawn on
Massagetae and Arabians !

XXXVI   *Et ture et fidibus*

On the return of his friend Numida, from the Spanish war.

WITH frankincense and with music and with
duly paid blood of a young calf would I seek
the favour of the gods that watch over Numida, who
now safely returned from the furthest West has many a
kiss for one and another of dear comrades, for none

more than for his sweet Lamia as he thinks of boyhood passed under one and the same king's rule and of gown changed together. The fair day must not lack a chalk-stone to mark it—the wine-jar must be brought out and there must be no stint of it—no rest for the feet in Salian [1] fashion. Bassus to-day must equal Damalis, for all her strong head, in Thracian drinking feats. Roses must not be wanting to the feast, nor long-lived parsley nor short-lived lily.

XXXVII   *Nunc est bibendum*
The death of Cleopatra.

NOW we must drink, now beat the earth with free step: now, my comrades, 'twas the fitting time to lay on gods' cushions a feast worthy of the Salii [2]. Ere this it had been a sin to have brought out the Caecuban from our grandsires' bins, while the Queen was plotting in her frenzy ruin for the Capitol and a grave for our Empire, with her polluted crew of shamed creatures, giving the rein to the audacity of her hopes, and drunken with fortune's sweet cup. But her madness abated when scarce a ship escaped the fire; and her reason, panic-stricken after her draughts of Mareotic wine, Caesar brought back to the fears of soberness, hotly

---

[1] The *Salii* were priests of Mars. Dancing was part of their worship, and, in the general belief, the origin of their name (from *salire*.)

[2] See the last note. The Colleges of priests had a reputation for luxurious banquets; see the end of Ode 2. 14.

pursuing her as she fled from Italy, like a hawk after
tender wood-pigeons or swift hunter after hare on the
plain of snowy Haemonia, that he might consign to
chains that portent of disaster.   But she, set on a nobler
end, shrank not with womanly terror from the sword,
nor sought to win by her swift ships some shore of
hiding, but dared with calm brow to visit her ruined
palace, and was brave to handle fell serpents so that she
might drink into her veins the deadly poison, more
defiant for her resolve to die.   Yea, she grudged to the
cruel Liburnian sloops their will that she should be led,
no tame-souled woman, unqueened in a proud triumphal
procession.

XXXVIII   *Persicos odi*

Simplicity [1].

PERSIAN luxury, boy, I hate.   I have no taste
for garlands twined with linden bark.   Cease your
efforts to find where the last rose lingers.   I would
have you take no thought or trouble to add anything to
plain myrtle.   Myrtle misbeseems neither you as you
serve nor me as I drink under the trellised vine.

[1] Notice the effect of this little Ode and its subject as a relief
after the last one.

Book II

I   *Motum ex Metello*

*Addressed to C. Asinius Pollio (the Pollio of Virgil's
Fourth Eclogue) one of the most accomplished men of the
age. He wrote tragedies of which Virgil, as well as Horace,
speaks in the highest terms. He founded the first public
library at Rome out of the spoils of his Dalmatian campaign. He is said to have introduced the practice, which
had such a large place in the subsequent history of Roman
literature, of an author reading a new work to an audience.
There is probably allusion to this practice in the present Ode.
He is now writing a history of the Civil War which
Horace is eagerly looking for.*

THE stir of civil strife from the consulship of
Metellus [1] downwards, the causes of war and its
crimes and its fashions, the game of Fortune, leagues,
deadly in issue, of chief leaders, and weapons dyed in
streams of blood not expiated yet—such is the theme,
full of the die's hazard, which you take in hand, treading
over fires hidden under a treacherous crust of ashes.

For a little while yet suffer the theatres to miss the
Muse of solemn Tragedy. By-and-by when you have
set in order your tale of state affairs, you shall go back to
the great task of the buskin worthy of Athens, O chiefest
stay of the accused in their mourning and of the senate-
house at its counsels, my Pollio, to whom the laurel of

[1] B.C. 60, the year of the league between Pompey, Crassus,
and Lepidus (spoken of in the following words) to which such
fatal issues were attributed.

Dalmatian triumph has won everlasting honour. Already
we are deafened with the blast of threatening horns,
already the clarions begin to bray, already the gleam of
arms is scaring the horses till they would fain fly and the
bold front of the horsemen. Already methinks I am
hearing of mighty captains begrimed with no inglorious
dust, and all the world humbled save Cato's stubborn
soul. Juno and any other of the gods who, though
they loved the Africans, had yet retired in impotence and
left their land unavenged, now have paid, to appease
Jugurtha's spirit, the children's children of his con-
querors. What plain fattened with Latin blood bears
not witness by its barrows to fratricidal battles, and to
the sound of Hesperia's downfall which has been heard
afar by the Mede? What deep, what rivers, have
known nothing of our sad warfare? What sea is not
stained with Daunian carnage? What shore is clean
from blood of ours?

Nay, wanton Muse, leave not thy sportive themes to
take up the unfinished task of the dirge of Ceos [1].
Come away, and in the grot of Dione's daughter [2] find
some measure for a lighter quill.

II   *Nullus argento*

*The right use of wealth. The Ode is addressed to Sallustius
Crispus, but the person most in view is Proculeius, who
is named as an example of such a right use. He was
brother-in-law to Maecenas, and the story went that*

---

[1] i.e. of Simonides of Ceos.   [2] i.e. Venus.

when his brothers had lost their property in the civil war
he had divided his own portion with them.

SILVER has no shine while it is hidden in the miserly
earth, my Sallustius Crispus, no friend to bar of
gold unless it gets brightness from a wisely guided use.
Proculeius will live beyond the term of life, for the world
knows him for his heart as that of a father towards his
brothers. He shall be borne on wings that dare not
droop by fame which dies not with him. You may rule
a broader realm by taming a greedy spirit than if you
could join Libya to distant Gades and the Carthaginian
of either shore owned one master. The dread dropsy
grows by indulging itself. It never gets quit of the
thirst till the cause of the malady has been driven from
the veins and the weary weight of the water from the
blanched body. Virtue is at issue with the crowd in
striking from the roll of the happy Phraates just set
again on Cyrus' throne. She would fain unteach the
world the false use of titles. She offers to one and
one alone the kingdom and the diadem in safety and the
bay for his own—the one, whoever he be, that can
see huge treasure-heaps and never turn to look again.

III   *Aequam memento*

To Dellius.   An Epicurean Ode, to match the Stoicism
of the last one.   The thought of death as a motive for
' letting no flower of the spring pass us by.'

REMEMBER when life's path is steep to keep your
mind even, and as much when things are prosperous to keep it chastened from extravagant joy, O

Dellius, who have still to die, whether you have spent
all your days in mourning, or flung at your length on some
quiet grass-plat from holiday to holiday have made yourself happy with the oldest bin of Falernian! To what
end, think you, huge pine and white poplar love to join
in partnership their hospitable shade? Why frets the runaway water in its haste to escape down its tortuous
channel? This is the spot; bid bring wine and unguents
and the too shortlived flowers of the lovely rose, while
fortune and our years and the black threads of the three
sisters allow us. You will leave the forest pastures
that you have bought up, and town mansion, and
country house by yellow Tiber's stream, you will leave
them, and the riches piled so high will belong to an heir.
It matters nothing whether rich and born of old Inachus'
line [1], or poor and of the dregs of the people, you linger
out your span under heaven, the victim due to Orcus
who has no pity. We all are driven one road. For
all alike the lot is being shaken in the urn and, be it
sooner or later, will leap out and place us in Charon's
bark for everlasting exile.

IV   *Ne sit ancillae*

*The situation described and the irony of its treatment are as
clear as Horace meant them to be, whether we suppose
'Phocian Xanthias' to be a Greek in Roman society,
or a shadow, or a literary name for some one whom
contemporaries would recognize.*

YOUR love for a handmaid need cost you no blushes,
Phocian Xanthias. Remember that Achilles long

[1] i.e. of ancient, even mythical, ancestry.

ago for all his arrogance was won by the snowy tints of
the slave-girl Briseis. Ajax, Telamon's son, was won
by the fair form of Tecmessa, though he was lord and
she his bondwoman. The son of Atreus in the midst
of his triumph was fired by love of a captive maiden
after the barbarian hosts had gone down before the
Thessalian conqueror, and Hector's loss had given
Pergamus an easier prey to the tired Greeks. You
may be pretty sure flaxen-haired Phyllis has wealthy
parents to whom you may be proud to be son-in-law.
A royal house at the least she mourns and unkind
household gods. Believe that in her you have not
loved one of the rabble crowd; that one so constant,
one who so scorns gain, could not be born of a mother
whom you need blush for. I am heartwhole when I
praise her arms and face and shapely ankles. Fie! suspect
not one whose age has been hurrying to close its eighth
lustre.

VI   *Septimi, Gades*

*To Septimius (see Epist. 1. 9).   Praises of Tibur and
    of Tarentum.*

SEPTIMIUS, that would go with me to Gades,
and to the Cantabrian who has not learnt yet to
bear our yoke, and to the savage Syrtes where the
Moorish surf for ever boils, give me rather for the
home of my old age Tibur founded by Argive settler;
give me—for I am weary of them— some limit to wander-
ings by sea and land and to campaigning. If that place
be forbidden me by unkind destinies, then I would make

for Galaesus' stream that the skin-covered flocks love well, and the country-side where Laconian Phalantus ruled. That nook of earth's surface has a smile for me before all other places. Its honey yields not to Hymettus, and its olive rivals green Venafrum. There Jove grants long springs and mild winters; and Aulon, the favourite of fruitful Bacchus, has least reason to envy the grapes of Falernum. That is the spot, that the happy strong-hold that invites us both. There you shall drop the tributary tear on the hot ashes of your poet-friend.

VII   *O saepe mecum*

To Pompeius. A reminiscence of Philippi.

O FRIEND that many a time faced fearful odds with me when Brutus led the war, who has given you back a citizen once more to the gods of your sires and the sky of Italy? Pompeius, chiefest of my comrades, with whom many a time when the day lagged I have broken it with a drinking-bout, a garland on my hair all shining with Syrian nard! We were together when I felt the shock of Philippi and the headlong rout, my poor shield ingloriously left behind me, what time Virtue [1] broke and those who threatened high bit the dust in defeat [2]. But for me, swift Mercury

---

[1] *Virtus*, lit. 'the quality of a man,' has on it here from the context the special colour of 'Valour': but the more general sense is necessary also, for there is a reference to the dying words of Brutus, 'Poor virtue!' &c.; see Introduction, p. 10.

[2] For the bearing and sober meaning of all this see in the same place.

lifted and bore me away all trembling through the foemen in a thick mist; you the wave's downdraught in
that boiling surf carried back again into the war. So
then you must pay to Jove the bounden sacrifice, and lay
your limbs, wearied with the long warfare, safe beneath
my bay-tree, and never spare the wine-jars which have
been set apart for your use. Fill up the polished
beakers with the Massic that brings forgetfulness.
Pour unguents from large shells. Who is seeing to
wreathe a hasty garland of dewy parsley or of myrtle?
Whom will the Venus throw[1] name president of the
feast? For me, my revel shall be as wild as the
Edonians'. To have recovered a lost friend is to me
a sweet excuse for madness.

VIII   *Ulla si iuris*

An incorrigible. To Barine.

IF ever, Barine, you had felt the smallest punishment
for perjury, if you were less fair by one discoloured
tooth or by one nail, I would believe you. But in your
case, so soon as you have laid on your head the burden of
broken vows, you sparkle out much the fairer for it, and
come abroad to break the hearts of all our youth. You
find it to your profit to swear falsely by the ashes of
a mother's tomb and the silent markers of the night
with all the stars of heaven and the gods whom

---

[1] See the end of Ode I. 4. The highest throw of the four
tali, a special kind of dice, was when all four turned up the same
face.

death's icy hand touches not. Venus herself laughs, laughs, I say, at it. The Nymphs laugh for all their simplicity, and Cupid for all his fierceness, sharpening all the time his burning arrows on bloodstained whetstone. You may say too that all our youth, as they grow up, grow to be slaves to you; nor do your former ones desert the home of their perjured mistress, often as they threaten it.

IX *Non semper imbres*

A dissuasive from too much grief. To Valgius, the poet.

THE rains drop not always from the clouds on drenched fields, nor gusty storms still vex[1] the Caspian sea. The dull ice stands not stiff the whole year through, good friend Valgius, in Armenian coasts, nor north winds strain the oak forests of Garganus, and widow the ashes of their leaves. But always with your tearful strains you pursue your lost Mystes; your passion gives you no respite when the evening star rises, nor when he flies before the striding sun. Yet the old man who lived thrice the life of men did not lament all his years for his darling Antilochus : his parents and sisters in Troy did not weep always for young Troilus. Cease —it is time—weak wailings, and let us rather sing the new triumphs of Augustus, and icebound Niphates, and how the Median river added to the conquered world rolls its waters more humbly, and the Geloni ride their narrowed steppes within bounds set to them.

[1] 'The still-vex'd Bermoothes.' *The Tempest.*

X   *Rectius vives*

The golden mean.   To Licinius.

YOU will live a happier life, Licinius, by neither
steering always for the deep sea nor in cautious
dread of storms hugging too close a dangerous shore.
Whoso loves well the golden mean avoids the squalor of
a ruinous hovel and is safe, is sober and avoids the palace
that attracts envy.   It is the giant pine that rocks the
oftener in the wind, and the tall towers that come down
with the heavier fall, and the mountain summits that the
lightnings strike.   The heart that is well forearmed hopes
when times are adverse, and when they are favourable fears,
a change of fortune.   Jove brings back again the unlovely
winters.   The same hand removes them.   If things are
ill to-day, they will not therefore be so presently.   Apollo
wakes sometimes the music that lies silent in his cithern,
nor keeps his bow for ever strung.   In straits of fortune
show front of courage and endurance, and no less you
will be wise to shorten your bellying sail when the
wind follows too freely.

XI   *Quid bellicosus*

*Counsels of an Epicurean.   Addressed to Quinctius
Hirpinus.*

WHAT the war-loving Cantabrian intends [1],
what the Scythian beyond the broad barrier
of Hadria, a truce to asking, Quinctius Hirpinus !
Weary not yourself for the provision of life, which needs

[1] 'And what the Swede intend, and what the French.'   Milton,
Sonnet 21.

but little.   Youth with its smooth cheeks and grace of form is flying behind us, as grey hairs and wrinkled skin banish love and play and sleep that came at will.   Spring flowers keep not their pride unchanged for ever, nor does the blushing moon shine always with the same face. Why overtask with plans for the far future a soul that is no match for them?   Why are we not drinking, stretched beneath some tall plane-tree or, if you will, just as we are, under yonder pine, while still we may, our grey hairs perfumed with rose garlands and anointed with Assyrian nard?   Evius [1] can scatter the cares that prey on us.   Ho! a boy with speed to quench with water from the running brook the fire of Falernian cups, a boy to entice Lyde the truant from her home! Bid her come quick with her ivory lyre, her hair bound up in a neat knot like a Spartan maid.

XII   *Nolis longa ferae*

To be compared with Ode 1. 6.   Here it is Maecenas that has asked Horace to write historical Odes on Caesar's exploits.

YOU would not wish that the long war of stubborn Numantia or hard Hannibal or the Sicilian sea crimson with Punic blood should be set to the soft measures of the cithern, any more than the fell Lapithae and Hylaeus overcharged with wine and the taming by Hercules' arm of the sons of Earth, at the peril of whose onset all ancient Saturn's shining home had rocked with fear.   And so you, Maecenas, will better tell in the prose

[1] Bacchus.

of history the tale of Caesar's battles and of the necks of threatening kings dragged in triumph along our ways. For me, the sweet Muse has willed that I should tell of the singing of your queen Licymnia, her brightly shining eyes and her heart loyal to mutual love, whom it has not misbeseemed to foot it in the dance, nor to mix in the skirmish of wit, nor to link arm in sport with the maidens in trim array on the sacred day that fills Dianà's temple. You, would you take all that rich Achaemenes held, or Mygdon's wealth in fat Phrygia, or the well-stored homes of the Arabs for a single lock of your Licymnia's hair, when she bends her neck to the warm kiss, or with playful cruelty refuses what it is her pleasure more than the asker's to have snatched from her, what sometimes she is the first to snatch?

XIII   *Ille et nefasto*

The thoughts suggested by the poet's narrow escape from death by the fall of a tree on his Sabine farm.

IT was on an evil day that he planted thee, whoever he was, in the old time, and with an impious hand that he reared thee, O tree, to be the bane of his children's children and the scandal of the village. I could believe that he wrung his own father's neck and sprinkled his hearth with a guest's midnight blood. He handled poisons of Colchis, and every wicked thing that is conceived all the world over, who set thee up upon my land, thee, ill-omened bit of timber, thee so ready to fall on the head of thy innocent master.

What special danger to avoid, man is never fore-

warned from hour to hour as he need be. The Punic
sailor dreads with all his soul the Bosphorus, nor
beyond that fears the blind blows of fate from any other
quarter. The soldier dreads the arrows of the swiftly
flying Parthian, the Parthian the chains of an Italian
prison-house. But it is a blow of death not foreseen
that has snatched and will snatch away all the world
alike.

How nearly were we seeing the realm of dark Proserpine, and Aeacus on his seat of judgement, and the
separate abode of good souls, and Sappho on Aeolian
strings making plaint of the maidens of her people, and
thee, Alcaeus, with golden quill sounding in richer
strains the hardships of shipwreck, the sad hardships of
exile, hardships of war! Round both stand the shades
in wonder at strains worthy of sacred silence; but most
the tale of battles and of banished tyrants the crowd,
shouldering close, drinks greedily. What marvel, when
spellbound at that singing the hundred-headed monster
droops his black ears and the snakes twined in the
Furies' hair take rest! Nay, Prometheus too and
Pelops' sire forget their woe at the sweet sound; and
Orion cares not to pursue his lions and frightened lynxes.

XIV   *Eheu fugaces*

A sad view of the shortness of life. To Postumus.

AH me, Postumus, Postumus, the fleeting years are
slipping by, nor will piety give a moment's stay to
wrinkles and hurrying old age and death the unconquerable:—no, my friend, not if with three hecatombs for

every day that passes you should try to appease Pluto the tearless, who holds fast Geryones the triple giant and Tityos beyond the sad water, aye, the water on which we must all take the final voyage, all we that eat earth's fruits, whether we be kings or needy peasants. It will not help us to have kept clear of the bloodshed of Mars and the breakers of hoarse Hadria. It will not help us to have shunned, the autumn through, the sirocco deadly to the human frame. Cocytus we needs must visit, wandering black with sluggish stream, and Danaus' ill-famed family, and Sisyphus, son of Aeolus, sentenced to long toil. This earth we needs must leave, and house and wife of our choice; nor of the trees which you tend shall any save the hated cypresses go along with their short-lived master. An heir who will put it to a better use shall drain to the dregs the Caecuban you hoarded under a hundred padlocks, and dye the pavement with the titled wine more choice than pontiffs drink at their banquets.

XV   *Iam pauca aratro*

A complaint of the growth of private magnificence and luxury.

PILES of royal magnificence will soon leave but few acres to the plough. On every side there will be fishponds to be seen of wider extent than the Lucrine lake, and the unwedded plane-tree will drive the elm from the field [1]. Violet-beds too and myrtles and

---

[1] i.e. trees that were for ornament only would supersede those which were used as supporters for vines.

the fulness of all that pleases the nostrils will scatter
fragrance where oliveyards were fruitful for former
masters, and the laurel boughs will make a thick screen
from the sun's fiery shafts.   Not such was the lesson
taught by the example of Romulus and bearded Cato
and the rule of old days.   In their time private revenues
were small, the common stock large.   Private citizens
had no colonnades measured out with ten-foot rules
and opening to the shady north; nor did the laws
allow them to despise the chance-cut turf, though they
bade them adorn their cities at the public cost and the
temples of the gods with new-hewn stone.

XVI   *Otium divos*

To Grosphus.   (See Epist. I. 12.)
*Peace and happiness depend on ourselves, not on things
outside us.*

PEACE is the prayer of one caught in a storm on
the open Aegean, at the moment when black
clouds have hidden the moon, and the stars on which
to rely no longer shine.   Peace is the prayer of Thrace,
though it is raving mad for the battle—peace of
the Mede, though his adornment is the quiver—peace,
Grosphus, which we cannot buy for gems nor for
purple nor for gold.   For no treasures, no consul's
lictor can bid disperse the miserable insurgent crowds of
the mind and the cares that flit round panelled roofs.
A happy life is his, though his means are small, on
whose modest board shines bright the heirloom salt-
cellar, and whom no fears nor mean desires rob of

untroubled sleep. Why, with our short years, are we so bold to aim our shaft at many marks? Why change our home for lands warm with another sun? What exile from his country finds that he has left himself also behind? Care that comes of fault boards the brazen trireme, nor is outridden by the squadrons of horsemen, swifter than stag, swifter than Eurus when he drives the storm clouds. When happy for the moment, the heart should shun all thought for what is beyond: and if the cup is bitter, sweeten it with the smile of patience. No lot is happy on all sides. Achilles in his glory was taken away by an early death. His long old age wore Tithonus to a shadow. And to me perhaps time in its course will proffer something that it has denied to you. You have a hundred flocks and Sicilian kine lowing all round you. You have a whinnying mare now fit for the chariot race. You are clothed in wool twice dipped in African purple. To me Fate, who breaks not her promise, gave the modest farm, and with it the fine inspiration of the Grecian Muse, and the power to rise above the spiteful crowd.

XVII   *Cur me querelis*

The poet consoles Maecenas in illness and protests that they must die together.

WHY take heart and life from me by your complaints? It is not as the gods will, nor as I will, that you should die first, Maecenas, mighty pride and pillar of my estate. Ah! if any untimely blow snatches you away, you the half of my own life, what

care I to stay, the other half, that could not love myself
as before, that should not be myself still? That day
shall usher in the fall of us both. I have sworn a soldier's oath, and will not break it. We will go, we will
go, whensoever you shall lead the way, comrades ready
to make the last journey together. For my part, neither
the breath of fiery Chimaera nor, could he rise from his
chains, the hundred-handed Gyas shall ever tear me
from you. So wills it Justice, whose will is law, and
the Fates. Whether it be the Balance or the Scorpion
that has me under his eye, more stormy presence at the
hour of nativity, or Capricorn tyrant of the western
waters, the horoscope of us two agrees in a marvellous
manner. You the guardianship of Jove, flashing in the
face of wicked Saturn, snatched from his power, and
stayed the wings of flying fate, what time the crowded
people thrice repeated the glad applause in the theatre.
Me the tree had slain, falling on my skull, had not
Faunus lightened the blow, the guardian of Mercury's
favourites. Remember to pay the victims and the shrine
you vowed. For myself, I shall slay a humble ewe lamb.

XVIII   *Non ebur neque aureum*

*The general subject is the same as that of the fifteenth Ode—
the extravagant growth of the country houses of the rich,
with their parks and fishponds; but a new point is added,
the cruel eviction of small owners from their properties.*

NO ivory nor ceiling of gold glitters in my house:
no slabs of marble from Hymettus lie heavy on
columns quarried in utmost Africa. Nor have I found

myself, a stranger-heir, in a palace of Attalus[1]. Nor do well-born dependants weave for me Laconian purple. But good faith I have, and wit in no niggard vein, and poor as I am, the rich man seeks my friendship. I do not weary the gods for anything more, nor ask any larger boon of a powerful friend, blest abundantly in my single Sabine farm.

Day treads on the heels of day, and new moons wax to wane again. Thou at the threshold of death art contracting for marble pavements and building houses without thought of the grave, and art fain to thrust back further the shore of the sea that breaks on Baiae, not rich enough to thy taste with the coast-line of the mainland. Nay worse, thy next neighbour's landmark again and again thou tearest up, aye, and over the boundaries of thine own clients leapest in thine avarice. Out they go, wife and husband too, carrying in their bosom the household gods of their sires and their ill-clad children. Yet no mansion more certainly awaits the wealthy master than that which is traced out for him by the limit of Orcus, greedy as himself. Why seek anything further? Earth opens her arms impartially to poor man and to prince; and the henchman of Orcus did not ferry back Prometheus for all his cunning or his bribes. He has a prison-house for proud Tantalus and Tantalus' race. He hears and takes his burden from the poor man when his labours are over, when he calls for him, aye, and when he calls not.

[1] See note on p. 25.

XIX   *Bacchum in remotis*

*An imitation probably of a Greek dithyramb. The poet
imagines himself to have come on Bacchus among his
Satyrs. He describes the effects of the sight, and then
finds relief in singing the praises of the god.*

I SAW among the rocks far away Bacchus teaching
his strains (believe it, after-years!) and Nymphs
learning them, and goat-hoofed Satyrs with their
pointed ears.   Evoe! spare me, O Liber; spare me,
awful wielder of the dread thyrsus!   It is allowed me to
sing of the tireless Thyiads and the running fount of wine
and welling streams of milk, and to tell again and again
how honey dripped from the hollow wands.   It is allowed
me to sing of thy consort raised to heaven and her
crown set among the stars, and of the home of Pentheus
scattered in ruthless ruin,   and the destruction of
Thracian Lycurgus.   Thou turnest the rivers and
calmest the barbarian sea.   Thou on far hill-tops
drenched with wine bindest thy Bacchants' hair in
knots of serpents, and takest no harm.   Thou, when the
impious crew of Titans was clambering up the steep to
the Sire's throne, hurledst back Rhoetus with the lion's
claws and jaw of terror.   And yet they called thee
fitter for the dance and jest and play, and said that thou
wast not meet for fighting.   But thou wast the same
in the midst of peace and of war.   Thee Cerberus
saw, nor harmed thee, adorned with thine horn of gold,
but gently wagged his tail, and as thou wentest away
licked foot and ankles with his triple tongue.

XX   *Non usitata*

An Ode chosen for the end of a Book as containing the poet's anticipations of future fame. The best explanation of it seems to be that Horace speaks as from his own death-bed or funeral pile, his friends standing round and Maecenas as chief mourner.

ON no common wing nor weak one shall I mount into the clear air, a poet transformed, nor stay longer on earth, but leave the cities of men, victorious over envy. I shall not die, I the 'child of pauper parents [1],' I whom you are calling by name, beloved Maecenas, nor shall I be bound by the stream of Styx. Even now the skin is roughening and shrinking to my shrinking legs, and above I am changing to a white-plumed bird. The smooth feathers are growing over fingers and shoulders. Presently known more widely than Icarus who had Daedalus to help him, I shall visit the shore of the moaning Bosphorus, and the Gaetulian Syrtes, and the plain beyond the North, a bird of song. The Colchian shall come to know me, and the Dacian who would fain hide his fear of the Marsian cohorts, and the Geloni at the world's end. I shall be the study of the scholarly Spaniard, and of him who drinks the Rhone. Be there no dirge for me, for I shall not be there to bury—no dishonouring grief or lamentation. Check all cries, and let be the meaningless honours of the tomb.

[1] As his rivals named him.

Book III

I *Odi profanum*

An introduction to a new Book, and to the six stately Odes which are to give its special character to it by setting forth, more definitely than has been done, the moral and social ideals that are to be aimed at by the rule of Augustus. The present Ode paints the existing evils of society. It has lost the sense of proportion : life is spoilt by ambition, greed of wealth, and vulgar ostentation.

I HATE the uninitiate crowd and bid them avaunt. Listen all in silence ! Strains unheard before I, the Muses' hierophant, now chant to maidens and to boys.

Kings bear rule in awful majesty each over his proper flock ; over kings themselves Jove, in the glory of his triumph over the Titans, moving all creation with his nod. It may be that among his fellow men one plants his lines of vine-props over larger spaces than another ; one, when he comes down into the Campus to ask for votes, has the higher birth ; another rival brings higher character or wider fame, another a larger crowd of clients— by one and the same impartial law Doom assigns the lot of highest and humblest : every name alike is shaken in her roomy urn. The Sicilian tyrant who has a naked sword suspended over his guilty neck will find no taste of sweetness in elaborate banquets : no choir of singing birds or stringed instruments will bring back sleep to him. Sleep, soothing sleep, despises not the low-roofed homes of country folk, or the shady river-bank, or wind-fanned valley. One who desires only what is enough neither stormy sea disquiets nor the fierce violence of setting Arcturus or of the rising Kid: no vineyards battered by the hail, or promise-breaking farm, whose trees now throw the blame on the rains, now on the stars that parch the land, now on the unkind winter. The fishes feel the seas narrowed as pile after pile is flung into the deep. There is the contractor with all his staff busy sinking the stones and rubble, with the servants and the lord himself, to whom life on dry land is not worth living. But Fear and Forebodings clamber up the same way as the lord. Black Care has no awe of brazen trireme, and mounts on the horseman's pillion. But tell me, if when I am in pain neither marble of Phrygia nor the wearing of purples brighter than a star nor Falernian vines and Persian nard can make a pang easier, why should I pile up a lofty palace hall after the new fashion with gates to make the world envious? why should I exchange my Sabine valley for wealth which adds to trouble?

II *Angustam amice*

The old Roman character—endurance, courage, independence, reticence.

A BOY should learn thoroughly the lesson to bear and welcome the restraints of poverty, and should grow hardy in the sharp school of warfare. He should mount his horse and hang on the skirts of the defiant Parthians, and make them dread his spear. He should spend his life under the open heaven and amid scenes of danger. As they see him afar from the foeman's walls, the wife of some warrior king and the maiden ripe

for marriage should breathe the sigh, ah! that the prince
of her choice, all new to the battle, may not challenge
yon lion so dangerous to rouse, whose passion hurries
him through bloodshed where the slaughter is thickest!
To die for fatherland is a sweet thing and a becoming.
Death is at the heels even of the runaway, nor spares
the haunches and back of the coward and malingerer.
Virtue, which cannot know the disgrace of rejection,
shines bright with honours that have no stain on them,
nor takes nor resigns the rods at the shifting breath of
the people's pleasure. Virtue, which opens heaven to
those who have deserved something else than death,
mounts by a way denied to man, spreads her wings for
flight, and spurns the vulgar throng and the dank air
of earth.

Loyal reticence too has its reward secure. Who
has divulged the sacred secret of Ceres[1], him shall I
forbid to stand beneath the same roof or unmoor the
frail bark with me. Many a time Jupiter, when men
have slighted him, has involved the righteous with the
guilty. Rarely has Punishment, though halt of foot,
left the track of the criminal in the way before her.

III   *Iustum et tenacem*

Firmness and Justice.

*The rule of Augustus is to be resolute. That has been the
secret of success to all the heroes of civilization—to the
founders as to the refounder of the Roman state. It is
also to be moral. This qualification, which occupies the*

---

[1] The 'secret of Ceres' is a type of secrets generally.

greater part of the Ode, is put in the form of a myth. It was an antecedent condition of Roman greatness that Rome was not to be a second Troy—that is, it was to be free from Asiatic perfidy, luxury, greed. Horace is thinking, no doubt, of what Rome had escaped in avoiding what had come to be the alternative to the rule of Octavianus, viz. the rule of Antony and Cleopatra.

THE just man and firm of purpose not the heat of fellow citizens clamouring for what is wrong, nor presence of threatening tyrant can shake in his rock-like soul: nor Auster, disorderly ruler of the restless Adriatic, nor the hand of thundering Jove in its might. If the round sky should crack and fall upon him, the wreck will strike him fearless still. This was the art by which Pollux and Hercules the wanderer climbed up and won the starry stronghold, between whom Augustus takes his place and quaffs with rosy lips the nectar. It was for deserving by this, Sire Bacchus, that thy tigers drew thee, bending their stubborn necks to the yoke: it was by this that Quirinus fled safe from Acheron in the chariot of Mars, when Juno had first spoken to the gods in council this welcome word: 'Ilium, see, Ilium, one [1] whose judgement was ruinous as wicked and a strange woman [1] have turned to dust the city that was given over for vengeance to me and to chaste Minerva, people and fraudful prince alike, from the day that Laomedon failed the gods of their promised wage. To-day no longer the guest of evil fame adorns himself for the eyes of his Spartan paramour; nor has Priam's perjured

[1] Paris and Helen.

house the aid of Hector to break the onset of the
Achaeans' battle.   The war prolonged by our differences
has sunk to rest.   From this day forth my bitter
wrath alike and my hated grandson, child of the Trojan
priestess,—I will make Mars a present of both.   For
all that is between us I will permit him to enter the
bright abode, to quaff the juices of nectar, and to be
enrolled in the quiet ranks of heaven.   So long as
leagues of stormy sea roll between Ilium and Rome
the exiles may reign where they please, and be happy.
So long as herds trample on Priam's and on Paris'
tomb, and wild beasts hide their whelps there undisturbed,
the Capitol may stand in all its glory, and Rome be
mighty to impose laws at the sword's point on the
humbled Mede.   A terror far and near, she may spread
her name to furthest shores, where the sundering water
divides Europe from the African, where the swelling
Nile overflows the fields[1].   Only the gold unfound,
and so the better placed, be her fortitude shown in
despising rather than in gathering with hand that snatches
for mortal uses all that is sacred !   Whatever bounds
have been set to the world, she shall touch them with
her arms, and rejoice to go and see in what quarter fiery
heat revels unchecked, in what quarter the mists and
dews of rain.   But the destiny which I promise to
the sons of Quirinus I promise on this condition—
that never, in mistaken piety or confidence in their own
power, they should think to rebuild the homes of their
sires at Troy.   The fortunes of Troy, if under an evil

---

[1] i.e. from end to end of the Mediterranean.

star it wakes to life again, shall be repeated in a downfall as sad as the last: for I will lead the victorious host, I, the wife of Jove and his sister. Three times were the walls to arise in solid brass by Phoebus' building, three times should they perish utterly by the sword of my Argives: three times should wives in slavery mourn for slain husbands and boys.'

This will not suit a mirthful lyre. Whither away, my Muse? Cease in thy wilfulness to repeat the talk of gods and belittle high themes by thy puny strains [1].

IV *Descende caelo*

' *The rule of Augustus is to be the rule of the Muses—of moderation, refinement, literary culture. Those who still resist it are like the giants trying to overthrow the Olympian gods.*'

COME from the sky and give voice on the pipe, O queen Calliope, to a sustained melody—on the pipe, if to-day thou preferrest a higher key; if a lower, on the lyre or Apollo's cithern. Do you hear it? Or is it a delightful madness that makes sport of me? I seem to hear, and to be wandering through haunted groves into which sweet waters stray and sweet breezes.

'Tis ever so: when I was a babe as I lay on Apulian Vultur's side, a truant beyond motherly Apulia's bounds, tired out with play and sleep, the doves of legend covered me with young leaves, to be the marvel of all who dwell in high-nestling Acherontia or in the forest

---

[1] ' To dwarf high themes in puny strain.' Conington.

glades of Bantia or on the rich soil of low-lying Forentum, how it could be that I slept, my limbs kept safe from the poisonous vipers and the bears, that I was buried in a heap of sacred bay and myrtle, a brave babe, surely, and some god's special care. Aye, yours, O Muses, ever yours I am, when I am upborne to my Sabine farm in the hills, yours whether cool Praeneste or Tibur on the hillside or Baiae by the clear water has pleased my fancy. Because I was the welcome guest at your fountains and dances, neither the rout at Philippi quenched my light, nor the accursed tree[1], nor Palinurus[2] in Sicilian waters. So long as ye will be with me I will gladly face the raving Bosphorus on shipboard and the burning sands of the Syrian shore on foot. I will visit the Britons, savage though they be to strangers, and the Concan that revels in horse's blood; I will visit the quivered Geloni and the river of Scythia, and none shall lay hands on me.

Great Caesar too ye solace when, so soon as he has given retirement in the country towns to his war-wearied cohorts, he seeks repose from his own toils in your Pierian cave. Ye give him gentle counsels, and joy to further them as ye give them, kindly goddesses. We know the tale how with bolt ready to fall he swept away the impious Titans' monstrous host, who sways dull earth and windy sea, and orders under one calm rule cities of

---

[1] See Ode 2. 13.

[2] The promontory at the southern end of the gulf of Velia. The sea between Italy and the north coast of Sicily was called 'Mare Siculum.' There is no other notice of Horace's escape from shipwreck.

men and realms of gloom and gods and mortal routs.
Mighty terror had they struck to Jove's heart; that
band of youths trusting in their forest of arms, and the
brothers who strove to leave Pelion set on the top of
leafy Olympus. But what should Typhoeus avail, and
Mimas for all his strength, or what Porphyrion for his
threatening stride, what Rhoetus and Enceladus the bold
launcher of uptorn trunks, in their rush against the
sounding aegis of Pallas? On this side stood eager
Vulcan, on that matronly Juno and he that will never
lay aside the bow from his shoulder, he that in the
pure dew of Castaly bathes his loosened locks, that
haunts the thickets of Lycia and the forest of his birthplace, the god of Delos and of Patara, Apollo. Force
without mind falls by its own weight. Force under
control the gods also advance and further: but the same
powers hate strength with all crime stirring in its heart.
Be Gyas the hundred-handed witness of my judgements,
and Orion known as the assailant of the virgin Diana
who fell before her maiden arrow. Earth travails
hurled upon the monsters of her own breeding, and
bewails her children cast down to lurid Orcus. Neither
have the fire's swift flames yet eaten through Aetna
that lies on them, nor has the vulture, the warder
appointed for his crime, ever left the liver of Tityos
the incontinent. Three hundred chains hold fast the
lover Pirithous.

V   *Caelo tonantem*

*The restoration of the old military spirit. Two pictures
are contrasted—the disgrace of Carrhae and the heroism
of Regulus.*

FOR his thunder we have believed that Jove reigns
in the sky. Augustus shall prove himself a god
on earth by adding to the Empire the Britons and hateful Persians.

Has Crassus' soldier lived on, the disgraced husband
of a barbarian wife, and grown old (ah! for senate
changed and old manners overset!) in the ranks of his
new kinsmen—a Marsian or Apulian under a king, and
him a Mede, forgetful of sacred shields and name and
gown and Vesta's undying fire, while Jove's Capitol and
Rome still stand?

This was the fear that was in Regulus' far-seeing
soul when he said nay to the base conditions, and traced
from the precedent a stream of ruin for the ages to
come, if the captives were not left to die as past pity.
'My eyes have seen' he said 'standards nailed up in
Punic temples, and armour that had been·torn from
off soldiers without bloodshed. My eyes have seen
citizens, freemen, their arms turned and tied on their
backs, and gates no longer closed, and fields which
had been laid waste by our war again in tillage. Think
you the soldier bought back for gold will come home
the braver? You but add waste to disgrace. The wool
once dipped in the dye never regains its lost hue: no
more does true valour, when once it has fallen away, care
to be replaced in degenerate souls. When the doe that

you have set loose from the thick toils shall turn to
fight, then will he be a brave soldier who has trusted
himself to a treacherous foe, and he will trample on
the Carthaginian in a second campaign who has felt the
thongs on his close bound arms, the coward! and has
feared to die. The fellow has not known where to
owe his life, has confounded peace with war. Oh the
disgrace! O mighty Carthage, lifted higher for the
shameful downfall of Italy!' They tell us he put
from him, as one disfranchised, his chaste wife and little
sons, and fixed grimly on the ground his manly face,
till he could brace up the tottering resolve of the Fathers
by such counsel as speaker never gave before, and through
the ranks of his mourning friends could hasten his
departure to his glorious banishment. And yet he knew
full well what the barbarian torturer was preparing for
him. Yet he moved aside the neighbours in his way
and the people that would hinder his return, for all the
world as if he were leaving the tedious business of some
clients, the suit at last adjudged, for a journey to the
fields of Venafrum or to Spartan-built Tarentum.

VI *Delicta maiorum*
The restoration of religion and of the sacredness of marriage.

FOR the sins of your sires, albeit you had no hand
in them, you must suffer, O Roman, till you have
set up again the temples, the falling shrines of the gods
and their images foul with sooty smoke. It is because
you bow before the gods that you have Empire. From

them entirely is the beginning of it : to them look for its end.   It is the gods, because they have been forgotten, that have showered so many woes on Italy, the home of mourning.   Thrice ere now Monaeses and the horde of Pacorus have crushed our onset, for it was unhallowed, and triumph to have added to their petty necklaces spoils taken from us.   Our city, while its heart was in civil broils, the Dacian and the Ethiopian wellnigh destroyed —the one a terror for his fleet, the other more skilled in dealing arrows.   The ages, fruitful in births of evil, tainted first the marriage state, our blood, our homes. From that fountain-head flowed the stream of ruin on our country and our people.   Not from such parents sprang the young generation that dyed the sea with Punic blood and smote Pyrrhus and towering Antiochus and dread Hannibal.   They were the manly sons of countrybred soldiers, brought up to turn the soil all day with Sabine mattocks and then cut and carry firewood till a stern mother called 'enough,' when the sun was making the mountain shadows fall another way, and relieving the tired bullocks from the yoke and bringing, as his chariot departed, the welcome hour.   Destroying time ! what does it not make worse!   Our sires' age was worse than our grandsires'.   We their sons are more worthless than they; so in our turn we shall give the world a progeny yet more corrupt.

VII   *Quid fles, Asterie*

The trader's wife.

A light piece meant to relieve the seriousness of the preceding Odes. The names are Greek, the life Roman.

WHY tears, Asterie, for one whom with the first days of spring bright skies and gentle winds will bring home to you richly laden with Bithynian wares, that lover of loyal heart, your Gyges? He was driven to Oricus[1] by the south winds that follow the Goat's wild star. There through the winter nights he lies sleepless and weeping many tears. Meantime her messenger tells him how Chloe, his lovesick hostess, sighs and burns (poor heart!) with a passion which belongs only to you, and tempts him in a thousand crafty ways; recounts how Proetus was driven by the false charges of a woman, treacherous as he was credulous, to contrive for Bellerophon an untimely death as a return for his prudery; tells the story of Peleus all but done to death as he fled in his virtue from the arms of Magnesian Hippolyta, and with guileful intent recalls all stories that teach the heart to stray. But it is in vain. Deafer than the rocks of Icarus is the ear he turns to her words, to this hour unscathed. Only do you beware that your neighbour Enipeus find not too much favour in your eyes. Though there be not another as conspicuous as he on the grass of the Campus for skill in guiding a horse, nor one that swims as fast

---

[1] A port of Epirus. In winter all sailing was suspended. He has tried to cross late in the season and failed, and so is laid up at Oricus till spring.

down the Tuscan river, yet at nightfall shut up the
house, nor look into the street at the music of the
plaintive flute ; and if he call you hard-hearted again and
again, remain obdurate still.

VIII   *Martiis caelebs*
The first of March. Addressed to Maecenas.

WHAT I can be about, a bachelor [1], on the
Calends of March, what these flowers can
mean, and censer full of frankincense, and the charcoal
laid on the altar of fresh-cut turf, you are wondering,
my friend, learned though you are in the lore of either
tongue [2].   I had vowed dainty cakes and a white goat
to Liber when I was nearly brought to my death by the
stroke of the falling tree.   This day, as each year
comes round, will be a holiday.   It will remove the
pitch-covered cork from a jar which first was taught
to drink the smoke [3] when Tullus was consul.   Come,
Maecenas, a hundred toasts to your friend's preservation ! keep the lights alive till daybreak.   No clamour
here, no angry passion !   Let be a citizen's cares for
the city's weal.   Dacian Cotiso's horde is crushed :
the Mede has turned on himself in civil strife the
weapons which he and no one else will rue : the
Cantabrian, our old enemy on the Spanish shore, is our
slave, tamed at last to the chain : even the Scythians

[1] The festival of March 1 was the Matronalia.

[2] i.e. the myths, antiquities, and ritual of Greece and Rome.

[3] Wine, to mellow, was placed in an upper chamber through
which the flues passed.

have unstrung their bows and think of retiring from their steppes. Be careless for a moment : be a private citizen: spare your anxiety lest in any way the people should take harm. Take the gifts of the present hour and enjoy them. Leave more serious thoughts.

IX   *Donec gratus eram*

The reconciliation of two lovers.

HE. So long as I found favour in your sight, and no rival preferred to me laid his arms on your white neck, I bloomed in happiness greater than that of the Persian king.

SHE. So long as you felt no other and greater flame, and Lydia was not after Chloe, a proud and famous Lydia I bloomed in glory greater than that of Rome's Ilia.

HE. For me, my queen now is Thracian Chloe, learned in sweet measures and cunning with the cithern. For her I should not fear to die, if fate will spare her dear life to survive me.

SHE. For me, the lover now who kindles in me the answering flame is Calais, son of Ornytus of Thurii. For him I would suffer death twice over, if fate will spare my lad to survive me.

HE. What if the old love comes again and brings the divided pair under its yoke of brass—if flaxen-haired Chloe is shaken from her place, and the door opened to offcast Lydia ?

SHE. Though fairer than a star is he, you lighter

than a cork and more rough-tempered than Hadria in his worst mood, with you I should love to live, with you be ready to die.

X   *Extremum Tanain*

'*A serenade on a cold night.*

IF you drank the waters of Tanais at the world's end, Lyce, the wife of a stern husband, yet you might weep to expose me, stretched at your cruel doors, to the winds which inhabit there. Do you hear how the gates creak, how the trees planted within your fair palace walls groan in the blasts, how the Power of the clear sky freezes the lying snow? Lay down the pride which Venus hates, lest cord snap and wheel run back together. Your sire was a Tuscan—you are no Penelope to rebuff suitors. O lady, though neither gifts nor prayers can bend you, nor lover's face pale with violet stains, nor a husband himself hard hit by that Pierian girl, still spare your suppliants. O harder than the stiff oak, more cruel than Moorish snakes, my back will not for ever endure your threshold and the water of the sky.

XI   *Mercuri, nam te*

Lyde and the Danaids.

O MERCURY, for thou wast the Master whose apt pupil Amphion moved stones by his singing, and thou, O shell, cunning to give back sounds from seven strings, thou that hadst no voice erewhile nor power to please, now art the welcome guest at rich men's tables and in the temples of the gods, teach me some strain to which Lyde will bend her obdurate ear. Now like a three-year-old filly she frolics and frisks in the broad meadow and will let none touch her, unmated as yet and unripe for a husband. Yet thou canst lead tigers and forest trees to follow with thee, and canst stay the course of swift rivers. To thy winning wiles yielded the warder of the dreary palace, Cerberus, albeit a hundred snakes ring his Fury-like head, and foul breath and venomous foam stream from his three-tongued mouth. Aye, and Ixion and Tityos found their faces forced to a smile: the pitcher stood for a moment empty while with thy sweet music thou charmedst the Danaid maids.

Let Lyde hear those maidens' crime and famous punishment, the vessel that would never fill with the water which emptied itself through the bottom—the doom sure though late which awaits crimes even in the depth of Orcus. The impious maids—for what greater crime could they venture?—the impious maids! They ventured with ruthless steel to slay their bridegrooms. One only of the number worthy of the marriage torch, with glorious falsehood met her sire, a maid famous to all time. 'Arise' she cried to her young bridegroom, 'Arise, lest a hand thou fearest not bring thee too long a sleep! Fly from thy father-in-law and wicked sisters. Like lionesses that have found a herd of calves, they are rending each her own. I have a softer heart than they. As for me, let my sire, if he will, load me with cruel chains because I had mercy, and spared a husband in his piteous hour. Let him banish me on shipboard to the far distant Numidian's land. Go whither thy feet or the sea breezes are waiting to snatch thee away, while night favours thee and Venus. Go, and blessing go with thee, and grave on my tomb my sad tale to keep my name alive.'

XII   *Miserarum est*

The maiden's dilemma.
Neobule soliloquizes.

POOR maidens! who may neither let love have his way, nor wash away their troubles in sweet wine, under pain of fainting for fear of the lashing of an uncle's tongue[1]. Your wool-basket Cythereas' winged boy snatches away: your loom, Neobule, and all your zeal for Minerva's busy tasks the bright beauty of Lipara's Hebrus, when he comes fresh from washing his shoulders from the oil in Tiber's stream—a horseman he better than Bellerophon himself, nor to be vanquished for fault of hand in boxing or of foot in running; skilled too to hit the deer as the frightened herd flies across the open, and quick to receive on the spear-point the boar who skulks in the close thicket.

[1] An 'uncle' in a Roman's mouth represented the censorious disposition in the family circle. Cp. 'don't come the uncle over me,' Sat. 2. 3. 88.

XIII *O fons Bandusiae*

The Bandusian spring.
It is written on the eve of the ' Fontanalia.'

O SPRING of Bandusia, more brilliant than glass, right worthy of sweet wine, aye and flowers too, to-morrow shalt thou have the present of a kid whose brow now beginning to sprout with his first horns has presage of love and of battles to come. It is vain; for with his warm red blood he shall dye thy cool streams, the firstling of the wanton flock. On thee the blazing dog-star's hour of fury can lay no hand. Thou hast store of delicious coolness for the bull wearied from the plough and for the strayed sheep. Thou too shalt rank with the fountains of name, for I will be the poet to tell of the holm-oak that crowns the hollow rocks from whence thy waters leap, babbling as they go.

XIV *Herculis ritu*

The return of Augustus from Spain.

A FTER the fashion of Hercules, he of whom but now we were speaking, O people, as having gone in quest of the bay-crown which death buys—our Caesar—is coming back to his home-gods a conqueror from the Spanish shore. Let the lady [1] whose one joy is in her husband come forth and do sacrifice to the righteous gods, and the sister [2] of the glorious chief; and, adorned with the ribbons of suppliants, the mothers of maidens and of sons just returned in safety. For you,

---

[1] Livia.   [2] Octavia.

young brides and bridegrooms, a truce to words of ill-
omen. This day, to my thinking, a true holiday, shall
take from us all care. I am not the man to fear tumult
or death by violence while the world is in Caesar's
holding. Go, boy, seek perfumes and garlands, and
a jar that remembers the Marsic war [1], if by chance one
crock had the luck to escape the raids of Spartacus [1].
Bid sweet-voiced Neaera, too, to make haste and knot
her myrrh-scented hair. If any hindrance be made
by that odious porter, come away. Whitening hairs
soften tempers that loved strife and quarrelling. I should
not have borne it in my youth's hot blood when Plancus
was consul.

XV   *Uxor pauperis Ibyci*
An old woman who forgets her age.
*In its bitterness of satirical tone the Ode belongs rather to
the Epodes.*

THE wife of Ibycus, a poor man, put an end
once for all—it is full time—to your good-for-
nothing ways and scandalous employments. As you come
nearer to a not untimely grave, cease to play among the
maidens like a flying cloud over bright stars. What
becomes Pholoe well enough does not therefore beseem
you, Chloris. To storm young men's houses like a Thyiad

---

[1] The references are to the Social war, B.C. 90–88, and the Servile
war fifteen years later. It will be noticed that both the instructions
to the boy carry an allegorical suggestion: 'We have lived,
nationally and individually, out of a time of tumult and hot blood
into one of peace and good temper.' The Consulship of Plancus
was in the year of Philippi.

frenzied by the beating drum suits your daughter better than you. She cannot help gambolling like a young kid for the love of Nothus: you are an old woman. Wool from the famous flocks of Luceria is what becomes your hands—not lutes nor scarlet rose-blooms, nor wine-jars drunk to the dregs.

XVI   *Inclusam Danaen*

The power of gold, and the wisdom of moderation in respect of it.

WHEN Danae was in her prison-house, tower of brass and door of oak and surly guard of wakeful watch-dogs had fenced her well enough from nightly paramours, had not Jove and Venus laughed at Acrisius, the frightened jailor of the secluded maiden, because they knew that a path would be found safe and open when the god took the form of offered gold[1]. Gold loves to find its way through the midst of bodyguards, and breaks through stone walls with greater force than the lightning stroke. It was for gain that the Argive augur's[2] house fell, swallowed in a gulf of ruin. It was by gifts that the hero of Macedon[3] burst open city gates and sprang mines beneath rival kings. Gifts catch in their meshes fierce sea-captains.

As money grows, care follows it and the hunger for more. I am right in dreading to lift my crest into the world's sight (am I not?), Maecenas, pride of the

---

[1] *Pretium* almost = 'hard cash,' or 'a bribe.' Horace means to rationalize the legend.

[2] Amphiaraus.   [3] Philip.

knights[1]. The more a man denies to himself, the more shall he receive from heaven. I strip myself, and join the camp of those who wish for nought, and am fain to fly as a deserter from the side of the wealthy, more proud as the lord of an estate which the world despises than if the saying went of me that I hoarded in my own granaries all the produce of the sturdy Apulian's plough, while I was a pauper in the midst of wealth. A stream of pure water, and a wood a few acres broad, and crops which never break faith with me, are a happier lot than his, little as he thinks it, who glitters in the lordship of fertile Africa[2]. For all that no bees in Calabria are making honey for me, nor wine mellowing in jars at Formiae, nor thick fleeces growing in the pastures of Gaul, yet Poverty never comes to break my peace; nor if I would have more, would you refuse to give it. By narrowing my desires I may better extend my revenues than if I could lay the kingdom of Alyattes to the broad plains of Phrygia. Who ask for much always want much. Well for him to whom God has given with sparing hand, but enough!

XVII   *Aeli vetusto*

To Aelius Lamia.

AELIUS, whose nobility is from ancient Lamus[3]— (since the world has it that it was from him that

---

[1] Maecenas had deliberately remained a 'knight,' refusing the honour of the Senate.

[2] A hyperbolical expression for the owner of vast estates in the corn-growing country of N. Africa.

[3] The king of the Laestrygones in the Odyssey.

the Lamiae of old days took their name, and the whole
race of their children's children whose memory lives in
Fasti, he doubtless is the founder to whom you trace
your origin who, history tells us, first ruled the city of
Formiae and the Liris where it swims on the shores
of Marica[1], a lord of broad realms)—to-morrow a storm
descending from the East will strew the forest with
a carpet of leaves and the shore with useless seaweed,
unless my seer deceives me, the old raven who pro-
phesies rain. Whilst you may, house your wood in the
dry. To-morrow you will be treating your genius with
wine and a two months' porker, with your household
freed from their tasks.

XVIII   *Faune, Nympharum*

Hymn to Faunus.

FAUNUS, as thou pursuest the Nymphs, thy flying
loves, through the bounds of my sunny farm pass
gently to and fro without harming my little younglings, if
the tender kid falls duly in thy honour when the year is
full, nor flowing wine is wanting to the bowl, Venus'
mate, and the old altar smokes with heaped incense.
It is play for cattle of all kinds in the grassy fields when
thy day returns, the Nones of December. The village
makes holiday, and is free from toil in the meadows,
together with the idle ox. The wolf wanders among
the lambs and they are not frightened. The forest

---

[1] Marica was a nymph worshipped at Minturnae at the marshy
mouth of the Liris (Garigliano).

spreads its rustic carpet for thee.   The ditcher rejoices
to strike with his foot in triple time his old enemy, the
earth.

XIX   *Quantum distet ab Inacho*
The feast in honour of Murena, the new Augur.

HOW great the space from Inachus [1] to Codrus [1],
who feared not to die for his country's sake, and
all the pedigree of Aeacus, and the tale of the war fought
at the gates of sacred Troy, all this you are ready to
tell us.   What is the cost of a jar of Chian, who is to
find the warm water, who offers the house, and at what
hour I may hope to be quit of this Pelignian cold—on
all this you are silent.   A toast, boy, quickly to the
new moon—a toast to midnight—a toast to Murena, the
new augur!   The cups are mixed in proportions to suit
the taste, nine ladles to three, or three to nine.   The
rapt poet, votary of the Muses nine, will ask for thrice
three each time.   The sister Graces unveiled and hand
in hand will fear brawls, and forbid the further three.
Mad riot is my humour.   Why pause the blasts of the
Berecyntian pipe?   Why hangs the flute with the lyre
silent as itself?   For my part I hate grudging hands.
Fling about the roses.   Let morose Lycus hear the
riotous merriment, and our neighbour so ill matched
with old Lycus.   For you, Telephus, with your thick
glossy locks, for you, fair as the clear star of evening,
Rhode is looking, as young and as fair.   And I am
dying in slow fires for love of my Glycera.

[1] Mythical kings of Argos and Athens.

XX   *Non vides quanto*

A battle royal.

D O you not see at what peril you lay hands on
the whelps of a lioness of Gaetulia? A few
moments more and you will be flying from the unequal
combat too craven-hearted for a plunderer, when through
the jostling crowd of rivals she shall come to reclaim her
chosen Nearchus; and there shall be a battle royal whether
the prize is to fall to you rather, or to her. Meantime, while
you draw your swift arrows and she sets her formidable
teeth, he, they tell me, sits as umpire of the fray, with
the palm-branch under his bared foot, and lets the gentle
breeze play on his shoulder bespread with his scented
locks, fair as Nireus was, or he that was snatched from
many-fountained Ida.

XXI   *O nata mecum*

The power of good wine.

Addressed to a jar of wine thirty-five years old.

O BORN with me when Manlius was consul,
whether what you bring us be voice of complaint
or of mirth, whether strife and blind passionate love, or
rather, my gentle wine-jar, sleep that comes at will,—to
whatever issue the Massic grapes were gathered whose
juice you have in store,—you deserve to be disturbed on
a happy day; so come down now that Corvinus bids
broach a mellower wine. Think not that he, drenched
though he be in Socratic lore, will be Cynic enough to
despise you. They say that even old Cato, for all his

Stoic virtue, warmed his heart many a time with good
wine. You lay on the rack of gentle compulsion the wit at
other times stiff and taciturn. You make the wise confess
their secret burden of thought in the power of mirth
and freedom. You bring hope again to anxious souls,
and to the poor strength to lift up his horn. When
you have been with him he trembles at the anger neither
of crowned kings nor of armed soldiers. Liber and
Venus, if she will come with good will, and the Graces
slow to loose clasped hands, with night-long lamps shall
prolong the revel till the returning god of day routs
the stars.

XXII   *Montium custos*
The dedicated pine-tree.

GUARDIAN of mountains and woodland, O maid
who listenest to young wives in their travail, if
thrice they call thee, and snatchest them from death, O
three-formed goddess, to thee I dedicate the pine-tree
which hangs above my farm-house. As each year comes
round I shall be fain to honour it with the blood of a
young boar just dreaming of his first sidelong thrust.

XXIII   *Caelo supinas*
The modest offerings of the humble.
Phidyle's name is chosen to suit the character of a 'thrifty'
Sabine housewife.

IF at each new moon you have raised upturned hands
to heaven, country-bred Phidyle, if you have propi-
tiated the Lares with frankincense and this year's corn and

a greedy little pig, then neither shall your fruit-bearing vine feel the blighting sirocco, nor your crop the barren mildew, nor your sweet younglings the sickly time when the year yields its fruits. The victim already doomed who is now browsing among the oaks and holms on snowy Algidus, or fattening on the herbage of Alba, shall dye at its throat the axe of some pontiff. No business is it of yours to besiege the gods' goodwill with piles of slaughtered sheep, so long as you crown their little images with rosemary and a sprig of myrtle. Though your hand when it is laid on the altar has held no gift, it has softened the displeasure of the Penates with the pious offering of meal and crackling salt, and would please no more with a costly victim.

XXIV   *Intactis opulentior*
Moral reformation.
The Ode travels over much of the ground of the great Odes at the beginning of the Book.

RICHER than the virgin treasure-houses of the Arabs and of Ind with all its wealth, though you fill with the foundations of your building all the sea on Tuscan and Apulian coasts, yet if Fate have set her hand to drive into the roof-tops her adamantine nails, you will not free your soul from fear or your neck from the noose of death. Better live the Scythians on their steppes, and the hardy Getae, whose acres which rod has never measured bear their produce of corn for the free use of all, nor care they to till for more than one year, and when one has fulfilled his toil a successor

relieves him on the same terms of service. There
a woman holds her hand from harming her motherless
stepchildren, nor does a wife on the strength of her
dower overrule her husband or trust the protection of
a sleek paramour. Their ample dowry is their parents'
worth and a chastity which in the inviolate bond shrinks
from touch of any man but one. They may not sin, or
if they sin the price is death[1]. Ho! whoso will away
with impious bloodshed and the fury of civil strife, if he
shall seek to have his name written beneath statues
'the Father of our cities,' let him take heart to put
a bridle on the untamed licence of the time, and he
shall be glorious to those who are born after us:
since (ah, sin and shame!) Worth, while still safely
ours, we hate, when lifted from our sight (such is envy)
we seek for it in vain. What avail sad complainings,
if the sin be not cut off by punishment? What profit
laws, which without lives are empty, if neither the
quarter of the world which is fenced in by burning heat,
nor the side which neighbours the North wind, with
its snows caked hard on the soil, frightens away the
trader; if, though seas are rough, seamen are cunning to
overcome them; and poverty, the one great shame, bids
men dare and suffer anything, while it leaves the road
which leads up the steep of virtue? For us, for us,
either to the Capitol whither the shouting calls us and
the applauding populace, or to the nearest sea, let us
convey our gems and precious stones and gold for which
we have no use, the occasion of the chief offending, if

[1] 'They dare not sin, or if they sin they die.' Conington.

we are truly tired of our wickednesses. The first lessons of depraved desire must be obliterated, and minds now too soft must be moulded anew in a rougher school. The free-born boy knows not—he has never been taught—how to sit a horse, and is afraid to hunt; he has his lesson better if you should bid him play with the Greek hoop, or, if you like it better, with the dice which the laws forbid: what wonder when his father is busy with his perjured word fooling the partner of his fortunes and his guests, and making haste to gather wealth for an unworthy heir? This is the end of the whole matter: money is shameless. It grows and grows; but the possession is always incomplete: something is for ever wanting.

XXV   *Quo me, Bacche, rapis*
A Dithyramb.

WHITHER, O Bacchus, art thou snatching me, filled full with thee? To what woods, what caves, am I carried in the speed, swift as thought, of my new self? In what grots shall my voice be heard as I seek to set Caesar's glory as a star for ever in the skies and at the council-board of Jove? Of something notable is my song, something new, untold before by other tongue. Even as on her mountain-top the sleepless Eviad gazes in rapt astonishment over Hebrus and Thrace glittering with its snows, and Rhodope trodden by savage footsteps, so I wander where I know not, and look with delighted wonder on river-banks and solitary woodland. O Lord of Naiads and of Bacchantes,

strong to uproot the tall ash-tree, nothing small or of
mean strain, nothing of mere man's utterance [1] may I
speak. It is a rapturous peril, O Lord of the wine-press,
to follow the god who wreathes his temples with the
green vine-shoot.

XXVI   *Vixi puellis*

An imperfect farewell to old pursuits.

THOUGH that life is past, I was but now still
meet for ladies' love, and fought my battles not
without glory. Now my armour and the lute, whose campaigns are over, will hang here on yonder wall which
guards the left side of Venus of the sea. Here, here
lay down the lighted links and crowbars and bow and
arrows that threatened the doors which were shut
against me. O goddess who dwellest in happy Cyprus
and Memphis which knows nothing of Thracian snow,
lift high thy lash and give Chloe for her haughtiness
one little touch of it.

XXVII   *Impios parrae*

Galatea and Europa.

LET omen of hooting owl go with the wicked on
their way, and bitch in pup and tawny wolf
descending from the hill by Lanuvium, or mother vixen.
Their journey, ere it is well begun, let serpent break off,
darting like an arrow across their path and frightening
the ponies. For myself, if I am anxious for any one,
I shall use my augury to forestall the future: before the

[1] Conington.

raven with her prophecies of coming storm can fly
back to the stagnant pools, I will call her by my prayers
to give good omens by her voice from the east.   Go and
be happy wherever you like best, Galatea, and think
sometimes of me.   Your journey may neither pie on the
left nor restless crow forbid !   Yet you see amid what
commotion Orion is hasting to his setting.   I know
myself what the gulf of Hadria is when it blackens, and
what the treachery of Iapyx [1] for all his clear skies.
May the wives and sons of our enemies feel the dark
movements of the rising south, and the blackening
water's roaring, and the shores quivering under the lashing surf !

It was even so that Europa laid trustfully her snowy
side on the cheating bull's back—even so that she saw
the water seething with monsters, and the treachery
when she was in the thick of it, and paled at the sight,
for all her boldness.   A moment ago in the meadows
hunting for flowers and making the garland she had
promised the Nymphs—now in the darkling night she
saw nought but stars and heaving water.   So soon as
she set foot on Crete, the lordly land of a hundred cities,
' My father ! ' she cried, ' ah ! name a daughter has left
behind her ! ah ! childly duty by madness overborne !
Whence, whither am I come ?   Too light a single
death for maiden's faults !   Am I awake and weeping
for a deed shamefully done ?   Or am I innocent, and is
it an empty phantasy that brings a dream from the ivory

[1] See Od. 1. 3 : the wind most looked for by those who crossed
from Brundisium to Greece.

gate ? Whether was it better, to be traversing the weary
waves or plucking the fresh flowers ? Ah ! if one
would give to my anger now the accursed bull, I would
use all my strength to wound him with steel and break
his horns, the monster but now caressed so fondly.
'Twas shameless to leave my father's home. 'Tis
shameless to keep death waiting. Oh, of all the gods
if one hears me, that I might wander naked among lions !
Before the marring hand of decay touch my comely
cheeks and the sap withers from the delicate prey, I
would my beauty were food for tigers. "Worthless
Europa," my father's voice rings in my ear, though he is
far away : "why delay you to die ? It is easy from
yon ash with the kirtle, that has happily come with you,
to let swing your neck and break it. Or if the cliff and
its rocks set sharp for death please you better, come,
trust yourself to the speed of the storm-wind—unless
you choose rather to card your portion of wool for a
mistress, you the child of kings, and live a concubine at
the mercy of a barbarian queen ! "' As she wailed,
Venus stood by her, with a smile of treachery on her
face, and her son with his bow unstrung. Presently
when she had enough of play, 'Hold,' she cried, 'from
anger and hot words of strife ; for the hated bull shall
give thee once again his horns to tear at thy will.
Thou knowest not that thou art the wedded wife of
almighty Jove. Let be thy sobs : learn to bear wisely
thy mighty fortune. Half a world shall bear thy name.'

XXVIII   *Festo quid potius die*
The Neptunalia.

WHAT better could I do on Neptune's holiday?
Quick, Lyde, bring out from its secret bin
the Caecuban, and push the siege of our deep-entrenched
seriousness.   You see the noonday past its full, and yet
as though the flying day were standing still you spare
to snatch down from the store-room that loitering jar
of Bibulus' consulship.   We will sing in turns—of
Neptune and the Nereids' sea-green tresses.   To your
curved lyre you shall sing in answer of Latona and the
arrows of flying Cynthia.   Ere our singing cease we
will remember her who rules Cnidus and the shining
Cyclades and visits Paphos on her car of swans.
Night too shall find place in the hymn which is her due.

XXIX   *Tyrrhena regum*
To Maecenas.

Written, as much as the following Ode, for its place at the
end of the three Books.   It repeats their dedication to
Maecenas, and the expression, the more graceful that it
is indirect, of affectionate admiration.   And it sums up
with force and dignity the philosophy of life, such as it is,
which under all the irony of form has been at the heart
of the Odes.   English readers will be familiar with
Dryden's noble paraphrase of the Ode.

HEIR of Tuscan kings, all has long been ready for
you here—the mellow wine in a jar never tipped
yet, with rose-blooms and the oil of the balm-nut pressed
specially for your hair.   The delay is on your side—snatch
yourself from it.   Gaze not for ever dreamily on moist

Tibur and the upland fields of Aefula and the ridge of
the parricide Telegonus. Give the slip to the abundance that only tires, the massy pile that nears the clouds
on high : abate for a time your admiration for the smoke
and the grandeur and the noise which make the happiness of Rome. Often a change of life has a zest for the
rich, and neatly served suppers under the humble roof of
the poor, though there be no hangings or purple tapestry,
have rubbed wrinkles from the brow of care. Now
Andromeda's sire shows brightly forth the fire he hid :
now Procyon rages and the sign of the furious Lion,
as the sun brings back the days of drought. Now the
shepherd makes for the shade and the stream, with his
fainting flock, and for the thickets of uncouth Silvanus,
and not a breath of wandering wind stirs the quiet of
the river-bank. You only are still full of thought what
constitution best fits the State, of anxious fears for the
City, what the Seres may have in store for us, and
Bactra, Cyrus' old realm, and Tanais which has quarrels
of its own.

In his good providence God whelms in the darkness
of night the issues of the coming time, and laughs if
mortal man frets himself beyond the just limit. What
is at your hand be mindful to order with equal mind.
All else is like the course of a river, that now runs peace-
fully between its banks to the Tuscan sea ; presently is
whirling wave-worn boulders and uptorn trunks and cattle
and homesteads all together amid the echoing of the hills
and neighbouring forests, when a wild deluge wakes to
frenzy quiet streams. He will through life be master

of himself and a happy man who from day to day can have said, 'I have lived: to-morrow the Sire may fill the sky with black clouds or with cloudless sunshine; he will not undo aught that is left behind me, nor change or make as though it had not been aught that the hour, fast as it flies, has once brought.' Fortune, who joys in her cruel business, nor ever tires of her tyrannous sport, shifts from one to another her fickle honours, now bounteous to one, now to some one else. While she stays I praise her: if she shakes her pinions for flight I return all she gave, and wrap myself in my own virtue, and seek the hand of honest, undowered Poverty. It is not my way, if my mast groan in African storm-winds, to fall to abject prayer and bargain in vows that my wares of Cyprus or Tyre may not add their wealth to the greedy sea. In that hour, safe in the guardianship of my two-oared shallop, I shall be carried through the turmoil of the Aegean by the wind and Pollux, the twin brother.

XXX   *Exegi monumentum*
The Epilogue.

MY work is done, the memorial more enduring than brass and loftier than the kingly building of the pyramids—something that neither the corroding rain nor the wild rage of Aquilo can ever destroy, nor the numberless succession of years and flight of ages. I shall not all die: a large part of me will escape the Funeral-queen. I shall grow for ever, fresh in the praise of the aftertime, as long as pontiff with silent maid shall climb the Capitol. I shall be spoken of as one who, where Aufidus is rough and loud, where Daunus in a thirsty land ruled over his rustic tribes, rose from humility to greatness, and was first to find a home among Italian measures for the lyric poetry of Aeolia. Assume the proud place thy deserts have won, and crown, of thy grace, my locks, Melpomene, with the Delphic bay.

Book IV

[It will be remembered that this Book was added after a considerable interval, during which Horace had laid aside lyric composition. Several attempts had been made, as we gather from Epist. 1. 1 and 2. 2, to induce him to resume it. In B.C. 17 he was appointed to write the hymn for the Secular Games, with which the sixth Ode of this Book connects itself; and eventually he yielded to the personal desire of Augustus that he should celebrate the victories of his stepsons, Tiberius and Drusus, which occupy the fourth and fourteenth Odes. To these are added Odes 5 and 15, to give Augustus himself his proper place.

The first three Odes form together an apologetic prelude to the Book.]

I   *Intermissa, Venus*

Two purposes are on the face of the Ode: (1) to form a link with the preceding Books by the reference back both to 1. 19, the first of the love-poems, and to 3. 20, in which Horace had declared his love-campaigns to be at an end; (2) to suggest with characteristic irony that the purpose of the resumption of lyric poetry is only to write more love-songs.

WHAT, Venus, dost thou wake again the war after long truce? Spare me, I pray, spare me. I am other than I was when poor Cinara [1] was queen.

[1] Cinara is the one female name of Horace's Odes to which something more than a shadowy existence seems to be

Try no more, 'imperious mother of sweet loves[1],' to bend to thy soft behests a heart which nigh on ten lustres[2] have hardened. Get thee gone whither the coaxing prayers of young voices are calling thee back. It will be more timely to lead the revel on thy winged car of lustrous swans to the home of Paulus Maximus, if thou seekest to fire a fitting heart. For he is high-born, and he is handsome, and no tongue-tied champion of trembling prisoners at the bar. The young hero of a hundred accomplishments, he will bear far abroad the standards of thy warfare. And so soon as he has laughed triumphant over the gifts of a large-handed rival, he will make thee stand in marble near the lakes of Alba under a roof-tree of cedar-wood. There thy nostrils shall drink clouds of frankincense, and thou shalt delight thyself with the mingled strains of lyre and Berecyntian flute and pipe besides. There twice each day boys and tender maids shall praise thy deity and beat the ground with their white feet in triple measure after Salian[3] wont. For me, no fond hope of answering heart, no drinking-bout has charms, nor fresh flowers to bind my brow. But ha! what is this? Why, Ligurine, why steals once and again the tear down my cheeks? why, when I would speak, falters in awkward silence my voice of ready utterance?

given by his references to it in his other writings (Epist. 1. 7 and 14).

[1] A line purposely repeated from the beginning of Od. 1. 19.
[2] Horace was fifty in the December of B.C. 15.
[3] See note on p. 58.

In dreams of the night now I have caught thee, now I am following thee as thou fliest thee down the grassy Campus Martius, hard heart, thee down the rolling river.

II *Pindarum quisquis*

To Iulus Antonius, son of the Triumvir, and eventually the husband of Octavia, the niece of Augustus.
Like 1. 6 and 2. 12 it is an Ode in professed deprecation of the task set him. 'Not I, but you. I am no Pindar to write Odes about great victories. I can only shout with the crowd.'

WHOSO would rival Pindar, Iulus, is poising himself on wings that some Daedalus has fastened for him with wax, and will give his name to some glassy sea. Like a stream down a mountain-side, when storms have swollen it above its wonted banks, Pindar boils and rushes in a flood of deep-mouthed utterance. Apollo's bay must be his, whether[1] through the daring dithyramb he roll his novel words as he pours along in lawless rhythms; or sing of gods and kings, the children of gods, by whose hands fell the Centaurs in well-earned death, fell the terrors of the fiery Chimaera; or tell of those whom the palm of Elis sends to their home very denizens of heaven, boxer or charioteer, and so give them a gift better than a hundred statues; or bewail the young husband snatched from his weeping bride, and lift to the stars strength and courage and life all golden, which he grudges to see the prey of black Orcus. Strong are the winds, Antonius,

[1] The following lines characterize the different kinds of Pindar's poems.

that upbear the swan of Dirce [1] as oft as he soars into the cloudy spaces.   For me, after the fashion of a Matine bee, that through incessant toil makes boot [2] upon the fragrant thyme about the woods and river-banks of streaming Tibur, I humbly build my laborious verse. You, a poet of loftier quill, shall sing of Caesar by-and-by when he shall drag along the sacred hill the fierce Sygambri, his brow decked with the well-earned bay-leaf. No greater or better gift than him have the fates and the good gods given to the world—no, nor will give, even though the times go back to the gold of the first age. You shall sing of the days of joy, Rome's common holiday, in honour of the return of the gallant Augustus granted to our prayers, and the courts empty of suitors. Then my voice too, if aught I can say merits hearing, shall add its part ungrudgingly, and 'O fair, O glorious day !' I will sing, in the delight of having received Caesar home again.   And for you, as you go in the procession ('Ho! Triumph!' again and again, 'Ho! Triumph!' will we cry, the whole city, as we offer frankincense to the kind gods), ten bulls and as many cows will be your discharge; mine a tender calf just weaned which is fattening in the rich pastures to pay my vow, on whose brow is the resemblance of the crescent brightness of the moon on her third day's rising, there, where the mark is, snowy white to the eye, the rest all red.

[1] The famous fountain at Thebes, Pindar's home.
[2]   the honey-bees . . .
    Make boot upon the summer's velvet buds.
                                Henry V, Act I. Sc. 2.

III   *Quem tu, Melpomene*

The Poet's calling.

Confidence is represented as returning to him in the thought of his poetic calling and its recognition in Rome.

ON whom thou, Melpomene, hast cast once for all in his birth-hour thy kindly glance, for him no Isthmian training shall win renown as a boxer, no spirited horse shall drag him in Grecian car of victory, nor war's business display him crowned with Apollo's bay to the Capitol as having crushed the vaunting threats of kings. But the waters that flow past green Tibur and the tangled tresses of the forest shall mould him to win a name in Aeolian song. The sons of Rome, the queen of cities, deign to place me among the sweet choirs of poets ; and now less fiercely bites the tooth of envy. O Pierian maid, who rulest the dulcet sounds of the golden shell, O lady, that couldst give, if so thou pleasedst, to the dumb fishes the notes of the swan, it is all of thy free gift that the finger of the passer-by points me out as the tuner of a Roman lyre. Breath of song and power to please, if please I may, are alike of thee.

IV   *Qualem ministrum*

The Victory of Drusus.

Drusus, the younger of the two sons of Livia by her former husband, Ti. Claudius Nero, had defeated the tribes in the neighbourhood of the Brenner pass (see Merivale's Roman Empire, vol. iv, ch. 35). Horace attributes his prowess to the blood of the Neros and to

*his bringing up in the home of Augustus. The glory of
the house of Nero is summed up in the victory won by
C. Claudius Nero over Hasdrubal at the river Metaurus
in* B.C. 207, *the turning-point of the second Punic war.*

SUCH as the winged bearer of the thunderbolt, to
whom the king of the gods granted to be king over
the fowls of the air when on golden-haired Ganymede he
had proved him faithful; whom erewhile his young
blood and the force of his race drove forth from the
eyrie when yet he knew not life's labours, then the
spring-breezes, when the storms had cleared, teach his
timorous wings their first strange efforts; soon with
lightning-rush he is swooping as a foe on the unresisting
sheepfolds; presently his thirst for the feast and the
fight is driving him on the serpents who will struggle
hard—or such as the lion fresh weaned from his tawny
dam whom a kid, her whole heart in the rich pasture,
looks up and sees, a moment before she dies by his
unfleshed tooth—just such seemed Drusus to the
Vindelici of Raetia when they saw him waging war
beneath their Alpine heights. Whence comes through
immemorial time the custom that arms their hands in
war with Amazonian axe, I have not found time to
inquire—man cannot know all things. Be that as it
may, their hosts, long victorious over all the country-
side, were vanquished in their turn by the young hero's
skill, and learned to know what is the force of a mind
and heart duly nurtured in heaven-blest homes, of the
fatherly care of an Augustus for young Neros.

Gallant sons spring from the gallant and good.   Good

blood tells even in bullocks and horses, nor do bold eagles breed the timid dove. But teaching quickens the native power and right training fortifies the heart. If ever it be that the public manners fail, faults discredit even the nobly born. How great thy debt, O Rome, to the house of Nero, witness Metaurus' stream and routed Hasdrubal and that fair day which scattered the darkness of Latium, the first day that smiled with Victory's cheer from the time when the dread African first rode his foray through the towns of Italy like flame through a pine-forest or the east wind across Sicilian waters. From this day forth the young strength of Rome grew in ever more victorious efforts, and the shrines desolated by the sacrilege of Punic invaders saw their gods once more on their pedestals ; till at last false Hannibal outspake, 'Weak deer, the doomed prey of robber wolves, we venture to assail those from whom to steal away were a rare triumph. That race which, sprung from the fires of Ilium, through the tossing of Tuscan waters bore safely its sacred treasures, its sons and aged sires, home to Ausonian cities, like the holm-oak shorn by ruthless axes on Algidus where black leaves grow thick, through loss, through havoc, from the very edge of the steel draws new strength and heart. Not more persistently, when he lopped its limbs, the Hydra grew sound again in face of Hercules, chafing at the foil[1] ; not stranger portent did the soil of Colchis breed, or Thebes in Echion's day. Plunge it in the depth—it comes forth the fairer. Close with it—mid loud applause it will lay

---

[1] From Conington.

low its conqueror, though his powers were still unbroken, and will wage a war for wives to tell of. Not to-day can I send proud messages home to Carthage. Fallen, fallen is all our hope and the fortune of our name in the death of Hasdrubal.'

There is nothing that Claudian hands cannot perform, when Jove with his kindly blessing protects them, and a wise providence guides their way through the rocky channels of war.

V   *Divis orte bonis*

The absence of Augustus.

Augustus left Rome in the autumn of B.C. 16 in consequence of a serious defeat of Lollius by the Sygambri, a tribe living on the Rhine. The barbarians on the approach of reinforcements made peace, but Augustus remained in Gaul till the summer of B.C. 13.

O BORN in an hour when the gods were good, best guardian of the race of Romulus, thou art absent already too long. Thou didst promise the sacred conclave of the Fathers a speedy return—keep now thy promise. Give back the light, dear chief, to thy country. For, like spring-tide, when thy presence has shone upon thy people the days pass more pleasantly and the suns beam more brightly. As a mother for her boy whom the south wind's unkindly blast keeps lingering beyond the waters of the Carpathian sea far from his dear home past the term of his yearly absence—with vows and omens asked and prayer she calls for him, nor can shift her eyes from the windings of the shore—so for Caesar longs his country, smitten with loyal yearning. For in conscious safety now the ox stalks about the countryside, the countryside that Ceres nurtures and kindly Plenty. Sailors fly to and fro across the seas now at peace. Faith shrinks from breath of blame. Purity of home is never stained by deeds of shame. Habit and law have vanquished the taint of vice. The sire's likeness in her babe's face is the mother's glory. Punishment follows close on the heels of crime. Who now would fear Parthian or frozen Scythian, who the teeming brood of rough German forests, while Caesar still is ours, or give a thought to fierce Hiberia's warriors? On his own hillside each sees the sun down as he is wedding the vine to long-widowed trees, and then goes home to the wine-cup with glad heart, and when the cloth is drawn invokes thy name among the gods. To thee he prays often, to thee pours the libation, ranks thy power divine among the gods of his hearth, even as Greece in her pious memory of Castor and mighty Hercules. Long be the happy time of holiday, dear chief, that thou grantest to Italy. So say we in the sober morning before the day begins, and say again at mellow evening when the sun has sunk under the sea.

VI   *Dive, quem proles*

To Apollo.

An invocation to the God of Greek poetry, the God to whom Rome owed her existence, to help the poet in the composition of the hymn which he has been selected to prepare for the Secular Games.

O GOD, whose hand Niobe's children knew in the punishment of a vaunting tongue, and Tityos the ravisher, and Phthian Achilles, stayed in the moment of victory over lofty Troy; a greater warrior than all else, but no match for thee, though he was the son of the sea-nymph Thetis and made the Dardan towers quake before the repeated onset of his terrible spear. Like a pine smitten by the biting steel, or a cypress under the force of the east wind, he bowed and fell at all his length and laid his neck in Trojan dust. He was not one to lurk within a horse that falsely feigned Minerva's rites, and surprise the Trojans in the midst of foolish merrymaking and Priam's palace when it was blithe with dancing. His foes were taken in open day; but his heavy hand (ah, horror!) had burnt in Grecian flames lisping children and the babe yet in its mother's womb, had not the Sire of gods, won by thy voice and kindly Venus, pledged to Aeneas walls to be built under happier omens. Oh, thou that taughtest Thalia her sweet voice and lyric music, Phoebus, that lavest thy locks in Xanthus' river, protect the honour of a Daunian Muse, O young Agyieus[1]! Yes—'tis Phoebus that has given me the breath and the art of song and the poet's name. O flower of maidens and boys sprung from noble sires, wards of the Delian goddess who stays with her bow the flying lynxes and the deer, come, keep the measure of Lesbos to the time of my thumb, singing in due course of Latona's boy, in due course of her who lights the night with crescent lamp, that prospers the fruits

[1] A Greek name of Apollo.

of earth and speeds the rolling months on their way.
Some day, when you are a wedded wife, you shall say,
'I too to please the gods, when the Secular holiday
came round, performed the hymn and learned well the
measure of the poet Horace.'

VII   *Diffugere nives*

Spring lessons.
The line of thought is the same as that of Od. 1. 4.

THE snows have scattered and fled; already the
grass comes again in the fields and the leaves on
the trees.   Change passes on the dry land, and the rivers
dwindle and flow within their banks.   The Grace with
the Nymphs and her own twin sisters ventures unrobed
to lead the dance.   That you hope for nothing to last
for ever, is the lesson of the revolving year and of the
flight of time which snatches from us the sunny days.
Cold softens before the Zephyrs.   Advancing summer
tramples spring before it, to die itself so soon as apple-
laden autumn has emptied its store of fruits: and then
dull winter rolls round again.   Yet change and loss
in the heavens the swift moons make up again.   For us,
when we have descended where is father Aeneas, where
are rich old Tullus and Ancus, we are but some dust
and a shadow.   Who knows whether the gods' will be
to add to-morrow's hours to the sum as it stands to-day?
That will all of it escape the greedy hands of your heir
which you have given to your own dear soul.   When
once you are dead and Minos has passed on you the
doom of his august tribunal, no high blood, Torquatus,

no eloquent tongue nor piety, will reinstate you. For neither does Diana set free from the darkness of Hades Hippolytus the chaste, nor can Theseus break the chains of Lethe from off his dear Pirithous.

VIII   *Donarem pateras*

The ' deathless powers ' that ' to verse belong.'

I WOULD send to my friends goblets and nice bronzes, Censorinus, to suit their taste, I would send tripods, the prizes of Greek heroes, and you should have the best of my presents, if I were rich, you understand, in works of art such as Parrhasius gave to the world, or Scopas, masters in representing now a man, now a god, the one of them in marble, the other in liquid colours. But my force lies not there; nor are yours the circumstances or the taste that you should desire such dainty gifts. Verse is what you love, and verse is what I can offer, and tell you the value of the gift. Not marbles engraved with inscriptions by order of the State, which give breath of life to dead captains of good service —a second breath of life—not the swift flight of Hannibal and his threats flung back in his teeth, not the flames of sacrilegious Carthage, show forth more brilliantly the praises of him who came home with a name won from the conquest of Africa, than do the muses of Calabria. If the poet's page should be silent of your good deeds you will miss your reward. What should we know of the son of Ilia and Mars, if churlish silence shrouded Romulus' great deeds? 'Tis by his virtue— yes, and by the goodwill and by the tongue oi poets, to whom that power belongs—that Aeacus was rescued from the waves of Styx, and blest in the happy islands. The hero who is worthy of her praise the Muse will not let die,—the Muse makes happy in heaven. That is how the strenuous Hercules attained his wish and is a guest at Jove's table; how the sons of Tyndarus, as a star of light, rescue shattered barks from the depths of the sea; how Liber, his temples wreathed with the green vine-shoot, guides his votaries to happy issues.

IX   *Ne forte credas*

What the lyric poet can and will do for Lollius.

THAT you believe not, as mayhap you do, the words must needs die which, by art till now a secret, I speak, whose birthplace was by far-sounding Aufidus, words to be wedded to the lyre-strings, bethink you that, if Maeonian Homer holds the first place, this does not mean that Pindar's verse is lost to sight or that of Ceos [1], Alcaeus' threatening or Stesichorus' stately Muse. Nor has time blotted out a playful line of Anacreon's. Still breathes the love, still lives the passion, which were told as secrets to her strings [2] by the Aeolian maid. Homer's Helen is not the only woman that was ever fired by a lover's smooth locks, or admired gold-bespangled robes and kinglike adornments and train of followers. Nor was Teucer the first to send arrows straight from Cretan bow. Not once only was an Ilium besieged. Huge Idomeneus and

---

[1] i.e. of Simonides.   [2] From Conington.

Sthenelus were not the only heroes who ever fought battles worth the Muse's telling. Hector the defiant and keen Deiphobus were not the first to meet rough blows in defence of chaste wife and boys. Gallant heroes lived before Agamemnon, not a few: but on all alike, unwept and unknown, eternal night lies heavy because they lack a sacred poet. When they are in the grave the difference is little between cowardice and valour, if they be hidden. I do not mean to leave you in silence unadorned by my pages, Lollius, nor to allow all your strenuous life to be the prey of envious oblivion. A soul you have of foresight, that holds its balance in times of success and of doubt, quick to punish greed and wrong, and proof against the charms of money which tempts all the world——the soul of one who has been consul not in a single year, but so often as, on a judgement-seat, generous and leal he has set honour before expediency, has flung back with lofty mien the gifts of the guilty, has carried his arms victoriously through opposing hosts. It is not the possessor of many things whom you will rightly call happy. The name of the happy man is claimed more justly by him who has learnt the art wisely to use what the gods give, and who can endure the hardships of poverty, who dreads disgrace as something worse than death. He will not fear to die for the friends he loves, or for his country.

XI   *Est mihi nonum*

Maecenas' birthday.

This is the only recognition of Maecenas in this Book.
The old regard is still existent, but Maecenas is no longer
the prominent figure he was when the first three Books
were written.   He is out of favour with Augustus, and
Horace has a more independent position.

HERE I have a jarful of Alban more than
nine years old; here in my garden, Phyllis, is
parsley for twining garlands, is good store of ivy, to be
the bright adornment of your knotted hair.   The house
gleams cheerily with silver: the altar ready bound with
sacred boughs waits eagerly for the sprinkling of the
slain lamb's blood.   All the household is astir, the
mixed throng of boys and girls is bustling to and fro.
The very flame is in a tremble as it rolls up in whirling
column of dingy smoke.   That you may understand all
this time to what merrymaking it is that you are bidden,
know that you must keep the Ides, the day that halves
sea-born Venus' month of April, by good right to me
a holiday and more sacred almost than my own birthday,
for that from its shining my Maecenas dates the years
as they add themselves to his tale.   Telephus, on
whom your heart is set, is no youth of your degree
and another has forestalled you, one rich and of
manners free, and holds him fast in chains which
he hugs.   Scorched Phaethon's doom should scare us
from too greedy day-dreams; and winged Pegasus,
that could not brook Bellerophon his earth-born rider,
gives stern lesson that you pursue always what befits

you, and, by counting it sin to hope beyond what is allowed, avoid an ill match. Come now, last of my loves—for never again shall my heart take fire at woman's face—come, learn well the melody which thy sweet voice is to render. Black care will grow less as we sing.

XII   *Iam veris comites*

An invitation to Vergilius (not the poet).

NOW spring's companions that make calm the sea, the breezes from Thrace, are swelling the sails : the meadows no more are hard frozen nor the streams roaring, swollen with winter's snow. Now lays her nest, making sad moan for Itys, the unhappy bird, the eternal shame of Cecrops' palace for her ill revenge on barbarian princes' crime. Now they that tend the fattening sheep in the soft young grass discourse music on the pipe, and pleasure the god who loves the flocks and black hills of Arcadia. The year has brought the thirsty time, Vergilius ; but if you fain would quaff Liber's juices from the press of Cales, O client of noble youths, you shall earn your wine with some nard. One little box of nard shall coax forth a jar which now lies resting in the Sulpician stores, the generous giver of new hopes and the power that washes all their bitterness out of cares. If such delights make your mouth water, come quick with the wares that you are to bring. I have no mind to let you see the bottom of my cups and not pay your share, as if I were a rich host in a house of abundance. Away with excuses and covetous thoughts : now while you may, remember the black funeral fires, and mix with your sage counsels some brief folly.   In due place to forget one's wisdom is sweet.

XIII   *Audivere, Lyce*

Revenge.

Like the first Ode, this is a sequel, taking up the imagined story of 3. 10 in which he complained of Lyce's high airs.   This may exempt us from the necessity of supposing that the situation is more than an imaginary one.

THE gods have heard, Lyce—Lyce, the gods have heard my prayers.   You are turning into an old woman and yet you are wishing to be thought beautiful, and you play and you drink without shame, and in your cups you appeal with your trembling ditties to the inattentive ears of the young god of love.   His sentry-post is on the fair cheeks of Chia, still in the green leaf and skilled with the cittern.   Aye he flies without ruth past the sere oak trees: he will have nothing to say to you, disfigured by the blackened teeth, by the wrinkles and snows of age.   No purple gauzes of Cos, no precious jewels bring back the days of old, when once flying time has prisoned them in calendars which all can read.   Whither has fled the charm, whither—ah me!—the tints, whither the graceful movement?   What have you left of her, of her whom I remember, in whose breath was love, who had stolen me from myself, that face, next only to Cinara, divine, so well known, so full of winsome wiles?   But to Cinara the fates gave short years, while Lyce they meant to keep long alive, to match the times of an ancient crow, that young men with their hearts still warm might gaze and laugh at the torch burnt down into a heap of ashes.

XIV   *Quae cura patrum*
The victorious campaign of Tiberius.

HOW can Senate or Roman people by largess of honours ample enough immortalize in graven titles or records for all time virtues such as thine, Augustus—O thou, in all the space over which the sun lights coasts where men can dwell, greatest of princes! What thy might in war, the Vindelici have just learnt, who had never known the rule of Latium before. For thine was the soldiery with which Drusus by his vigorous onset repaid with heavy interest the Genauni, that turbulent race, and the fleet Breuni, and flung their fortresses down their terrible Alpine heights. Soon the elder of the Nero brothers joined shock of battle, and under a happy star drove in rout the giant Rhaetians. A brave sight he was in Mars' contests, for the mighty earthquake-shocks with which he shook that line of breasts that offered themselves so readily to a freeman's death (much as Auster drives, but cannot tame, the waves, what time the dancing Pleiads are shining through torn clouds), unwearied in assailing the foeman's squadrons and setting his foaming charger through the midst of the fires. Even so rolls down bull-like Aufidus, who skirts the realm of Apulian Daunus, when he grows furious and plans dread deluge for the well-tilled lowlands, as Claudius by his devastating onset laid in ruins the steel-clad lines, mowing down the first rank and the last, like corn before the reaper, a conqueror without cost of blood. And it was thou that gavest the force, that gavest the plan, and gods all thine own. Aye, it was for thee that on the self-same day that Alexandria on her knees had opened to thee her port and empty palaces, prosperous fortune, five lustres after, crowned the war with success and claimed one more glory, one envied laurel to thy past campaigns. To thee the Cantabrian who could never be tamed before, and Mede and Indian, to thee the Scythian of the steppe, look with awe. O present guardian of Italy and of Rome, the queen of the world, thee Nilus, who keeps secret the springs of his waters, and Ister, thee rushing Tigris, thee the monster-teeming Ocean that roars round distant Britain, thee the Gauls, fearless of death, and hard Hiberia's land, obey. The Sygambri, whose joy is in bloodshed, lay to rest their arms, and worship thee.

XV *Phoebus volentem*
The rule of Augustus.
An Epilogue to the Book, the final answer to Augustus' request.

'TWAS Phoebus who, when I was thinking to tell of battles and conquered cities, thundered at me on his lyre and bade me not set my puny sail across a Tuscan sea. Thine age, Caesar, has brought back plenteous crops to our fields, and to our own Jove has restored the standards plucked down from the proud

portals of the Parthian, and has closed the gate of
Ianus Quirinus, for the war was over, and has put
a bridle in the mouth of licence that would stray beyond
right order, and has banished vices and recalled the old
ways of life through which the name of Latium and the
strength of Italy grew, and the majesty of the empire
was spread to the sun's rising from his bedchamber in
the west.   While Caesar guards the world, no civil
madness or violence shall banish peace, no anger which
forges swords and sets at variance wretched cities.
Neither those who drink the deep Danube shall break
the edicts of the Julian house, nor Getae nor Seres nor
faithless Persians, nor those whose birthplace is by the
river Tanais.   And for ourselves, on working days and
on holidays, amid the bounty of mirthful Liber, with
our children and our wives, when we have duly prayed
to the gods, with song accompanied by Lydian pipes we
will sing after our fathers' fashion of chiefs who have
lived their lives like true men, and of Troy and of
Anchises, and of the offspring of kindly Venus.

THE SECULAR HYMN

Phoebe, silvarumque

In the Museo Nazionale at Rome there are some frag-
ments of a column pieced together which were dug up in
the year 1890 near the Tiber during the formation of
the new embankment. The inscription upon them gives an
account of the celebration of the Secular Games by Augustus
in the year B.C. 17. *According to this, sacrifices were*
offered by the Emperor in person on three successive
nights to 'the Fates, the Ilithyiae, and Mother Earth,'
and on three successive days to Jupiter and Juno on the
Capitoline and to Apollo and Diana on the Palatine. On
the last day, when the sacrifice was finished, twenty-seven
boys and the same number of girls sang a hymn, and it is
added that the 'hymn was composed by Quintus Horatius
Flaccus.'
It was to be sung both on the Palatine and on the
Capitoline. It is mainly addressed to Apollo and Diana,
but it gathers up the ideas of the whole celebration.

PHOEBUS, and queen of the woodland, Diana,
lucent glory of the heavens, to be honoured even
as ye have been honoured in all time, grant ye now what
we ask at this sacred season, at which the Sibyl's verses
have taught us that maids and boys, chosen and chaste,
should sing a hymn to the gods who have loved well
the Seven Hills.

O life-giving Sun, that with thy chariot of light
bringest forth and hidest away the day, and art ever
born anew other and yet the same, mayest thou never
find aught to look on mightier than Rome city !

O thou whose gentle hand, after thine office, can open the way for the birth when the ripe hour is come, guard, Ilithyia, our wives and mothers, whether 'the Bright One' be the name thou lovest to hear, or 'the Mother of life.' O goddess, nurture our children, prosper the Fathers' decrees on the marriage yoke and the law of wedlock, that is to be the fruitful seed of a young generation! So without fail the revolution of ten times eleven years shall bring back the songs and games that gather crowds thrice in the bright daytime and as often in the pleasant night hours.

And ye, Parcae, whose song is truth, as once and for aye has been promised (and Time's landmark, that may not be removed, protect the promise!), link happy destinies to those already accomplished. May Earth, bounteous in increase of fruits and of cattle, dower Ceres with garlanded corn-ears : may wholesome waters and Jove's breezes nurture all that grows from her !

Listen with gentle heart and kindly, thy quiver closed, to the boys' prayer, Apollo ! Queen of the stars, with horned brow, listen, Moon-goddess, to the girls ! If Rome is of your handiwork, if from Ilium came the cohorts that settled on the Tuscan shore, a remnant bidden to find a new home and city after a heaven-directed wandering, for whom, uninjured through the fires of Troy, clean-handed Aeneas, saved alive when his country perished, found safe and free passage on his way to give them more than all they left behind—then grant, Powers Divine, to youth teachable hearts and honest lives, grant to old age peace and rest, grant to

Romulus' race wealth and increase and all that is bright and happy; aye, and what with sacrifice of white oxen the glorious son of Anchises, Venus' lineage, prays of you, may he win, ever master of the fighting foeman, ever gentle to the vanquished!

Already the Mede trembles at the arms puissant by sea and land and the rods that came from Alba: already the Scythian asks as of an oracle our bidding, and the Indian a moment ago so proud: already Good Faith and Peace and Honour, and the Modesty of old days, and Virtue long dishonoured, take heart to return, and Plenty with the blessings of her full horn is seen amongst us. Phoebus, the Seer, whose adornment is the shining bow, the welcome friend of the nine Muses, who with his art of health brings relief to the body's heavy-laden limbs, as surely as he looks with kindly eye upon his altar on the Palatine, bids advance Rome's greatness and the happiness of Latium for another lustre and for ages that grow ever better. And the goddess who owns the Aventine and Algidus, Diana attends to the prayers of the Fifteen[1] and lends friendly ears to the vows of the young choir.

That this is the will of Jove and of all the gods, good hope and sure we carry home, we the chorus that have learnt to sing the praises of Phoebus and Diana.

[1] The Commission whose business it was to arrange for the Secular Games and the rites belonging to them.

EPODES

[THE name 'Epodes' was given to these poems by the Latin grammatical and metrical writers, and meant properly couplets consisting of a longer and a shorter verse. Horace's own name for them was '*Iambi*,' which not only described their metre, but also their character; for the metre itself had been named from its use by Archilochus and others in the poetry of invective.

They are amongst Horace's earlier poems.]

I   *Ibis Liburnis*

Before the battle of Actium. Maecenas is expecting to go and Horace protests that he will go too. Whether they really went is not quite certain. (See Epode 9 and Introd. p. 18.)

SO you will go, dear friend Maecenas, in the light galleys among the ships' towering bulwarks, with your heart set to meet at peril to yourself every peril that awaits Caesar. And what shall we do? we to whom life, if it be while you live too, is a delight, if otherwise, a burden. Say, shall we obey you and live on in ease, ease which has no charm save in your company; or face this toil, and bear it with the soul with which heroes should? We will bear it, and in your train, whether over Alpine ridges or the unharboured[1] Caucasus, or even to the furthest gulf of the West, we will follow with staunch hearts. Would you ask how with my poor efforts I could second such as you, no warrior

[1] See note on p. 46.

I, nor man of might? If I am with you, I shall be less in
fear.   Fear haunts us with more power when we are
apart.   Even as a bird, when she is sitting on a callow
brood, fears more for them the sliding serpent's approach
if she have left them; though, for all her presence, she
could give no whit more aid if they were by her.
Gladly will I fight through this campaign and every
other for the hope of your favour—not that ploughs may
struggle behind more teams of bullocks on my land, or my
cattle move from Calabrian to Lucanian pastures before
the dog-star's heat, nor that I may have a shining white
villa close on the Circean[1] walls of Tusculum on its
hill.   Enough and to spare, your bounty has enriched
me already.   Far be it from me to gather in order to
bury the hoard in the earth like a miserly Chremes[2], or
to scatter it like a dissolute spendthrift.

II   *Beatus ille*

*Praises of country life.   The Idyll, as has been said, is
turned into an Epode by the irony of the conclusion,
which has the force of 'so men say—but their acts show
how little they believe it.'*

'HAPPY the man who far from schemes of
business, like the early generations of mankind,
ploughs and ploughs again his ancestral land with oxen
of his own breeding, with no yoke of usury on his
neck! He is not wakened like a soldier by the fierce
clarion; he dreads no angry sea.   He avoids the

[1] Built, according to legend, by Telegonus, son of Circe by
Ulysses.   [2] A character in some unknown Comedy.

Forum and the insolent portals of the great.　And so
he is either wedding the tall poplar to the full-grown
vine-plant, or looking forth on his herds of lowing
cattle as they stray in the shady valley, or cutting
off with the pruning-hook useless boughs and grafting
in those of happier fruit.　He is either storing in
clean pitchers the squeezed honey, or shearing the
unresisting sheep.　Or when Autumn has lifted over
the land his head wreathed with mellow fruitage, what
joy it is to gather the pear from the tree he grafted, and
the grape that vies with the purple dye, to present to thee,
Priapus, and thee, Sire Silvanus, guardian of his bounds !
Now it is his fancy to lie under some aged holm-oak,
now on the soft deep grass, whilst the streams slide
along in brimming courses, birds make moan in the
woods, and springs babble with gushing water, sounds
to invite light slumbers.　And then when the wintry
months of Jove the Thunderer gather storms and snow,
he either drives this way and that with his pack of dogs
the wild boars into the toils set for them, or spreads on
smooth pole the wide-meshed nets to catch the greedy
fieldfares, or sets snares for the timid hare and the
crane from over seas, sweet prizes.　In such a life who
does not forget any evil cares which belong to love ?
But if a chaste wife do her part and grace his house
with its sweet children (such as is a Sabine spouse
or the sunburnt partner of the sturdy Apulian) ; pile the
sacred hearth with old logs against the return of her
wearied lord ; and, as she shuts the glad cattle in the
wattled fold, drain dry their full udders, and broaching the

sweet cask's wine of the year make ready the unbought banquet, no Lucrine shellfish could give me more delight, no turbot or scar [1], if the storm that burst in thunder on Eastern waves should direct any to our waters. The bird of Africa would not cross my palate, nor the woodcock of Ionia, with more pleasant flavour than the olive gathered from the tree's richest boughs, or the sorrel plant that loves the meadow land and the mallows that give health to the laden body, or, it may be, the lamb slain on the festivals of Terminus, or the kid snatched from the wolf's jaws. While we sit at such a banquet, what delight to look out and see the well-fed sheep hastening home, to see the wearied bullocks dragging with tired neck the reversed plough, and the home-born slaves, the swarm that makes a wealthy home, all gathered round the glowing images of the home gods !'

So spake the usurer Alfius, on the point of turning farmer. He got in on the Ides all his money that was on interest : next Kalends he is seeking to put it out again.

III   *Parentis olim*

A mock heroic invective against garlic which Horace has unwittingly eaten in the seasoning of some dish at Maecenas' table.

HENCEFORTH if any one with impious hand shall have wrung an aged parent's neck, make him eat garlic ! It is more deadly than any hemlock.

---

[1] The *rhombus* is traditionally rendered ' turbot,' but neither it nor the *scarus* is identified as a Mediterranean fish.

O iron stomachs of the harvesters! What poison is this that is burning in my vitals? Had the cook put viper's blood without our knowledge in that dish of herbs? or had Canidia handled the poisonous mess? When Medea fell in love with the chieftain, of young beauty beyond the other Argonauts, ere he went to fasten the novel yoke on the bulls' necks this was the unction with which she protected Jason. With this she smeared the gift by which she took her vengeance on his paramour ere she fled on her winged serpents. Not of such power was ever the star's vaporous heat that settles on thirsty Apulia, nor with such fervour burnt his wife's gift on the shoulders of stalwart Hercules. Oh, if ever you set your fancy on any such dish, Maecenas, may you find, in return for this pleasantry, that you cannot get a kiss when you ask for one!

IV   *Lupis et agnis*

A violent attack on some wealthy freedman who had risen to the command of a cohort, and who affronted Horace and the citizens by his arrogance and display.

GREAT as the quarrel which fate has set between the wolf and the lamb is the quarrel betwixt me and you, O Sir, whose back has been scored with Spanish rope-ends, whose legs with the iron fetters. Though you may strut in the pride of money, Fortune cannot change the blood. See you how, as you march from end to end of the Sacra Via with your gown twice three ells broad, frankest indignation marks the faces of those that pass you to and fro?—'This fellow, once flayed by

the lashes of the triumvirs till the crier was tired, now
ploughs a thousand acres of Falernian soil, and drives his
ponies on the Appian way, and sits in state as a knight
on the front benches, and snaps his fingers at Otho [1].
What mean we by launching all these beaked and heavy-
weighted ships of war against a gang of brigands and
slaves [2], when such as he, aye he, commands a cohort of
our soldiers ! '

V   *At O deorum*

Canidia.

*Compare Epod. 17 and Sat. 1. 8.   Canidia is repre-
sented as a witch engaged in drawing to herself by spells
of magic a wretched old man, who is named Varus.
The Scholiasts tell us that under the pseudonym of Canidia
Horace attacked a lady named Gratidia.   That the form
of the attack is not to be taken quite seriously is clear
from the Satire (probably the earliest of the three poems),
but the feeling behind it cannot be fully measured.*
*The Epode opens with the cries of a boy who has been
set in the midst by the hags and sees that they have some
dreadful purpose.*

' OH, every god in heaven that rules the earth and
the race of man ! what means this tumult, and
what so many eyes all glaring fiercely on one poor boy ?
Oh, by thy own children, if in true pangs Lucina has

---

[1] One among several references to the law of L. Roscius Otho,
which set apart fourteen rows in the theatre for the knights and
those of ' equestrian *census*.' It was intended to be exclusive in its
effect : but this man has got the money and so cannot be excluded.

[2] In reference to the war against Sextus Pompeius (see
Epod. 9 with note).

heard and helped thee, by this purple's empty adornment [1]
I pray thee, by Jove, who will surely disallow thy deed,
why dost thou gaze on me like a stepmother or like
a wounded wild beast?' When, despite these piteous
cries from his trembling lips, the boy is set, stripped of the
emblems of boyhood, a childish form such as might
soften the hard hearts of Thracians, Canidia, with short
vipers entwined in her dishevelled hair, bids bring wild
fig-trees rooted up among the tombs, bids bring funereal
cypresses, and eggs and feathers of the nightly screech-
owl smeared with the blood of a hideous toad, and
herbs sent from Iolcus and Hiberia, the fruitful gardens
of magic drugs, and bones snatched from between the
teeth of a starving dog, and burn them all in the witches'
flame. Sagana meanwhile, girt up for the task, sprinkles
all over the house waters of Avernus, her hair on end
like a sea-urchin or a boar as she bustles about. Veia,
not deterred a whit by the full knowledge of her crime,
was scooping out of the ground with the stubborn spade,
groaning as she dug, a hole where the boy might be
buried and die within full sight of food changed twice
or thrice in the long day, his head standing above
ground just so much as a swimmer's body is above
water when it floats by the chin, that they might take
out the marrow and the liver, when it had dried up, to

---

[1] The Romans expressed the reverence due to childhood by
clothing boys in the bordered gown which belonged to the
highest civil offices. This and the *bulla*, an ornament hung
round the neck, are the 'emblems' spoken of in the following
lines.

make a philtre, so soon as his eyeballs, fixed on the forbidden food, had withered in their sockets. That Folia of Ariminum had her part to play is the belief of gossiping Naples and all the towns near to it, Folia who can charm from their places by her words of witchcraft the stars and moon and snatch them from the sky. Just then Canidia, gnawing in jealous rage her talon-like nails, what said she and what said she not? 'O witnesses not unloyal to my purposes, Night and Diana, who rulest the silence when mystic rites are performed, now, even now be present; now turn your wrath and your power on the homes of our foes; while every beast is in its lair in the awful woods overcome with sweet sleep, let the dogs of the Subura bark at the fond old lover, that all may laugh at him as he comes dripping with unguent, the masterpiece of my skill!—— What has happened? Why fail to-day the dread sorceries of barbarian Medea, with which ere she fled she took her revenge on her haughty rival, great Creon's daughter, what time the robe, her present, dipped in poison, took off in fire the new-made bride? Surely no herb, no root, though it lurked in rough places, has escaped me. The bed he sleeps on has been smeared with that which brings oblivion of all other loves. Ha! I see it now. He goes free, for he is loosed by the spell of some witch of greater skill. It is no vulgar philtre that shall bring thee with speed back to me, O Varus, poor soul that must shed many tears, nor are they Marsian spells at whose summons thy heart shall return home. I have a more potent plan to try, a more potent cup to brew for thy haughtiness; and sooner shall the heaven sink below the sea, and the earth be spread above it, than that thou shouldst not burn with love for me even as the pitch in yon smoky flame.'—When he heard this, the child no longer as before with gentle words would soften the ruthless hags, but doubting only how first to break the silence, uttered prayers as of Thyestes: 'Sorceries may overset the mighty laws of right and wrong: the law of human retribution they cannot. With my curses I will follow you: for the curse once pronounced no victim can make atonement. Nay, when you have bidden me die, and I have breathed my life away, I will meet you as a fury of the night, a ghost with hooked talons will I claw your faces— such power have the spirits of the dead—and sitting as a nightmare on your hearts that know no peace, I will take sleep from you for terror. The mob from street to street shall assail you on all sides with stones till they crush you for filthy hags. Afterwards your unburied limbs shall be torn by the jackals and birds of the Esquiline. Nor shall my parents, who (ah me!) must survive me, miss the pleasure of the sight.'

VI   *Quid immerentis*

The right and wrong use of the poetry of invective.

WHAT mean you, O watch-dog, who fly at the harmless guest though you dare not attack a wolf? Nay turn, if you have the heart, on me your impotent threats, and assail one who can bite back again. For like a Molossian or tawny Spartan hound, the shepherd's sturdy friend, I shall prick my ears and through the deep snow shall run home any beast in whose track I follow. For you, sir, after making the forest ring with your terrible voice, you stop to snuff the meat thrown in your way. Beware, beware! Of sternest purpose towards the bad, my horns are lifted and ready, as was the son-in-law [1] whom faithless Lycambes had spurned, or the keen enemy of Bupalus [1]. Think you that if one assails me with a venomous tooth I shall take it and whimper like a child?

VII   *Quo, quo scelesti*

One of the earliest of the poems in which Horace expresses his horror of the aimless prolongation of civil war.

WHITHER rush ye, O wicked people? Why are hands grasping again the swords that had been sheathed? Has too little of Latin blood been shed on dry land and on Neptune's realm, not that Romans might burn the proud towers of rival Carthage, or that the Briton yet untamed might walk in chains down the sacred way, but that the Parthians' prayers might be granted and Rome might perish by her own hand? This was never the wont of wolves or lions, to turn their fierceness save on some other kind. Is it madness or some overmastering power that hurries you on—or wickedness? Make answer. They are mute; and ashy paleness dyes their faces; and their conscience-stricken hearts sink within them. So it is. A bitter doom pursues the Roman race, the sin of brother's murder,

[1] Archilochus and Hipponax, both Greek writers of lampoons.

from the day when the blood of innocent Remus flowed on the ground to be the curse of children's children.

IX *Quando repostum*

It has been usually thought that this Epode was composed when the news of the victory at Actium first reached Rome; but recently it has been held more likely that it was written on the spot, perhaps for an extempore banquet on board Maecenas' galley (see Introd. p. 18).

WHEN shall I drink with you, O happy Maecenas, in our joy at Caesar's triumph, under your lofty hall, so Jove has pleased, the Caecuban stored for such a banquet, while the lyre gives forth its notes mingled with the pipes, the one a Dorian, the others a barbarian strain ! Even as we did so lately when the Neptune-born chief [1] fled, driven from the sea and his ships burnt, after threatening the city with the chains which he had struck off from his friends the traitor slaves. To think of Romans—after-ages will not credit it— sold as bondsmen to a woman, carrying stake and arms of a soldier and yet brooking to slave at the bidding of wrinkled eunuchs, while amid the warriors' standards— O sight of shame—the sun looks down on a mosquito tent ! Chafing at sight of them twice a thousand Gauls turned their horses' heads and raised the cry of ' Caesar ! '; and the foemen's ships back to the left and hide themselves in the haven. Ho, Triumph-god, is it thou that delayest the golden chariot and the unyoked heifers ? Ho, Triumph-god, he was not such a captain whom

---

[1] Sextus Pompeius, defeated by Agrippa at Naulochus B.C. 36. He is said to have given himself out to be a son of Neptune.

thou broughtest home from the war of Jugurtha [1], nor he of Africa whose monument his valour built him on the ruins of Carthage [2]. Vanquished by land and sea, the foe has changed his scarlet for a cloak of mourning. He is making either for Crete, with her famous hundred cities—but he will not command the winds which carry him—or for the Syrtes, still vexed by the south wind, or he drifts on the pathless sea. Bring, boy, bring hither larger goblets and wine of Chios or Lesbos; or rather, to check any rising qualms [3], measure out for us the Caecuban. All care and fear for Caesar's state we would cast free by help of the sweet Enfranchiser [4].

X *Mala soluta*

We only know the poet Maevius from this Epode and from Virgil's contemptuous wish for one who does not hate Bavius that he may love the poems of Maevius. In Ode 1. 3 Horace wishes Virgil a good voyage, so in the Epode he wishes Maevius a bad one.

UNDER an evil star she slips her moorings and goes forth, the ship whose stinking cargo is Maevius. Forget not, O south-west wind, to lash both her sides with ugly waves. May the black south-east strew the upturned sea with cables and shattered oars! May the north wind rise as high as when on the mountain-tops he breaks the trembling holm-oaks! May no friendly

[1] Marius.

[2] A difficult line of which neither the reading nor the meaning can be considered as settled.

[3] It is difficult to think that these words do not imply that the writer was at sea or thinking of people at sea.

[4] See note on p. 33.

star appear all through the black night on which Orion
sets in gloom! May he ride on a sea no calmer than the
conquering Grecian host, when Pallas turned her wrath
from Ilium in ashes on to Ajax' impious bark! Ah me,
how shall your mariners soon be sweating, and yourself turning pale and yellow, and crying out in that
womanish fashion, and praying to Jove's averted face,
when the Ionian gulf, roaring before the rainy south wind,
has sprung a leak in your hull! But if a dainty morsel
be flung on the curving shore to glut the cormorants, a
lusty goat and a ewe lamb shall be slain in sacrifice to
the Tempests.

XIII *Horrida tempestas*

*Lessons of Epicureanism drawn from winter (very much
in the vein of Ode 1. 9).*

THE sky is lowering with hideous storms and
Jove descending in rain and snow: now the sea,
now the forests roar in the north wind: let us snatch
opportunity, my friends, ere the day passes, and whilst
our knees have still sap in them [1] and we fitly may, let
us clear our brows at least of the clouds that old age
gathers. Go, dear friend, broach the wine that was
pressed under my own consul Torquatus [2]. Speak not
now of aught else. Heaven, may be, by some kindly
change will bring it all back as it was before. To-day

---

[1] The Latin suggests a contrast hard to indicate in English
between the winter outside, and the freshness of spring and freedom
from clouds which it is still possible to keep within.

[2] Od. 3. 21. 1. L. Manlius Torquatus, consul in the year of
Horace's birth, B.C. 65.

our one joy is to be drenched in Persian perfumes, and
with the music of Cyllene's lyre to make the heart light
of hateful care.   As the glorious Centaur sang to his
mighty pupil[1]: 'Hero, mortal though the son of a
goddess-mother Thetis, thou must yet see the land of
Assaracus, which the icy stream of tiny Scamander
furrows and the sliding Simois.   Return from thence
the sister Fates have cut off from thee by the fixed
length of the thread they spin: nor shall thy sea-nymph
mother be able to bring thee home again.   There lighten
all the ills of life with wine and song, the sweet con-
solations of grim melancholy.'

XIV   *Mollis inertia*
Why the Epodes are so long in finishing.

WHY soft sloth has steeped my inmost sense in
such forgetfulness as though I had drained
into a parched throat some cup that brought the
slumbers of Lethe, O truth-loving friend, Maecenas,
you kill me by your often asking.   A god—I can only
answer—a god forbids me to complete the roll of my
iambics, the poem so long promised.   Even so they
tell us Anacreon of Teos loved, and oftentimes wailed
over his passion on the hollow shell in artless measures.
You yourself feel the fire and its pain.   Yet rejoice in
your happy lot.   She that fired beleaguered Troy was
not more lovely.   She whom I pine for is Phryne,
a freed-woman with a score of lovers.

---

[1] The story of Chiron (the Centaur) and Achilles.

XV   *Nox erat et caelo*

Inconstancy.

'TWAS night and the moon was shining in a cloud-less sky amid the host of lesser stars, when, with the heart to wrong the majesty of mighty gods, you swore after my words, clasping me all the while with clinging arms closer than the ivy clasps the tall holm-oak, that while wolves were the foes of sheep, and Orion of sailors when he troubled the winter sea, and while Apollo let his unshorn hair toss in the winds, this our love should be mutual.   Alas, Neaera, you shall be sorry that I am the man I am; for if Flaccus has in him aught of a man, he will not bear your favours shown to a rival, but in his anger will seek a heart as constant as his own.   Nor will his resolution yield to the charms of a beauty which has once become odious, if the pain has entered and fixed itself.   And for you, sir, whoever you are, my happier rival who now triumph in my pain—though you may be rich in cattle and broad acres, or own Pactolus' stream, and though no secret be unknown to you of Pythagoras and his second birth, and though in beauty you surpass Nireus—alas for you! you shall yet mourn over love that has fled elsewhere, and then in my turn I shall have the laugh.

XVI   *Altera iam teritur*

To be set with Epode 7 as a lively expression of weariness and disgust at civil war, but before Horace had seen in the rule of Octavianus the escape from it. 'Let us sail off to the Happy Islands' is a way of saying 'there is no escape.'

A SECOND age already is wearing away in civil wars, and Rome is tumbling under the strength of her own arms. The city which neither the neighbouring Marsians could destroy, nor the Etruscan bands of threatening Porsena, nor the rival valour of Capua, nor keen Spartacus and the Allobroges faithless to revolution [1], nor fierce Germany with her blue-eyed sons could tame and Hannibal, the loathing of parents' hearts—that city we shall destroy, an impious age and a doomed race; and the ground it stands on shall be tenanted once more by wild beasts. Ah me, a barbarian conqueror shall stand over its ashes, and trample the city under his horse's ringing hoofs, and scatter in contumely (O sight of horror!) the bones of Quirinus that lie sheltered from winds and suns.

May be you are asking with one voice, or the better part of you, what can help you to get quit of your sad troubles. Let no advice be preferred to this: even as the whole state of the Phocaeans [2] having sworn an oath went forth in exile from their lands and the homes of their sires, and left their temples to be the lairs of wild boars and robber wolves, even so to go whithersoever our feet shall carry us, whithersoever over the waters the south wind or the wild south-west shall invite us. Is it your pleasure so? Or has any aught better to

[1] This refers to the part played by the embassy of the Allobroges in respect of the Catilinarian conspiracy.

[2] Herodotus tells (1. 165) the story how half the population of Phocaea in Ionia, when pressed by the Persians, sailed away westward to Corsica and Italy. Aristotle adds that eventually they founded Massilia (Marseilles).

advise ? Then, since the omens favour, why delay to
embark ? Only let us swear to this : So soon as stones
shall rise from the water's depth and swim on the surface,
then let it be no sin for us to come back ; no shame to
turn our sails and set them for home when the Po shall
wash the Matine hill-tops or lofty Mount Apennine
shall run out into the sea, when strange loves shall
make monstrous unions of unheard-of passion, when tigers
choose to mate with stags and the dove with the kite,
when cattle grow trustful and fear not the tawny lion,
and the goat grows smooth and learns to love the salt
seas. Such an oath let us swear, or any other that may
cut off for ever all sweet returning, and let us go—the
entire state, having sworn our oath, or at least the part
better than the wilful crowd—leave softness and
despair to hug still their ill-starred bed of sloth. You
who have men's hearts, put aside womanish wailing, and
spread your sails along the Tuscan shore. For us is
waiting the ambient Ocean. Let us look for the land,
the happy land, the islands of wealth ; where the soil
unploughed gives its corn-crop year by year, and the
vineyard ever blooms unpruned, and the olive shoot
buds and never breaks its promise, and the dark blue
fig adorns its own ungrafted tree. Honey drops from
the hollow holm-oak, light streams dance down the
mountain-side with tinkling foot. There the she-goats
come unsummoned to the milkpail, and the flock for
love brings home its full udders ; no bear of the evening
roars around the sheepfold, nor the ground heaves high
with vipers. And many another wonder shall our happy

eyes see—how neither the watery east wind sweeps the land with floods of rain, nor the fruitful plants are burnt in a dry soil, for that the king of heaven tempers either extreme. Hither nor the sturdy rowers of the Argo brought their pine bark, nor the shameless Colchian set her foot. Hither sailors from Sidon never turned their yard-arms, nor Ulysses' toil-worn crew. No taint of plague destroys their herds, no dog-star's furious rages fever their flocks. These shores Jupiter severed from the world for a people of the good, when he debased with brass the times of gold—with brass and then with iron he made hard the ages, from which now a happy escape is offered to the good through my prophetic mouth.

XVII   *Iam iam efficaci*

Under the form of a recantation offered by himself and rejected by Canidia, Horace repeats and aggravates his attack upon her in Epode 5 and Sat. 1. 8.

Horace. I YIELD, I yield to the power of thy science, and on my knees I pray—by the realm of Proserpine and by the might of Diana that none may provoke; aye, and by the book of magic spells that can draw the stars from the sky and bring them down to earth—Canidia, stay at length thy mystic words, and let go, loose and let go, the spinning wheel. Telephus touched the heart of the Nereid's son [1], though he had marshalled against him in defiance the hosts of Mysia and hurled sharp-pointed weapons. The Ilian matrons anointed for burial man-slaying Hector's body, though

[1] Achilles.

it had been sentenced to birds of carrion and to dogs, when the king left his city and fell on his face at the feet (ah me!) of the hard-hearted Achilles. Ulysses' toil-worn rowers by Circe's grace put off their swinish shape and hard and bristling hides; then mind and speech slipped back, and the wonted beauty into their faces. I have suffered thy vengeance enough and to spare, O best-beloved of sailors and pedlars. My youth is gone, and the blushing pink has left me, mere bones covered with yellow skin. My hair is white from your magic perfumes: no rest gives me respite from my pain. Day treads on the heels of night and night of day, nor can I draw the breath that would ease my strained lungs. So I am constrained to believe to my sorrow, what I denied, that Sabellian charms can ring through and through the heart and Marsian incantations make the head burst asunder. What wish you more? O sea and earth, I burn as neither Hercules in the unction of Nessus' poisonous blood, nor the Sicilian flame that ever lives in fiery Aetna. You are a laboratory of magic drugs whose fires will not slacken till I am burnt to ashes for the winds to scatter in their rough play. What end, what composition may I look to? Speak! I will pay loyally any penalty you name. I am ready to offer expiation if you shall ask a hecatomb, or desire that I shall tune my lyre to falsehood and sing of you. You the modest, you the good, shall walk among the stars a golden constellation. Castor when he was wroth for defamed Helen's sake, and mighty Castor's brother, were overcome by prayer and

gave the poet back the eyes they had taken from him.
Even so do you—for you have the power—loose me
from my madness.   O lady that never went in rags
from a father's meanness, no hag cunning in groping
among the nine-day ashes of a pauper graveyard, your
heart is kindly and your hands are clean, and Pactu-
meius is the child of your own womb.

Canidia.   Why pour prayers to sealed ears? Not
more deaf are the rocks to the naked sailors' cry,
when the winter sea lashes them with high-running surf.
To think that without suffering for it you should
have divulged and laughed at the rites of Cotytto,
and the mysteries of free love, and after playing the
pontiff at my witcheries on the Esquiline should have
made me with impunity the talk of the town!   What
profit then should I have for having made the fortune
of Pelignian hags and brewed a poison-bowl of quicker
powers?   But the fate that awaits you is slower than
you would pray for.   You must drag on a hateful life
for this one purpose, to be for ever the food of fresh
pangs.   The sire of faithless Pelops longs for rest,
Tantalus, as he hungers ever for the boon of food.
Prometheus longs, as he lies bound, the prey of his
bird.   Sisyphus longs that he may fix his stone on the
mountain-top; but the laws of Jove forbid it.   You
shall wish now to leap from tower-tops, now to pierce
your breast with a sword of Noric steel.   In vain shall
you twist nooses for your throat in the anguish of your
weary sorrow.   Then shall I ride in triumph astride my
foe's shoulders, and the earth shall bow to my insolent

triumph.   What, though I can make waxen images feel, as you know through your prying, and can snatch the moon from the sky by my spells, can call up the dead from their urns and brew a philtre of desire, must I mourn the issue of an art powerless against you?

SATIRES

BOOK I

I   *Qui fit, Maecenas*

Wishing and enjoying.

The subject of the Satire is the weakness which Horace is always attacking, that of wishing *for what we have not, instead of enjoying what we have. The folly is seen in its extreme form in the hoarder of money. His case, his unreasonableness, and the vanity of his excuses, are set out at length; but the Satire begins and ends more generally.*

HOW comes it, Maecenas, that, whether it be self-chosen or flung to him by chance, every one is discontented with his own lot and keeps his praises for those who tread some other path? 'O happy traders [1]!' cries the soldier, as he feels the weight of years, his limbs crippled with hard service. Hear the trader, on the other hand, when his ship is tossing in the south winds: 'Soldiering is the better business. Do you doubt it? There is the battle shock, and in a few minutes' space comes a speedy death or the joy of victory.' The adept in law and statute, when a client is battering at his door before cockcrow, has a word of praise for the farmer. That poor fellow yonder who

---

[1] The *mercator* in Horace is the trader who sails his own ship.

has been dragged into town from the country to keep his surety cries that they only are happy who live in town. The other instances which I could add—so many are they—are enough to tire out the tongue of Fabius. To cut it short, hear the moral that I draw. If some god were to appear and say, ' Look you, I will grant your desires this moment. You who were but now a soldier shall be a trader, you who were a counsel a countryman. Now, sirs, change your places ; your parts are changed. Quick ! why do you stand still ? ' They do not wish it. Yet bliss is theirs if they will. What reason can be pleaded why Jupiter should not puff both his cheeks with anger at them and say that never again will he be so easy as to open his ear to vow of theirs ? Once more (not to dismiss the question with a laugh like a mere jester—and yet, why may not one be telling truth while one laughs, as teachers sometimes give little boys cakes to coax them into learning their letters?—still, let us put play aside and treat the question seriously) yonder fellow laboriously ploughing the heavy sod, my cheating host here, the soldier, the sailors who cross so boldly every sea, all say that this is the purpose with which they bear their toil, that when they are old they may be able to retire and securely take their rest, when they have gathered enough (their phrase is) to give them their ' rations,' just as (it is the proverbial example) the tiny toilsome ant is to be seen dragging whatever she can get hold of with her mouth, and adding it to the heap which she builds, because she knows and plans for what is to come. Yes, but in her

case, so soon as the Water-carrier [1] saddens the inverted
year, she stirs no more abroad, but uses that store of
which you speak, the store which she has gathered before-
hand, for she is wise; while as for you, neither summer's
heat nor winter's cold, fire, sea, nor sword, can turn you
from the pursuit of gain—nothing stops you, if only
there may be no rival richer than yourself. What profit
is it to have gathered a vast weight of silver and gold
and then in stealth and in terror to hide it in a hole in
the ground?

'If once you were to break in on it, it would soon
dwindle to the last worthless brass coin.'

But if you do not, what beauty has the heap you
have piled? Your threshing-floor has threshed, suppose,
a hundred thousand bushels: you cannot for that reason
swallow more than I can, any more than if you chanced
to be the one in a train of slaves to carry on your
shoulders the heavy bread-net you could get more of it
for yourself than the slave who carried nothing. Or
again, tell me, what does it matter to the man who
lives within the limits which Nature sets whether he
ploughs a hundred acres or a thousand?

'It is so delightful to take from a large heap.'

Provided you let me take from a small one exactly
the same quantity, why should you laud your granary
above my bin? It is as if you required not more than

---

[1] The sun was in the sign of Aquarius from the middle of
January to the middle of February. The phrase 'inverted
year' has been adopted into English poetry by Dryden, Thomson,
and Cowper.

a pitcher, or even a ladleful, of water, and were to say, 'If I had the choice I would rather draw from a broad river than the same quantity from this mean little spring.' That is how it happens to those who set their fancy on quantity beyond the bounds of good sense to be swept away, with the bank which they stand on, by Aufidus in his fury; while the man who asks only for the little that he needs neither finds his draught fouled with mud nor loses his life in the waters. But half the world says (such are the illusions of greed) 'Enough you can never have; for the more you were to have, the more you would be thought of.' What can you do to a man who talks so? Bid him be miserable, since so he chooses. He is like a man at Athens, as miserly as he was rich, who, they tell us, was wont to pour contempt on what the people said after this fashion: 'The people hisses me, but I applaud myself, as often as I gaze on the moneys in my chest.'

Tantalus, ever thirsty, catches at the streams that fly from his lips: why do you smile? Change but the name, and it is of yourself that tale is told. When you have ransacked the world to fill your money-bags you put them under your pillow and sleep with parted lips, but you do not dare touch them any more than if they belonged to a god, or take any pleasure in them save as pictures to look at. Do you know what money is meant for, to what uses it may be put? You may buy a loaf with it, garden stuff, a pint of wine, and other things which our human nature would feel pain at being denied. Perhaps it is a pleasure to you to lie awake half-dead with terror, to spend nights and days alike in fear of those wicked thieves, of fire, of slaves that may rob you and run away. In such blessings as those I for my part should wish all my life to be poor indeed.

'But if you have caught cold and are racked with pain, or some accident has made you a prisoner in bed, you have some one to sit by you, prepare the applications, beseech the doctor to raise you from your bed and restore you to your children and dear relations.'

Why, even your wife does not wish you well again, nor your son: every one hates you, neighbours and acquaintances, man and maid. Can you wonder, when you rank everything after your money, that no one renders you the love which you do not earn? You can hardly think, when Nature at no cost to you gives you kinsmen, that to take a little trouble to keep their love would be as sad a waste of pains as if one tried to break an ass to obey the rein and show its paces in the Campus.

The sum of my answer is, let us end our money-getting somewhere. As what you have increases, let your fears of poverty diminish; begin to bring your toil to a finish when you have gained that which you desired; lest that befall you which once on a time befell Ummidius,—it is not a long story—so rich that he measured his money by weight, so miserly that he was never dressed better than a slave; down to his last hour he was always in terror lest he should die of starvation. But his end was that a freedwoman split him down the middle with an axe, a second Clytemnestra.

'Well, what then would you have me do? live the life of a Naevius or a Nomentanus [1]?'

You insist on pitting opposites against one another as though you were making up a fight. I certainly, when I bid you not be a miser, am not bidding you turn fool and spendthrift. There is some mean between a Tanais and Visellius' father-in-law. There is measure in everything. There are fixed limits beyond which and short of which right cannot find resting-place.

I return to the question with which I set out, how it comes that, [2] like the man of avarice, every one is discontented, and rather gives his praise to those who tread other paths, pines with jealousy because another's goat gives more milk than his own, and, instead of comparing himself with the greater crowd of men poorer than himself, is bent on surpassing first one and then another. Once start on that race, and there is ever a richer in your way. Just as, when the barriers are slipped and the chariots are flying behind the horse-hoofs, a charioteer gives his whole thought to the team in front of him, recking nothing of that poor fellow whom he passed just now and left in the ruck. This is how it comes to pass that we can seldom find one to confess that he has had a happy life, and rise contented, when his time is up, like a satisfied guest from the banquet. But enough. If I add a word more you will think that I have been plundering the portfolios of Crispinus.

[1] Nomentanus in Horace is a name that represents a spendthrift.
[2] Or 'no one, like the miser in my story, approves himself, but every one rather gives &c.'

II   *Ambubaiarum*

A fool's way of avoiding one folly is to fall into another [1].
*This Satire, only part of which is translated, was without
doubt among the earlier work which Horace's maturer
taste prevented him from eventually giving to the world.
It is conjectured that its preservation was due to the
desire of Maecenas, who had been amused by a personal
jest in it at his own expense, 'Maltinus walks about
with his tunic down to his heels;' for tradition tells
us that 'Maltinus' meant 'Maecenas.' Another line in
it 'Rufillus smells of perfumery, Gargonius of the goat,'
is made in Sat. 1. 4 a type of his personal and censorious
Satire.*

THE guilds of street players, the drugsellers,
beggars, mime-actresses, buffoons, and all their
kith and kin are in mourning and distress at the death of
Tigellius.   He was ' so generous,' they will tell you.
On the other hand my neighbour here, for fear he should
be called a prodigal, would not give to a friend in want
the wherewithal to keep at arm's length cold and the
pains of hunger. Another, if you should ask him why, to
gratify his thankless gluttony, he is stripping bare the
inheritance of two generations, buying up every costly
dainty in the market with borrowed money, answers
that it is because he does not wish to be held mean and
poor-spirited.   He wins praise from one side at cost of
blame from another.   Fusidius, rich in lands, rich in
moneys on loan, fears the repute of a fool and a spendthrift; so, when he lends, he deducts from the sum lent

[1] Another doctrine habitual with Horace. In the Art of Poetry
he gives it a literary application.

five payments of interest [1]; the nearer one is to ruin the harder he presses him; he touts for borrowers among raw youths just in the gown of manhood and with strict fathers. 'Mighty Jove!'— who does not cry as soon as he hears it ?—' but such a man surely spends on himself proportionately to his gain?' You would scarcely believe how poor a friend he is to himself. The father in Terence's play [2], who lived such a miserable life after banishing his son, never tormented himself worse than he.

If any one should be asking by this time 'to what does all this tend?' to this: *Fools in avoiding a vice run into its opposite.*

III   *Omnibus hoc vitium*
          Satire and personal censoriousness.

The main subject is personal censoriousness — its frequency, its inconvenience, its unfairness, the need of mutual forbearance, of some discrimination of the relative gravity of faults. This last point leads to an attack on the Stoic doctrine of the equality of offences. But there is a further purpose in the Satire. The first paragraph is a satirical picture of Tigellius as the type of a character made up of inconsistencies. Horace supposes himself to be interrupted with the question, ' Have you no faults of your own ?' ' Yes,' he answers, ' not that particular fault, possibly smaller ones, but I am not like Maenius (the representative of self-righteous censoriousness in private

---

[1] The words may mean rather 'he gets out of his capital (though it takes a knife to do it) five times the usual interest.' The usual Roman interest was 1 p.c. per month, i.e. 12 p.c. per annum.

[2] The Heautontimorumenus, or Self-tormentor.

life), who shuts his eyes to his own faults.' As in Sat.
4, while he strikes at a common vice, he is defending the
position of the Satirist.

ALL singers have this fault: when they are begged to
sing in a party of friends they can never persuade
themselves to do it ; when they are not asked they never
leave off. This was the way with Tigellius, that true Sardinian. Caesar, though he could compel him, if he be-
sought him by his father's friendship and his own, could
make no way with him. If the fellow was in the humour
for it, he would sing over and over, from the eggs to the
apples [1], 'Io Bacche ! ' up and down the whole scale.
There was nothing in him on one level. You would
often see him running as though he had an enemy at his
heels, very often stalking as though he were carrying
Juno's sacred vessels. Often he would keep two
hundred slaves, often ten. At one moment his talk
was kings and tetrarchs, all on the grand scale; at another
'Give me a three-footed table and a shell of clean salt,
and a gown as coarse as you please if it can keep out the
cold.' Suppose you gave a million to this pattern of
thrift and contentment, in five days he had nothing in
his purse. He was awake all night till broad daylight
and snoring all the day. Never was a creature so incon-
sistent.

Now some one will say to me, 'What of yourself ?
Have you no faults ? ' Yes, I have, not the same ones—
it may possibly be less ones. When Maenius once was

[1] i.e. from the first course to the last. See introduction to Sat.
2. 4.

picking Novius to pieces behind his back, 'Ho, sir,' said some one, 'do you not know your own faults? Or do you think, as though we did not know them, that you are imposing on us?' 'I shut my eyes[1] to my own faults,' answered Maenius. Such self-love as that is foolish and outrageous, and deserves to be branded for what it is. Your eyes, when they are cast over your own faults, are weak and still smarting from the ointment. Why to those of your friends are you as keen of vision as an eagle or as a serpent of Epidaurus? The return you get is that they again look closely into your faults.

'He is a little too hot-tempered. He does not quite suit our exquisite modern taste. He may even raise a smile by the rustic cut of his beard, the ill sit of his gown, his loose shoes that will hardly stay on his feet.' Aye, but he is a good man, none better—but he is your friend—but under that uncouth outside are hidden vast gifts of mind[2]. Lastly, give yourself a good shaking[3]: see whether nature, or even (it may be) bad habit, have sown in you any seeds of fault; for once neglect land, and fern grows in it for the bonfire.

Let us aim first at the lover's practice, whose eyes are blind to his mistress's blemishes, or even find them beauties, as Balbinus did with Hagna's large nose. I could wish that we made that mistake in friendship, and that virtue had given the mistake an honourable name.

---

[1] There is a play, impossible to keep, on *ignoras, ignotum, ignosco*.

[2] The Scholiasts have a story, most probably an invention, that the Dominie Sampson portrayed is Horace's friend, the poet Virgil.

[3] As if you were searching a thief's pockets.

† w. t. h.

But at least we might do for a friend what a father does
for his son—not be disgusted for a single blemish.
Of a boy who squints his father says that he has a little
cast[1]; if he has one who is as dwarfish as the misbe-
gotten Sisyphus, that he is a chicken.   One with bandy
legs he fondly calls his little 'Varus,' one that can
scarcely stand on his twisted ankles his 'Scaurus.'
Has a friend thrifty habits? Let us say he is 'steady.'
Another is deficient in tact and is a little given to brag:
he claims that his friends should set it down to the wish to
be good company.   Or again, he is more bluff and free-
spoken than he need be, let him be taken for frank and
courageous. He is too hot-headed; let him be reckoned
a man of energy. This, I believe, is what both makes
friends and keeps them when made.   But we turn even
virtues the wrong way upwards, and want to foul a clean
vessel.   Have we among us a worthy fellow more un-
assuming than others? We nickname him slow and stupid.
Another is on his defence against snares and bent on
offering no exposed side to malice, seeing that we live
in a world where envy is keen and slanders are rife: instead of speaking of his sense and caution we call him
artful and deep.   Is one somewhat simple, and such
as I dare say I have often shown myself to you, Maecenas, interrupting you perhaps when reading or resting
with some troublesome chatter: 'he is utterly without

---

[1] There is a double point in some, if not in all, of the names
supposed to be used by the father.   In some cases they certainly
designated a less extreme form of the blemish. But they were
also all names of more or less distinguished Roman families.

the social instinct' we say. Ah me! how rashly do we
give our sanction to a harsh law which will recoil upon
ourselves! For none in this world is without failings:
he is best who labours under the smallest ones. My
friend who wishes me to love him must be indulgent, and
weigh, as is fair, my good qualities against my failings,
and turn the balance in favour of these as the more numerous—if, as I hope, the good are the more numerous.
On this condition he shall be weighed in similar scales.
He who expects his friend not to be annoyed at his
wens will excuse the other's warts. It is fair play that
one who asks indulgence for shortcomings should give
it in return. In fine, since no knife will cut away the
failing of anger and all the others that cling to us poor
fools[1], why does not Reason employ her own weights
and measures, and apportion the severity of punishment to the reality of each offence? If one were to
crucify a slave who, when bidden to remove a dish, has
been tempted to taste the half-eaten fish in its lukewarm
sauce, sane men at least would call him more insane than
Labeo. How much madder and greater a crime is this:
a friend has committed some small offence, which it
would seem ungracious not to excuse; you hate him
bitterly and shun him, as Ruso is shunned by the poor
wretch, his debtor, who, if by the time the sad
Kalends come he cannot hunt up from somewhere either

---

[1] Horace humorously accepts for himself and the mass of mankind
the title which the Stoics would give to all but the perfect man or
philosopher. He is going presently to have his revenge upon
them.

interest or principal, has to offer his throat like a captive in war and listen to his odious histories. Say a friend has had an accident, knocked off the table a salt-cellar which Evander had fingered [1], for this offence, or because when hungry he snatched before me a chicken set on my side of the dish, is he therefore to be less pleasant in my eyes? What shall I do if he commits theft or betrays a trust or repudiates a pledge?

Those [2] whose creed is that all offences are pretty nearly on a par are in difficulty when they come to face facts. The moral feelings rebel, and even utility, the mother, or next to it, of justice and right.

[3] When living beings first crawled on earth's surface, dumb brute beasts, they fought for their acorns and their lair with nails and fists, then with clubs, and so from stage to stage with the weapons which need thereafter fashioned for them, until they discovered language [4] by which to make sounds express feelings. From that moment they began to give up war, to build cities, and to frame laws that none should thieve or rob or commit adultery. For there had been wantons before Helen who had been the shameful cause of war;

[1] See Sat. 2. 3 (p. 217). There seems to have been a considerable sale in Rome for 'old curiosities.'

[2] The Stoics.

[3] This sketch (after the Epicurean doctrine as set forth especially in Lucretius 5. 925 foll.) of the origin of society is intended to justify the statement that utility, and not any transcendental distinction of right and wrong, is the origin of law. If this is so it is evident that, tried by that test, all offences are not equal, for they are not equally injurious.

[4] Literally 'verbs and nouns.'

but in those days they died inglorious deaths whom, snatching the pleasures of lawless love after the manner of beasts, some superior in physical strength struck down like the bull in a herd. If you examine the dates of the world's history you will have to confess that the source of justice was the fear of injustice. As Nature can draw no line between the unjust and the just, in the way that she does between what is advantageous and the reverse, what is to be sought and what is to be avoided, so Reason will never prove to us that the offence is one and the same to cut a tempting cabbage in a neighbour's garden and to rob a temple in the night-time. We need a rule to assign fair punishments to offences, lest you assail with the executioner's scourge what deserves the schoolmaster's strap. For that you will chastise with the cane one who deserves severe stripes, that is not what I fear when you say that larceny is on the same level as robbery with violence, and threaten that you would cut back small crimes and great with much the same pruning-hook if men would make you king. Nay, if the wise man, and he alone, is 'rich and a good cobbler and beautiful and a king [1],' why are you sighing for that which you already have? 'You do not know' he answers 'what our father Chrysippus [2] means. The wise man has never made a slipper for himself of Greek cut or of Latin; yet the wise man is a cobbler.' How? 'As Hermogenes, though he may not be singing a note, is still the best of singers and musicians; as the

[1] See the end of Epist. I. I.
[2] Chrysippus, the second founder of Stoicism.

versatile Alfenus[1], after he had thrown away every tool of his art and shut up his shop, was a barber; so the wise man is the only master of every craft, so he is a king.' Wanton little boys pluck at your beard, and unless you beat them well with your staff you have a crowd of them swarming round you and teasing you, while you snarl in impotent rage, O mightiest of mighty kings. To cut it short, while your majesty goes to your farthing[2] bath without a single attendant except the foolish Crispinus, my indulgent friends will pardon me if I make a slip—for I am 'not a wise man'—and in return I shall gladly suffer their shortcomings, and in my private station shall have a happier lot than you as a king.

IV   *Eupolis atque Cratinus*
An apology for writing Satire.

The purposes are (1) to indicate Horace's attitude towards his great predecessor in Satire, Lucilius (compare the 10th Satire of this Book); (2) to justify and determine the position of Satire (in Horace's sense of the word) as a form of literature; (3) to defend himself against the charge levelled against Satire as the expression of misanthropy or malignity.

It is to be noticed that he repudiates the intention of publishing his Satires. He composes them for his own pleasure and profit, and only reads them to friends and when pressed to do so.

[1] According to the Scholiasts he migrated to Rome and became an eminent jurist.

[2] *Quadrans*, the fourth part of the *as*, was the recognized fee at the public baths.

EUPOLIS and Cratinus and Aristophanes, those
poets indeed, and the other true men to whom
the Comedy of old days belongs, if any one deserved to
be drawn as a rogue and a thief, as a rake or cut-throat,
or as infamous in any other way, branded him with
great freedom. It is to them that Lucilius owes what
he is. They are the masters whom he followed in all
but their metre. He was witty, of keenest perception,
harsh in the construction of his verse. His defect was
this : he often as a feat would dictate without effort two
hundred verses in an hour. In the turbid stream there
was much which you would desire away. He was
garrulous, and slow to bear the trouble of writing—of
writing correctly, I mean : for quantity I do not count.
See, Crispinus is ready to challenge me at long
odds : ' Take your tablets, if you please, and at once !
Let place be fixed for us, and time and arbiters ; and
let us see which can write the most.' Thank Heaven
which, when it moulded me, gave me few ideas and
a poor spirit and a tongue of rare and scanty utterance !
I leave it to you, as you prefer it, to be like the air
imprisoned in the goat-skin bellows, which puffs and puffs
till the fire softens the iron.

What a happy man is Fannius[1] when he has sent

---

[1] A poetaster named also in Sat I. 10, but unknown otherwise.
The meaning of the following words can only be guessed. They
should imply his self-sufficiency and love of publicity. Pliny tells
us that when Pollio founded the first public library at Rome he
put into it *imagines* or waxen masks of great authors, but only
admitted Varro of living ones. It is suggested that Fannius
volunteered for some such honour.

unasked his books and his mask to the library! My
writings no one reads, and I fear to read them in public,
for the reason that there are people who particularly
dislike my style of composition, knowing well that
more than half the world deserves the satirist's lash.
Choose whom you like from out of a crowd: he is
suffering either from avarice or some miserable ambition. One is mad with love for somebody else's wife.
One is attracted by the sheen of silver: Albius'
whole soul is in bronzes. Another is busy trading from
the rising sun to that which warms the lands of evening;
nay, rushes headlong through pains like a column of dust
before the whirlwind, in terror lest he lose an atom of his
earnings or in hope of adding to his wealth. All of these
dread verse-writing, hate the name of poet: ' He carries
hay on his horns [1], give him a wide berth: provided he
can raise a laugh he will spare neither himself nor any
friend, and whatever he has once daubed on his paper he
will rejoice to have known to every boy and old dame
as they come home from the bakehouse and the tank.'

Come, now listen to a few words in answer. First
I must strike my name from the list of those whom
I shall admit to be poets. For you must not call it
enough to make a verse scan, nor give a man the name of
poet while he writes, as I do, in the style of common
talk. Who has the native gift, who has the inspired
soul and tongue of lofty utterance, to him you may give
the honour of that name. And so some have ques-
tioned whether even Comedy is or is not poetry; since

[1] A wisp of hay on the horns was the mark of a dangerous bull.

it lacks the fire and force of inspiration both in diction and matter, and, save that it differs from talk in the fixity of rhythm, is mere talk. 'But surely,' you say, 'there is fire when a father is storming because his spendthrift son, mad after a worthless mistress, refuses a wife with a large dower, or in a drunken fit parades the town (a great scandal) with torches in the day-time.' Would Pomponius hear words less vehement than those if it were a father in real life? It is clear that it is not enough to make up your verse of plain words such that, if you broke it up into its materials, any father you choose would express anger in the same style as the one in your play. With the verses which I write, or which Lucilius in old days wrote, if you took away the regularity of quantity and rhythm, and altered the order of the words, you would not, as you would if you decomposed such lines as

> 'When foul Discord's jar
> Had burst the steel-clad doors and oped the gates
> of war [1]'—

recognize, even in his dismembered state, the limbs of a poet.

But enough of this. Whether this kind of composition be proper poetry or not is a question for another time. At this moment I am asking only whether you are justified in looking so jealously on it. Sulcius [2] with his keen scent and Caprius [2] go up and down with hoarse

---

[1] From Ennius.

[2] Professional accusers. The names are probably literary, from some comedy or from Lucilius.

ill-omened voices and armed with their note-books, the
terror, both of them, of robbers. If a man's life is
honest and his hands clean he may think scorn of both
of them. Even suppose you are like Caelius and
Birrius, the robbers, while I am not like Caprius or
Sulcius, why should you dread me? It does not follow
that shop or pillar [1] displays my books to be thumbed by
the crowd and Hermogenes Tigellius [2]. Nor do I read
them to any save to friends, and to them only when
I cannot help it—not anywhere or before every one.
There are men who read their books in the middle of
the Forum, men who read in the baths: 'It is such
a good place' they say 'for sound.' That is what the
empty-headed like. They do not ask whether what
they do is out of taste, or out of season.

'You delight in giving pain' my critic says, 'and do
it purposely from some crook in your nature.'

Where did you find that to throw at me? Does
a single person with whom I have lived vouch for it?
The man who backbites an absent friend, nay, who
does not stand up for him when another blames him,
the man who angles for bursts of laughter and for the
repute of a wit, who can invent what he never saw, who
cannot keep a secret—that man is black at heart: mark
and avoid him, if you are a Roman indeed. You may
often see out of a party, with four upon each of the

---

[1] i.e. a pillar in an arcade against which booksellers exposed
their wares.

[2] He is, with Horace, the representative of the effeminate and
foppish taste of the day in music and poetry.

three couches, one who loves to bespatter with water
clean or foul every one except the host, and him also
presently, when he has well drunk and the truth-telling
god of freedom unlocks his heart.   This man you
think a good fellow, well bred and frank—you who so
hate the 'black-hearted.'   For me, if I have had a laugh
at 'the foolish Rufillus for smelling of perfumery,
Gargonius like a goat[1],' do you think I have poison in
my fang?   Suppose the talk turned in your presence on
the thefts of Petillius Capitolinus, you would defend
him after your fashion: 'Capitolinus is an old comrade
of mine, a friend from boyhood; he has often done me
a good turn when I have asked him, and that he is
alive and at large in Rome is a joy to me—yet how he
ever came safe out of that trial, I own, I marvel!'
That is the very blackness of the cuttlefish, the sheer
poison of verdigris.   That vice I promise you, if I can
promise anything truly, will be, as before, far distant
from my pages, and from my heart.

If my words perhaps are rather frank and rather playful, you will be kind and grant me this licence.   The
best of fathers taught me the habit by the way he had of
branding one by one by means of examples the vices
which I was to avoid.   When he would exhort me to
live thriftily, frugally, and content with the provision he
had made for me, 'Do you not see' he would say
'what a bad life young Albius has of it, and how Baius
has come to beggary?   A great warning to you not to
squander your patrimony!'   When he would deter me

---

[1] Quoted from Sat. 1. 2.   See p. 164.

from base amours, 'Do not you be like Scetanus. The exposure of Trebonius is not a pretty story. Philosophers will give you better reasons than I can why one thing is better than another to avoid or to seek. It is enough for me if I can keep the rule which I inherited from my forefathers, and guard safely your life and name so long as you need a guardian. When years have brought strength to body and mind, you will swim without the corks.' With such talk he tried to mould me in my boyhood; and whether he were advising me to do something, 'You have a good pattern in so acting' he would say, and point to some one on the judges' panel; or forbidding something, 'Can you doubt whether this is dishonourable and inexpedient or not when such and such a man is in the full glow of ill repute?' When the greedy are feeling sick a neighbour's funeral frightens them, and drives them, from fear of death, to be careful of themselves. It is thanks to his training that I am whole from all the vices which bring ruin; that the faults which still entangle me are lesser ones and such as you would excuse. Perhaps even these may be largely reduced by length of years, honest friends, self-counsel; for when I retire to my couch or to a walk in the colonnade I do not forget myself: 'This course is right... By acting so I shall be a happier man... This is the way to be welcome to my friends... That is not pretty conduct of so and so... Is it possible that without knowing it I may some day do something like them?' So, with my lips shut tight, I talk to myself. When I find a moment of leisure, I waste some paper. This is one of those lesser faults of which I spoke. If you should not grant it indulgence, then there would come an army of poets to my succour—for we are more than half mankind—and, like Jews, make a proselyte of you.

V   *Egressum magna*
                    The Journey to Brundisium.

A humorous sketch of a journey taken by the poet in the company of Maecenas. Maecenas is going on state business, not indicated more particularly except that it concerned the relations between Octavianus and Antony.

One purpose of the Satire was, no doubt, to give a picture of the poet's relations to Maecenas, the freedom and absence of servility which characterized them, the literary circle with which they were shared, the absence of any political bearing in the intimacy. It is a comment on this last point that the poem so entirely lacks reference to political events that we cannot fix with any certainty the occasion or date of the journey.

It is to be remembered that to the Romans a journey to Brundisium (Brindisi) was what a journey to Dover was a generation or two ago to Englishmen, Brundisium being the port from which the passage to Greece was made. The journey begins on the Appian way. At Appii Forum the travellers leave the road and pass the night in a barge on the canal through the Pomptine marsh. From Anxur they journey by Fundi, Formiae, Sinuessa, to Capua. From there they strike into the Apennines by Caudium and Beneventum, descending into Apulia and so by the coast to Brundisium.

FRESH from Rome's grandeur I found a resting-place in a modest inn at Aricia; my companion Heliodorus the rhetorician, most learned of all Greeks.

Next Appii Forum [1], a place crammed full of bargemen
and close-fisted innkeepers.   In our laziness we made
two days' journey of what is but one to better travellers.
The Appian road is less tiring if you take it slowly.
Here for the water's sake, which was most vile, I
broke off all parley with my appetite, and sat in a bad
temper waiting till my companions had supped.   Night
was beginning to draw her curtain over the world and to
sprinkle her stars on the sky.   Then arises a babel of
voices—slaves slanging bargemen, bargemen slaves :
' Ho, boatman, thrust in here ! ' ' Are you putting three
hundred on board ?   Hold, there are enough already.'
In collecting the fares and harnessing the mule an hour
is spent before we are off.   Rascally mosquitoes and
frogs of the marsh frustrate all efforts at sleep, and meanwhile the bargeman and a passenger, both fuddled with
bad wine, sing maudlin love songs against one another.
At last the passenger tires and drops asleep, and the
lazy bargeman turns his mule to grass, tethers it to a
stone, flings himself on his back, and begins to snore.
Day was already breaking when we discover that the
barge is not moving, until one of the party who has a
temper leaps ashore, cuts a willow cudgel, and belabours
head and back of mule and man.   It is quite ten o'clock
before we land and wash face and hands in thy sacred
water, Feronia.   Then we breakfast, and crawl in carriages the three miles uphill to Anxur, perched on its far-
seen white cliffs.   It was here that Maecenas was to meet

[1] It will be remembered as a stage in St. Paul's road from
Puteoli to Rome, Acts 28. 15.

us, and Cocceius, best of men, envoys both of them on
high state affairs, and old hands at reconciling estranged
friends.   My business here was to smear my sore eyes
with the black eye-salve.   While I am so engaged,
Maecenas arrives and Cocceius, and with them Fonteius
Capito, the pink of accomplishment, and without a rival
in Antony's friendship.

Fundi we are not sorry to leave, with its praetor
Aufidius Luscus, laughing, as we go, at the high pre-
ferment of the crack-brained clerk, his edged gown and
broad stripe and shovel of hot charcoal[1].   After a long
day our next resting-place is the city of Mamurra[2] and
his like, where Murena finds the house and Capito stocks
the kitchen.   The next day's dawn was the most welcome of all, for at Sinuessa we are joined by Plotius with
Varius and Virgil[3], whitest-souled of earth's children,
and to whom none owes deeper debts than I.   How
we embraced, and how we rejoiced !   Never while I
keep my senses shall I compare anything to the delight
of a friend.

The little house by the bridge where you enter

[1] The *praetexta* or gown with a purple border belonged to
higher magistrates at Rome, the broad stripe down the front of
the tunic to senators.   What the purpose of the shovel of
charcoal was, is not known.   The jack-in-office at Fundi is
represented apparently as assuming both in title and in dress
distinctions which did not belong to him.

[2] The place is Formiae (now Mola di Gaeta).   Mamurra was
a favourite of Julius Caesar whose wealth and scandals had occupied
men's thoughts.

[3] Plotius and Varius were afterwards Virgil's literary executors.
For Varius see Od. 1. 6.

Campania gave us shelter, and the commissaries the due provision of fuel and salt. After the next stage our mules deposit their saddle-bags betimes at Capua. Here Maecenas goes off to play, Virgil and I to sleep; for a game of ball is equally bad for sore eyes and for the dyspeptic. Our next entertainment is at the well-stocked country house of Cocceius, which stands beyond the taverns of Caudium.

[1] Now, my Muse, I would have you recount in brief the engagement of Sarmentus, the trencherman, and Messius Cicirrus, and the parentage from which the two heroes sprung who joined the wordy fray. Messius was of right famous stock, an Oscan; the mistress of Sarmentus is still living—such the lineage with which they came to the fight. Sarmentus opens: 'I call you the very image of a unicorn.' We laugh, and Messius himself, 'Be it so,' and makes as though he would butt. 'Oh!' says the other, 'if only the horn had not been cut out of your forehead, what would you be capable of, seeing that you are so formidable without it!' The fact was he had a disfiguring scar on the left side of his bristly forehead. With many jests on the disease of Campania and on his face, he prayed him to dance the shepherd Cyclops: he would need neither mask nor satyr's buskin. Cicirrus had plenty to answer.

[1] A mock heroic commencement. Horace describes an encounter of wit between two buffoons, Sarmentus, a *scurra* travelling in the suite of Maecenas, and Messius, a native of the neighbourhood and probably belonging to the household of Cocceius. They figure as something like the jesters of feudal times.

Had he presented his chain yet, he asked, to the Lares, as he vowed? Clerk though he was, that did not make his mistress's right less good in law. His last question was why he had ever run away, since a pound of meal was enough for one so slim and puny. Full merrily we spent that supper-time.

Thence without a halt we journey to Beneventum, where the bustling host nearly burned himself out of house while turning some skinny fieldfares at the fire. For the Fire-god slipped abroad through the old kitchen, and the flame on its travels was well nigh catching the roof-tree. Then followed a scene—hungry guests and frightened servants snatching at the supper, and all trying to put out the flames.

From this point Apulia begins to show to my eyes the outline of its familiar hills [1], which the sirocco scorches, and up which we had never crawled had not a country house in the near neighbourhood of Trivicum given us a night's lodging, spoilt by smoke that drew tears as the stove was lighted with damp wood, the leaves still on.

Thence we bowl downhill in carriages four and twenty miles, to rest in a little town which I may not identify in verse by its name, though I may easily by these tokens: it is a place where water, the cheapest of things, costs money, but the bread is far away the best on the road, so that the old traveller is wont to load his slaves' shoulders with it for the next stage; for Canu-

[1] They were the hills at the head of the waters of his native Aufidus.

sium, which sturdy old Diomede founded, is not by a pitcherful better off for water, and its bread is gritty. Here Varius and his friends part company, he sad and they in tears. Next night we arrived at Rubi, wearied out, for it was a long stage to travel and the rain had broken up the road. Next day the weather was better, the road worse, right up to the walls of fish-famous Barium. Then Gnatia, built under the displeasure of the water-nymphs, gave us food for laughter and jests by its anxiety to persuade us that frankincense melts without fire when it crosses the temple's threshold. Apella the Jew must believe it, not I; for I have learnt the lesson[1] that gods live in careless ease, and that if Nature works some marvel it is not something sent down from the vault of heaven by gods out of humour. Brundisium is the end of a long story and a long journey.

VI   *Non quia, Maecenas*
The Freedman's son.

The starting-point of the Satire is the jealousy to which Horace felt himself to be exposed as the son of a freedman. This leads to several passages of personal interest—
  1. the narrative of his introduction to Maecenas ;
  2. the noble picture of his relations to his own father ;
  3. the description of his modest and happy life in Rome. But the Satire is intended also to touch at many points that which Horace ranks as (next only to avarice) a vice of Roman society, viz. ambition, both in the sense of pretending to, and of seeking, greater position than naturally belongs to us.

[1] i. e. the Epicurean doctrine of Lucretius.

THAT of all the Lydians [1] that are settled in Tuscan territory none is of better blood than you, or that you have had a grandsire on mother's side and father's too who commanded mighty legions in days of old, does not make you do, Maecenas, as the world does, hang on the crook of your nose those of unknown origin, such as me, the freedman's son.

You say that if a man be himself free-born it matters not what his parents were. When you say so, you argue rightly, that long before the reign of Tullius [2], the lowly born king, there lived many who, though they had no line of ancestors, were good men and true and were distinguished with offices of honour; that Laevinus, on the other hand, descendant of the Valerius at whose hands proud Tarquin was driven a fugitive from his throne, was never set at more than the value of a brass coin, even when the people acted as censor, a judge you know of what kind—how in its folly it gives high office to the unworthy and is the foolish slave of rumour, and is lost in admiration of titles of honour and waxen masks. What then ought you and I to do, who rank ourselves so far above the crowd?

For be it so that the people would prefer in the case of an office to give it to a Laevinus rather than to a Decius of no family, and that an Appius as censor would strike me off the list if I were not the son of a free-born father— and rightly too, since (like the ass in the fable) I had not rested content in my own skin.

---

[1] The Lydian origin of the Etruscans is a commonplace in Latin poetry.   [2] Servius Tullius, the son of a slave mother.

But, the truth is, glory drags bound at the wheels of
her triumphal chariot the unknown no less than the
well-born.   What did you gain, Tillius, by reassuming
the stripe [1] and becoming a tribune ?   Envy has gathered
to you which would be less were you in a private station.
For as soon as a man has been mad enough to embarrass
his leg up to the knee with the black thongs and has
dropped the broad stripe down his breast, forthwith he
hears : 'What fellow is this ?   What was his father ?'
Just as, if one suffered from the same weakness as
Barrus, of desiring to be thought handsome, wherever
he went he would make the ladies take the trouble to
ask about details, what his face was like, his ankle, his
foot, his teeth, his hair ; so if one offers to take the
charge of his fellow citizens and of the city, of the
Empire and of Italy, of the temples of the gods, he
compels all the world to care and to ask who his
father was, whether there is any flaw on his mother's
side.   'Do you, sir, the son of Syrus [2], Dama [2],
Dionysius [2], dare to fling from the rock or hand over to
Cadmus [3] a Roman citizen ?'   You say 'Novius, my
colleague, takes a place a whole row behind me, for he
is now what my father was.'   Do you therefore fancy
yourself a Paulus or a Messalla ?   You forget that he has
a stentorian voice which, if two hundred teams and three
funerals were all in the Forum at once, could be heard over
the horns and trumpets ; that is some claim at least on us.

[1] See note on p. 181.
[2] Common names of slaves.
[3] Said to be the name of an executioner.

Now to return to myself, the 'son of a freedman sire,' whom as the son of a freedman sire all carp at, now because I am your frequent guest, Maecenas; in old days it was because I was a tribune in command of a Roman legion. The present case is unlike the former. It does not follow that because it is open to any one to grudge me the office, therefore he may equally grudge me your friendship, especially as you are so careful to choose friends for merit, with no room left for crooked ways of winning favour. Lucky I cannot call myself, in the sense that it was by chance that I gained your friendship. It was no accident that threw you in my way. Virgil long ago, the best of men, and after him Varius, told you all about me. When I was first introduced to you I stammered out a few words, for tongue-tied shyness would not allow me to say more. Certainly I did not tell you that I was of distinguished parentage, or that I was used to ride a Tarentine pony round an estate of my own. I told you the truth as to what I was. You answered, as you usually do, in few words, and I went away. Nine months afterwards you sent for me again, and bade me consider myself one of your friends. For my part, I am proud to think that I pleased one who draws as you do the line between honour and disgrace, not by a father's renown but by the blamelessness of my own life and heart. But after all, if the faults are slight and few in a nature otherwise sound, as you might find a mole here or there to notice on a handsome person, if no one will truly charge me with avarice or meanness or debauchery,

if my life is without stain or harm (forgive my egotism),
and if my friends love me, for all this I have to thank
my good father, who, though a poor man with a hungry
little farm, yet would not send me to Flavius' school,
whither the sons of centurions, bigger and grander than
I, with satchel and tablet hung on left arm, used to go
carrying every Ides their fee of eight brass pieces each [1];
but ventured to carry off his boy to Rome to be taught
all the accomplishments that any knight or senator would
have his children taught. Any one who saw how
I was dressed, and what a train of slaves I had after
the fashion of a great city, would have supposed that
such expenditure was furnished from inherited wealth.
What he did for me himself was to come with me daily
from lecture to lecture, the safest of possible governors.
Need I say more? He kept me modest, which is
virtue's earliest distinction, and safe not only from deed
of shame but from breath of scandal. He had no fear
that by-and-by, if I should have to earn a small livelihood
as an auctioneer, or, as he was himself, a collector of dues,
some one would say he had wasted his money. Nor
in the event should I have made that complaint; but as
things have turned out I owe him the greater praise and
the greater gratitude. Never while I am in my sound
senses could I be ashamed of such a father. And so
I do not mean to defend myself, as a large part of the
world would do, by saying that it is not the fault of
malice prepense that they had not free-born or illustrious

[1] Or, acc. to the other reading, 'carrying their fee on the Ides
of eight months' (i.e. every month when schools were open).

parents. Such a reply is in a very different key from anything that I either say or feel. If Nature were to invite us after a cycle of years to live our lives over again and to select to the full of our pride fresh parents, each might choose for himself—content with those I had, I should have no desire for people distinguished by the rods and ivory chair; and, though the world pronounce me mad, I dare say you will still hold me sane for not wishing to undertake a burdensome load to which I am not accustomed. For forthwith I should have to get a larger income, to receive more visitors, to take with me one companion and another, for I must never go into the country or abroad alone. I must keep a stableful of grooms and horses, and take a train of wagons. As things are, I may ride if I choose as far as Tarentum on a bob-tailed mule, whose loins are sore with saddle-bags and his withers with the rider. No one will charge me with stinginess as he does you, Tillius, when as praetor you go along the road to Tibur with five boys behind you carrying a cooking-pot and wine-basket. This is a point in which my life is more comfortable than yours, my illustrious senator, and there are thousands besides. Wherever my fancy is, I go on foot and go alone. I ask the price of kitchen-stuff and grain: I often stroll about the cheating Circus and the Forum towards evening: I stop by the fortune-tellers. Presently I return home to my dish of leeks and pulse and macaroni. My supper is served by three boys, and a slab of white stone supports two drinking-cups with a ladle. By them stands a salt-cellar of

cheap material, a cruet and saucer of Campania ware.
Then I go off to bed, with no anxious thought that
I must rise early to-morrow and face poor Marsyas [1], so
distressed by the look of the younger Novius. I lie
still till past nine o'clock. After this, when I have read
or written in quiet as pleases my fancy, I take a stroll or
anoint myself with the olive oil of better quality than that
which filthy Natta steals from the lamps. But when
I am tired, and the fiercer sun has warned me to go to
the baths, I am off from the Campus and the game of
three. After a moderate luncheon, just enough to save
my going a whole day on an empty stomach, I amuse
myself at home. Such is the life of men set free from
the pains and burdens of ambition. In this way
I console myself with thinking that I shall live more
happily than if my grandfather had been a quaestor,
aye, and my father and uncle to boot.

VII   *Proscripti Regis*
Rupilius Rex.

*Probably, like the second Satire, one of Horace's earliest
compositions. It tells a story of the time in* A.D. 44 *or*
43, *when he was with Brutus in the province of
Asia. The main point is the play on the name Rex with
which it ends, a form of humour which the Romans highly
appreciated ; but the story is told in a lively way and
the different types of the two litigants are well marked—*

---

[1] Marsyas was the satyr who was flayed by Apollo. There
was a statue of him in the Forum. Horace humorously
attributes either a look of pain on his face or some gesture to his
displeasure at the frequent presence of the younger Novius,
according to the Scholiasts a moneylender.

the half-Greek trader, courtly, fluent, witty, and the
country-bred Italian, thick-skinned and heavy-handed in
his sarcasm.

HOW the half-breed Persius repaid the filth and
venom of Rupilius, that outlawed ' King,' is a
tale familiar I think to every sore-eyed man and barber[1].
This Persius was a rich man, with business in a large
way at Clazomenae, who had a troublesome lawsuit with
Rex ; he was tough, one who in offensive manner could
beat even Rex, bold and blustering, and of tongue bitter
enough to leave a Sisenna or a Barrus nowhere in the
running.   To come to the story of Rex.   When they
cannot settle their difference—(for men at law are always
troublesome to one another, or not, in virtue of the same
quality [2] as heroes who meet in single combat : between
Hector, Priam's son, and Achilles, the soul of courage,
the quarrel was mortal, so that nothing short of death
could part them, for no single reason but this, that in each
of them valour reached its highest point : if cowards had
the misfortune to quarrel, or if two met in war who were
ill-matched, as Diomede with Lycian Glaucus, the one
of least spirit would retire from the fight offering gifts
of propitiation)—well, when Brutus was praetor in
charge of the rich province of Asia, there was a fight
between Rupilius and Persius, a pair as well matched as
Bithus and Bacchius.   They rush into court keen com-
batants, each of them a sight to see.   Persius sets forth his
case, to the amusement of all the bystanders.   He praises

[1] Apothecaries' and barbers' shops are spoken of as the chief
places of gossip.

[2] Or 'all quarrelsome persons have the same right.'

Brutus, and he praises his staff. The 'sun of Asia' he
calls Brutus, and 'stars of good influence' all his suite—Rex
only excepted, for his coming was that of the 'dog-star,
the farmers' bane. So he rushed on, like winter torrent
down some ravine of uncleared woodland. In answer to
that copious flood of wit, the man of Praeneste has abuse
to hurl back like the juice wrung from a vineyard, as
though he were the vinedresser tough and unconquerable
who is often too much for the passer-by that calls
'cuckoo'[1] at him. But the Greek Persius, when he
was well soused with the Italian vinegar, cries aloud,
'By the great gods, Brutus, I adjure you, since it is your
wont to put kings out of the way, why do you not slay
this Rex? Believe me it is a task for you.'

VIII   *Olim truncus eram*
Canidia.

*The Satire must be read with the 5th and 17th Epodes. It
is probably in date the first of Horace's attacks on 'Canidia.'
The mock-heroic tone of the narrative and the farcical
catastrophe seem to forbid us to take it quite seriously.*

*The scene is the 'Campus Esquilinus,' on a site outside
the 'agger' of Servius Tullius, where there had been a
large burial place for the lowest class of the people.
Maecenas had recently bought it and laid it out as gardens,
but the transformation seems scarcely complete. There
are still 'sepulchral mounds' and bones to be found by
scratching the ground, and it is haunted by witches.*

*The speaker throughout the Satire is a rough wooden image
of Priapus, the god of gardens, which in the utilitarian
spirit of Roman religion serves in part as a scarecrow.*

[1] To call 'cuckoo' was to imply that the vinedresser was
still at work, which should be done before the cuckoo comes.

EREWHILE I was a trunk of figwood, a piece of useless timber, when the carpenter after doubting whether to make a stool or a Priapus made his choice for the god. And so a god I am, the special terror of thieves and of birds; for thieves are kept in awe by my right hand [1] and red pole, and the mischievous birds are frightened by the reed [2] set on my head from settling on the newly-made gardens. To this place in old days slaves paid some one to bring in a cheap bier the carcass of a fellow slave when it was tossed out of his narrow quarters. It was the common graveyard for the dregs of the people, Pantolabus the trencherman and Nomentanus the spendthrift. A boundary stone used to give here a thousand feet frontage and three hundred of depth, the burying place to go to no heirs or assigns. Nowadays men may live on the Esquiline and find it healthy, and take their walk in the sun on the rampart, from which before there was the sad look out over ground disfigured with blanching bones. For myself, my annoyance and trouble now is not so much the thieves and jackals which used to infest the place, as the witches who with spells and sorceries torment human souls—these I cannot make an end of or stay them in any manner, so soon as the moon on her travels has lifted her fair face above the horizon, from gathering bones and herbs of harm. With my own eyes I have seen Canidia come with black mantle girt high, with bare feet and streaming hair, howling in concert with Sagana, greater than herself, each of them terrible to look

[1] Which held a sickle.   [2] Apparently a rattle formed of reeds.

on. First they dug the ground with their nails and
tore a black ewe-lamb to pieces with their teeth; the
blood was collected in a trench that thereby they might
draw the spirits of the dead, souls to give oracular
answer. Then there was an effigy of wool, another
of wax; the one of wool the larger, that it might hold
the weaker in durance and punishment, the waxen one
standing in suppliant attitude as expecting sentence to a
slave's death. One witch calls on Hecate; the other
on fell Tisiphone. You might see serpents and hell-
hounds moving about, and the blushing moon that she
might not witness such sights hiding behind the huge
sepulchral mounds. Nay, if I lie in anything, may
my head be defiled by the crows and the worst of each
sex use me for basest purposes! Need I tell each
detail—how sad and shrill sounded the voices of the
shades in dialogue with Sagana—how they buried
stealthily in the ground a wolf's beard and the tooth of
a spotted snake—how the waxen image made fire blaze
higher—and how I avenged myself for being the shudder-
ing witness of the words and deeds of the two Furies?
With a noise as of a burst bladder my buttock of figwood split with a pop, and off they scurried into the
town. You might see Canidia drop her teeth and
Sagana her tall wig, and the herbs and the charmed
love-knots from their arms; and great was the laughter
and the mirth.

IX   *Ibam forte Via*

A morning stroll in Rome.

The subject, on the face of it, is the sufferings of Horace under the persecution of a man of strong will and thick skin who meets him during his morning stroll; but, as appears in the later part of the Satire, this is only the dramatic presentment of a more serious theme.   In Sat. 1. 6 Horace has given an account of his own introduction to Maecenas' friendship, how small a part he had himself had in it, and how consistent with self-respect every stage of it had been.   This Satire gives, in contrast, a picture of the way in which vulgar and pushing people sought, and sought in vain, to obtain an introduction.

IT chanced I was strolling in the Sacra Via, conning after my fashion some trifle I know not what, and wholly absorbed in it, when a man I just knew by name runs up to me and seizes my hand with 'How do you do, my dearest friend?' 'Pretty well, just now' I answered, 'I hope you are the same.' When I saw that he was following at my heels I turn on him with 'Is there anything I can do for you?' He: 'You surely know me, we are both men of letters.' 'Indeed' said I, 'that will be a recommendation to me.' Longing miserably to shake him off, I first quickened my pace, then stopped short, made as though I was whispering something in my slave's ear — in a fume all the time that made every pore stream. 'O Bolanus, you happy man,' I was saying to myself, 'if only I had your hot temper!' while the fellow rattled on upon anything and nothing, praising the streets, the town. When I made him no answer, 'I know you must be sadly wanting to get rid of me'

says he, 'but it is no good [1], I cannot let you go—
I shall attend you to your destination.' 'There is no
need to take you so far round. I am going to visit a
friend whom you do not know. He lives a long way
off, on the other side of the river, near Caesar's gardens,
and he is ill in bed.' 'I have no business and am in
the humour for a walk—I shall come all the way with
you.' Down go my ears like those of a sullen ass
when he is laden beyond his liking. He is the first to
speak next : 'We should be friends. If I know anything of myself you will not value Viscus more, nor
Varius. Who can write verses more in number or more
quickly than I can ? Who can dance more gracefully ?
My singing even Hermogenes might envy.' Here he
gave me a moment's chance of interrupting : 'Have you
a mother [2] or kindred to take care of you ?' 'Not one
—I have laid them all to rest.' 'Happy souls [3], I am
the only one left. Make haste and finish me, for the
hour is come for that sad fate which when I was a boy
the Sabellian crone foretold for me, after shaking the
lots in her divining urn :

> No sword shall kill, no poison injure him,
> Nor aching side nor cough nor crippled limb :
> This lad a chatterbox alone will slay ;
> Talkers let him avoid, if he would live his day !'

[1] Of course this is meant as a jest. The man cannot conceive
that his company is really displeasing.

[2] Possibly Horace means to hint that the man is out of his
mind and should be taken care of by his relations.

[3] Evidently an 'aside,' for no reply is made.

We had come now to Vesta's temple[1] and it was past
nine o'clock, and it so chanced that at that hour he was
bound on his recognizances to appear in court under
penalty, if he failed, of losing his suit. 'If you love
me' says he 'wait a little to give me your countenance.'
'Nay, I protest I am not strong enough to stand so
long, and I know nothing of law matters, and besides
I must hasten whither you know.' 'I am in a strait' he
says 'what to do, to desert you or my suit.' 'Oh!
me, please.' 'I cannot' says he; and begins to lead
the way. It is hard fighting with one who is your
master, so I follow him. 'On what terms is Maecenas
with you?' so he starts afresh, 'a man choice in
his friends and who knows what's what. No one
has played his cards more dexterously. You might
have a strong backer, and one quite prepared to take
a second part to you, if you would introduce your humble
servant. Hang me if you would not find that you
had cleared every one else from your way!' 'You
misunderstand the terms on which we live there.
There is no house purer or more free from such intrigues
as that. It never stands in my way' I say 'that one
is richer than I or more learned. Each has his own
place.' 'Dear me, what you tell me sounds like a
miracle.' 'Yet it is a fact.' 'You whet my desire for
his intimacy.' 'You have only to wish for it—your

---

[1] i. e. the corner of the Palatine where the Sacra Via entered
the Forum and where Horace's path would diverge to the left if he
were going to cross the river in the direction of Caesar's gardens
on the Janiculum.

valour is such that you will storm the fort. He is to
be won, and that is why he makes the first approaches
difficult.' 'I will not fail myself: I will bribe his
slaves : if the door is shut on me to-day I will not give
it up; I will watch my opportunity; I will fall in with
him in the streets and escort him home. The prizes
of life are never to be had without trouble.' While he
is so occupied Aristius Fuscus[1] met us, a dear friend
of mine, and one who, I felt sure, knew him only too
well. We halt. 'Whence come you and whither go
you?' is asked and answered. I tried plucking his
sleeve, squeezing his arm, but it showed no feeling. I
nodded, winked fiercely at him, as a hint that he
should save me. With cruel humour he smiled and
pretended not to understand. I was burning with wrath.
'You surely told me you had something you wished to
talk about privately.' 'I remember fully, but I will
tell you at some better time. Do you not know to-day
is the thirtieth Sabbath[2]—do you wish to insult the
Jews?' 'I have no superstitious scruple' say I. 'But
I have—I am not as strong-minded—one of the many—
you will pardon me—I will talk another day.' To think
so black a day as this has dawned on me ! He makes
off ruthlessly and leaves me with the knife at my throat.

At that moment it so happened that the plaintiff in
the suit came down the road and met my companion :

---

[1] Horace's intimate friend; see Od. 1. 22 and Epist. 1. 10.

[2] The phrase is probably a riddle without a key. It seems a
composition of the two phrases the 'Sabbath' and 'the thirtieth'
day of the month, i. e. the new moon : some words with a mystic
sound, but chosen at random.

' Where are you going, you scoundrel ? ' he cries, and to
me ' Witness my summons.' I offer my ear to touch [1]—
he drags him off towards the court, both shouting and
a mob collecting.   So Apollo bore me from the fray [2].

X   *Nempe incomposito*

   Lucilius and Horace.   Fair and unfair criticism.
*The Satire, as its last words testify, was viewed by
Horace as an Epilogue to the Book.   He reiterates and
defines his position with respect to Lucilius as he had
stated it in Sat. I. 4, defending himself from the contemptuous criticism of Demetrius and Hermogenes Tigellius
and their school, and appealing to the judgement of the
really good writers and critics of the time.*

IT is true I did say that the verses of Lucilius have
   a halting rhythm.   Who is such a silly partisan of
Lucilius as not to confess so much ?   But on the same
page he is also praised for having made the town smart
with his wit.   Only when I allow this merit I do not
mean to grant him every other ; for on that principle I
should have to admire a mime of Laberius as a beautiful
poem.   Take it then that it is not enough by itself to
make an audience grin with laughter (although there is
some merit even in that) : there must be the power of
terse expression, that the thoughts may flow on unim-
peded by the verbiage, which only tires the overladen

---

[1] The formality by which a person expressed his willingness to
witness the serving of a summons.
[2] As he bore Hector in Il. 20. 443 :
                him wrapt in clouds opaque
         Apollo caught with ease divine away.   Cowper.

ears : there must be the style that changes, now serious
and again playful, now suited to the part of the declaimer
or poet, now to the man of the world who husbands his
strength and says less than he means. Humour very
often cuts the knot of serious questions more tren-
chantly and successfully than severity. This was how
the true men who wrote the old comedy won success
and this is where they are to be imitated. They are
writers whom Hermogenes the fop has never read, nor
that ape whose one accomplishment is to drawl Calvus
and Catullus.

' But it was a great hit ' you say ' his mingling Greek
words with his Latin as he did ! '

O you dunces turned pedants ! How can you think it
a difficult or wonderful thing to do what was within
the reach of the Rhodian Pitholaus ?

' Language nicely compounded of the two tongues
gains flavour, as if you mix wine of Falernian brand with
Chian.'

When you are writing verses only ? I put the
question to yourself—or is it the case also when you
have a hard case to plead, like that of Petillius ? Doubtless you would forget fatherland and father, and while
Pedius Publicola and Corvinus were spending their
utmost strength in pleading their case in pure Latin,
prefer to adulterate your mother-speech with foreign
words like a bilingual Canusian [1].

I too, though born on this side of the sea, had a
thought of writing some poor Greek poetry, but Quirinus

[1] For Canusium and its Greek origin see in Sat. 1. 5 (p. 183).

himself appeared to me in the morning hours, when dreams are true, and forbade it with words like these : ' 'Twere no greater madness to carry timber into a forest [1] than, when you have the choice, to swell the crowded ranks of Greek writers.' So while the turgid hero of the Alps [2] murders Memnon and fits the Rhine with a ' head of mud,' I amuse myself with these trifles —neither poems to be read in the temple as offered for Tarpa's [3] judgement, nor plays to be put again and again on the stage in the theatres. You alone of living poets, Fundanius, can charm us with the chatter of the keen-witted slave-girl and Davus cheating old Chremes. Pollio sings of the deeds of kings in the measure of triple beat [4]. Varius builds the brave Epic with a spirit all his own. Tenderness and finished grace the Muses of the country have granted to Virgil [5]. Satire, which Varro of the Atax and some others had essayed unsuccessfully, was what I could write, better than they, but below the level of its inventor. I am not the man

---

[1] As we say ' coals to Newcastle.'

[2] Furius Bibaculus, a poet laughed at in Sat. 2. 5 (p. 241). He is called the ' hero of the Alps' on account of his verse ridiculed in that place. He had written apparently on the Death of Memnon (slain by Achilles). He incurs Horace's ridicule for speaking of the source of the Rhine as ' muddy.' It was no doubt unpoetical; but it was a truer epithet than probably either of them knew.

[3] The Scholiast identifies him with the Maecius of Ars Poet. 387, and with a person employed by Pompey to approve of plays for performance in his theatre.

[4] i. e. in tragic iambics; see Od. 2. 1.

[5] Virgil had at this time published only the Eclogues.

to rob that famous head of the garland which with the world's applause rests upon it.

But, you repeat, I said his was 'a turbid stream, often carrying with it more that you would desire to remove than to leave.' Come, I put it to you—you are a man of learning—do you find nothing to criticize in the mighty Homer? Does Lucilius, for all his good nature, wish nothing otherwise in Accius, the great tragedian? Does he not laugh at the verses of Ennius as wanting in dignity? But this does not mean that he reckons himself as greater than those whom he so criticizes. And so for us also when we are reading the writings of Lucilius, why may we not ask whether it was his own fault or the unkind 'nature of things' that prevented his verses from being better finished or running more smoothly than those of a man who, content with merely putting his thoughts into correct six-foot measure, should pride himself on having written two hundred verses every day before luncheon and the same number after dinner, after the way of Tuscan Cassius, with his genius like a stream in flood, who (the story goes) was burnt on a pile of his own works in their cases?

Grant, I say, that Lucilius had good-tempered and well-bred humour: grant even that in polish he was beyond what the creator of a new style such as the Greeks had never tried could possibly be, beyond what the ruck of the older poets was—still even he, if fate had deferred his birth to this age, would use the polishing-file freely on his own writings, would prune redundancies, and in perfecting his verses would often scratch his head and

bite his nails to the quick.   You must often use the blunt
end of your *stilus* [1], if you are to write what deserves
a second reading; you must not care for the admiration
of the many, but be content with readers fit but few.
You surely are not senseless enough to prefer that
your poems should be lesson-books in cheap schools.
I at least am not.   It is enough for me if the knights
applaud — I care not a fig for the rest of the house, as
bold Arbuscula said when she was hissed off the stage.
Would you have me care for Pantilius, who 'stinks and
stings [2],' or be in agony because Demetrius pulls me to
pieces behind my back, or because Fannius, the tasteless
boon companion of Hermogenes Tigellius, decries me?
No! Plotius and Varius, Maecenas and Virgil, Valgius
and Octavius, and Fuscus, best of men—let these approve
my writings, and the two brothers Viscus praise them.
I have no base interest when I name thee, Pollio, thee,
Messalla, with thy brother, and you, Bibulus and Servius.
Together with them thee, fair-souled Furnius, and
many more, men of taste and friends to me, whom I could
name if I chose.   In their eyes I hope these verses,
whatever be their value, may be pleasing; and I shall
be sorry if they please them less than I hope.   As for
you, Demetrius and Tigellius, I bid you go whine
among the armchairs of your lady admirers.

Go quick, boy, and write this as an Epilogue to my
little book.

[1] The sharp end of the *stilus* was used to write on the waxed
tablet, the blunt end to erase what was written.
[2] Pope.

Book II

I   *Sunt quibus in satira*

Trebatius: or The right and wrong of Satire.

An imaginary dialogue between Horace and C. Trebatius Testa, a great lawyer of the generation before, known to us from Cicero's correspondence with him. There seem to be some personal touches, for the devotion of Trebatius to swimming and his fondness for such 'night-caps' (l. 14) are subjects of raillery in one or two of Cicero's letters to him.

It is an illustration of the careful order in which the Satires are arranged that this apology for Satire, and for Satire which has given offence, is made to serve as the prologue to a Second Book.

Horace. THERE are who think that I am too fierce in my Satire and carry things beyond lawful bounds. The other half of the world thinks all my composition nerveless, and that verses as good as mine might be spun a thousand a day. Give me your advice, Trebatius, what I shall do.

Trebatius. Take a holiday.

Horace. Not write verses at all, you mean?

Trebatius. I do.

Horace. The best advice, after all—may I be hanged if it isn't! But I cannot sleep.

Trebatius. Those who would sleep sound must rub the oil in and swim thrice across the Tiber, and take a nightcap of good wine, or if the passion for writing is irresistible, be bold and tell of the heroic exploits of Caesar. You will receive full reward for your pains.

Horace. Fain would I do so, good father: but the faculty fails me. Battle-lines bristling with pikes, or Gauls dying with lances shivered, or Parthian slipping wounded from his horse, are not what every one can paint.

Trebatius. If so, you might paint himself, just and strong, as Lucilius, who was a wise man, drew his hero Scipio.

Horace. When occasion prompts I will be true to myself. Unless the time be propitious the humble words of Flaccus will not find with Caesar entrance in an attentive ear. If you try awkwardly to stroke him, he is on his guard in every direction and has his heels ready.

Trebatius. How much wiser this than to assail with ill-natured verse 'Pantolabus the trencherman and Nomentanus the spendthrift[1].' When you do that, you make every one fear for himself and hate you, though you have not touched him.

Horace. What am I to do? Milonius, so soon as the heat of the wine has touched his head and made the lamps look double, falls to dancing[2]. Castor finds his joy in horses, the brother, born from the same egg, in boxing. For every thousand souls there are a thousand tastes. My delight is to fit words into the

[1] A line quoted from Sat. 1. 8 as a specimen of Horace's personal satire.

[2] In men a great sacrifice of Roman decorum. Cicero in his defence of Murena (pro Mur. 6. 13) says that 'no one dances unless he is either drunk or mad.'

frame of feet after Lucilius' fashion, a better man than
either of us. He used of old to whisper his secrets to
his parchments as to trusty companions, never running to
any other haven, whether things had gone ill with him
or well. So it comes that the whole life of the veteran
lies open to our view painted as on a votive picture. It
is he that I follow, a son of Lucania or of Apulia—it is
hard to say which, for the settlers of Venusia plough
close to the borders of the two[1], sent there, as the old
tradition goes, when the Sabellians were dispossessed,
for the purpose that no enemy might find the gap empty
and make inroad on Roman lands[2], if either the Apulian
race or Lucania in mood of violence were at any time
threatening war. But *stilus*[3] such as mine will never
assail any man alive: it will protect myself, like
a sword safe in its sheath. Why should I attempt to
draw it while I am safe from the assault of robbers?
O Jupiter, Sire and King, that the weapon may be let
rust away where it lies, that none may ever attack one
who desires peace! But for him who rouses me
('Better not touch me!' I cry loudly) he shall weep
for it, and be the theme of talk and song throughout
the town. Cervius when he is angered threatens his
foes with the law and the jurors' ballot-box: Canidia
with the poison of Albucius: Turius with a bad time

[1] Cp. Od. 3. 4.

[2] A good description of the military purpose of a Roman
'colonia.'

[3] There is a play on the double use possible of the *stilus*, to
write on the waxed tablet and as a weapon like the modern
stiletto.

if you come into court when he is on the bench.
Every one, to frighten those he fears, uses the weapon
with which he is strongest, and does this by nature's
sovereign command. That is the principle, and you
may prove it thus: the wolf attacks with his teeth, the
bull with his horns—where did they learn that but from
instinct? Put a long-lived mother within spendthrift
Scaeva's power: his filial hand will commit no crime—
what a marvel! no, not any more than a wolf will attack
with his heels or an ox with his teeth; but the villainous
hemlock in some drugged honey will carry off the old
lady. To make a short story—whether a tranquil old
age is in store for me, or Death already is flapping its
black wings round me, rich or poor, at home or, if
chance so order it, in exile, whatever the colour of my
life, I shall go on writing.

Trebatius. My son, I fear your life is not a good
one. Some one of your great friends will smite you
with a frost that kills.

Horace. What! when Lucilius first dared to compose poems after this kind, and to tear off the skin in
which men walked with fair outside before the world's
eyes, though base within, was Laelius offended at his
wit, or he who drew his well-earned name from the
conquest of Carthage? Did they smart because
Metellus was hit hard, or Lupus pelted with lampoon-
ing verse? Yet he laid hands on the leaders of the
people and on the people in whole tribes. In fact, he
had fellow-feeling for none but Virtue and her friends.
Nay, when Scipio's virtue and Laelius's mild wisdom

had withdrawn from the crowd and public stage into privacy, they were wont to play like schoolboys with him while the cook was getting ready their supper of herbs. Whatever I am, however far below Lucilius in social rank as in native gift, yet envy will be fain unwillingly to confess that those whom I have lived with are the great, and, while thinking to close its teeth on something that will break, will strike on a solid substance. I say this, Trebatius, in submission to your judgement.

Trebatius. My teeth at any rate can break nothing off it [1]. But for all that, you should be cautioned lest you get into trouble from ignorance of the Twelve Tables. So let me remind you that if any have written 'ill verses upon any man' there are courts and an indictment holds.

Horace. Aye, if they be 'ill' verses, be it so; but what if they be good ones and Caesar has praised them— if you have but given tongue at the man who deserves abuse, while you yourself are clear?

Trebatius. In a tempest of laughter the Tables will go to pieces [2]. You will leave the court without a stain on your character.

---

[1] There is a question both of reading and of sense. The Scholiast took *diffindere* in a technical sense, and as meaning 'I cannot adjourn the question,' i. e. 'I assent at once to what you say.'

[2] Another expression to which possibly the clue is wanting.

II   *Quae virtus et quanta*

Ofellus: or Plain living.

This Satire is not a dialogue, although there are two speakers, Horace interrupting twice—at the beginning to explain that we are listening not to himself but to Ofellus, and again towards the end to give his remembrance of Ofellus' habits in old days and introduce the second imagined speech, in which the old countryman applied his philosophy to his own life and that of his sons.

Ofellus is represented as belonging to the country in which Horace's early boyhood was spent, and as having been dispossessed of his property at the same time as Horace himself or his father. He has lived on as a tenant under Umbrenus, the veteran to whom the land was assigned.

The general condemnation of luxurious living suits the character of the sturdy Apulian, but there is little attempt in detail to distinguish the style or the arguments from those of a Stoic lecturer, such as we have in the next Satire. Many of the special criticisms are such as an epicure would have found it not difficult to answer.

'WHAT the virtue, good sirs, and how great an one it is, of frugal living'—this is no talk of my own, but the teaching of Ofellus, the countryman, a philosopher, though not from the schools but of home-spun wit—'listen and learn, not amid sheen of plate and trim tables, when the eye is dazzled by meaningless brilliance, and the mind, having learnt to lean on what is false, loses its taste for what is better: but let us talk the question over now before breaking our fast.' 'Why so?' 'I will tell you, if I can. A bribed judge weighs truth in false scales. When you come tired from hunting the hare or breaking a horse—(if the soldierly exercises of Rome are too fatiguing for one accustomed to Greek ways, perhaps a game of ball, in which the interest takes out the taste of the toil, or of quoits, attracts you; if so, by all means fling the quoit through the yielding air)—then when toil has knocked niceness out of you, when you are thirsty and hungry, despise, if you can, plain food, and refuse to drink your *mulsum*[1] unless the honey is from Hymettus and the wine Falernian. Suppose the housekeeper is out, or the sea is rough and fish not to be caught, some bread and salt will suffice to appease the wolf inside you. Whence or how do you think it gets that power? The chief pleasure lies not in the smell of costly cookery but in yourself. If you want relishes, get them by hard exercise. The man who is bloated and pale from wrong living will get no help from oysters or rare fish or foreign bird. But I suppose I shall hardly root out the prejudice which makes you wish, if a peacock is on table, to tickle your palate with this rather than a barn-door fowl. You are misled by empty show; because it is a rare bird and cost gold, and the colours of its opened tail are a sight to see—as though that had anything to do with the matter! Do you eat those feathers which you admire so? Has it the same brave show when cooked? Yet, though there is nothing to choose between them in the eating, you crave for the one rather than the other because you are taken in by the difference in the outside! Well, be it so, but what sense tells you

[1] A drink of wine sweetened with honey.

whether the pike that lies here gasping was taken in the Tiber or in the sea, in the current off the bridges or at the mouth of the Tuscan river? You praise, foolish man, a mullet of three pounds, though, before you can help it, you have to cut it up into separate portions. It is the look, I see, that attracts you. But what then is the consistency of disliking pike if they are large? I will tell you: it is because nature makes the pike large and the mullet small. This contempt for things common belongs to the stomach which seldom feels real hunger. "O give me" cries a gullet worthy of the greedy Harpies "the sight of something vast lying at length in a vast dish!" Come in your power, O south winds, and cook the dainty dishes for these gentlemen! Yet that is not needed. The freshest boar and turbot have gone stale when the jaded stomach sickens at the food of which it has had enough, and turns for relief to some sharp-tasting salad.

The fare of humble life has not yet been entirely banished from the halls of princes; room is still left for cheap egg and black olive. It is not so many years since a sturgeon gave the table of Gallonius the auctioneer an ill notoriety [1]. Think you there were fewer turbots then in the sea? The turbot was safe, and the stork found its nestlings safe, till an authority of praetor's rank taught you the lesson. If one now with the same authority shall have pronounced that divers are nice

---

[1] The point is that the standard of luxurious living varies from age to age. It is a matter of fashion, and therefore not of reason.

roasted, the young generation, always ready to learn a mischievous lesson, will follow his lead.

There will be a great difference, if you trust the judgement of Ofellus, between simple living and mean living. It will be of no use to have avoided the one fault if you turn off the road in another direction. Avidienus, whose nickname of *Canis*[1] is no meaningless jest, eats his olives five years old and cornels from the woods, and is chary of opening a wine-jar till the wine is gone sour: as for his oil, you couldn't bear the smell of it, yet even if in freshly-cleaned gown he be keeping a wedding or a birthday feast or some other holiday, he drops it on his salad with his own hands, a drop at a time from the two pound horn: the only thing he does not spare is his old vinegar[2]. What style then will the wise man adopt? Which of these two will he imitate? There is a wolf, as the proverb says, on one side, a dog on the other. He will be neat enough to let no one complain of his meanness. His mode of living will be unhappy in neither direction. He will neither be hard on his slaves when they are taking their orders, like old Albucius; nor, like too easy Naevius, let them give his guests water with grease floating on it. This too is a serious fault.

Let me tell you now what and how great are the advantages that simple living offers. First, you may have good health. For how unwholesome is a variety of

---

[1] The dog of the Roman streets was a foul feeder.

[2] A receipt for a miser's salad—the oil bad, and even then sparingly measured, the vinegar good and in plenty.

dishes you may believe if you remember the plain meal
of old days and how lightly it sat.   But when once you
have mixed boiled and roast, shellfish and fieldfares,
what is sweet will turn acrid, and ill digestion raise in-
testine war.   Do you notice the pale faces with which
men rise from the supper with the puzzling bill of fare ?
Aye, and the body burdened by yesterday's excess
weighs down with itself the mind also, and makes fast
to earth the particle of heavenly breath.   The other,
after the refreshment that takes but a few minutes, goes to
rest and wakes in full freshness for his daily tasks.   Yet
he will be able to cross the line sometimes to better
fare, if an annual holiday comes round, or if he has
been brought low and wants to recruit, and as his years
increase and weakening age asks for softer treatment.
But in your case, what have you in reserve against the
chance of illness with its inconveniences, or the slackness
of old age, to add to the softness which you forestall
while still young and in good health ?

The ancients used to say that a wild boar should be
high—not, I suppose, that they had no nose, but with this
meaning, that it was more fitting that a guest, who might
come later, should eat it when it was over-kept, than the
greedy master of the house when it was fresh.   Oh that
I had lived in the young world amid heroes like those !

You make some count, I suppose, for the world's
voice.   It takes the human ear with more charm than
music.   Big turbots and big dishes mean big disgrace
as well as big expense.   Add the angry uncle [1], the

[1] See note on Odes 3. 12.

angry neighbours, the self-reproaches, the vain desire
for death, when you have not a penny left to buy a
halter with [1]. "You may justly scold Trausius in that
way," he answers, "but I have great revenues, riches
ample for three kings." Well then, is there nothing
better on which you could spend your superabundance?
Why is any in want who does not deserve it, while you
have wealth? Why are the ancient temples of the
gods in ruin? Why, shameless man, do you measure
nothing from that great heap for the country which you
love? You, of course, alone of mankind are secure
from possible reverse. Oh, how your enemies will
laugh by-and-by! Which of the two will meet the
chances of life with most self-confidence—one who
has pampered mind and body by accustoming them to
superfluities, or one who, content with little and distrust-
ful of the future, has, like a wise man, in time of peace
made ready for war?'

That you may give more credit to his words, let me
say, that I remember this Ofellus when I was a boy,
living as modestly on his full means as he does now
that they are clipped so closely. You may see him
any day on the land of which he has been dispossessed,
working sturdily as a tenant farmer with his team and
his sons, and he will tell you, ' I was never one in old
days to eat anything on a working day, without good
reason, beyond garden stuff and a knuckle of smoked
bacon; and if at rare intervals an old friend came to see
me, or a neighbour dropped in on a rainy day when

[1] A proverbial jest.

I could not work, a welcome guest, we made merry not
with fish sent for from town, but with a pullet or a kid;
and afterwards the dessert was made out with some
raisins from the string and nuts and split figs, and we
had our wine and our game of forfeits, and our prayer to
Ceres—so might she lift her head high on the stalks!—
and our brows were smoothed from every care. Let
fortune bluster and raise new troubles as she will, how
much can she knock off from all this? By how much,
my boys, have we been in worse case since this new
proprietor came? The truth is, Nature makes neither
him nor me nor any one else in a true sense owner
of the land. He turned us out: he will be turned
out by the villainy of some other, or by his own
ignorance of the subtleties of the law: and if he is not,
in the end he will be turned out by an heir whose life is
a better one than his own. The land goes now by the
name of Umbrenus: a few years ago it went by that of
Ofellus: but it will never belong to anybody. It will
yield its use now to one, now to some one else. So
live, my boys, as brave men; and if fortune is adverse,
front its blows with brave hearts.'

III   *Sic raro scribis*

Damasippus: or A mad world.

*The subject of the Satire is the Stoic paradox that every
one but the wise man is mad. Horace treats it after
his wont, laughing at it with others, but using it as a
weapon with which he can strike at practical follies.
The doctrine is applied successively to the vices of avarice,
ambition, extravagance, superstition. The bulk of the*

*Satire is put into the mouth of Stertinius, a lecturer
of the day. Damasippus, Horace's interlocutor in the
dialogue, is a character from Cicero's Epistles, in which
we hear of him as a clever go-between in the purchase
of estates and works of art. Horace represents him as
having been bankrupt and as having been saved from
suicide by meeting Stertinius, who preached to him the
Stoic doctrine, with the conclusion that as nearly all men
were mad, he need not be too painfully ashamed of
himself.*

*It will be noticed that Horace ends the Satire by good-
humouredly turning the laugh against himself.*

Damasippus. YOU compose so seldom that you
do not ask for the parchment[1]
four times a year, treating whatever you compose as
a Penelope's web, angry with yourself that, though you
are so generous of wine and of sleep, the amount of
poetry produced is not worth mentioning. What will
be the end? You reply that even in the Saturnalia
you have come here for refuge. Well, then, if you
are so sober, give us some utterance to match your
promises. Begin. Nothing comes. The blame is
laid on the undeserving pen: the innocent wall gets
the worst of it—poor thing, neither gods nor poets
smiled on its birth. Yet your face was as of one
threatening great and brilliant things if once the holidays came and you were safe under the warm roof
of your little country house. What was the good
of packing Plato tight against Menander, of carrying
into the country with you Eupolis, Archilochus, such

[1] For the purpose of making a fair copy of a completed composition.

grand travelling companions? Perhaps your idea is
to appease ill-will by leaving Virtue to her fate[1]. You
will only be despised, and will deserve it. No—you
must avoid the shameless Siren, idleness, or else be
content to give up all that in your better hours you
have earned.

Horace. The gods and goddesses grant you,
Damasippus, for your good advice, the boon of—a
barber! But how come you to know me so well?

Damasippus. Ever since all my fortune went to
pieces on 'Change I have made other people's business
my care, as I had been knocked overboard from my
own. Once on a time my inquiries were always
whether this brass pan were the one in which cunning
old Sisyphus had washed his feet, whether a marble
was chiselled inartistically or a bronze cast too roughly.
I posed as a connoisseur, and fixed the price of such a
statue at a hundred thousand. I knew better than
any one else how to buy gardens and choice town-
houses at a good bargain, whence the crowd that hangs
about auctions gave me the nickname of 'Mercury's
favourite.'

Horace. I know it, and I am marvelling to see you
cured of such a malady as that.

Damasippus. A marvel it is, but the truth is, a
new one drove out the old, as happens often when the
pain of suffering side or head shifts into the stomach;
or when a patient wakes up from a drowsy fit and
wants to fight his doctor.

---

[1] i. e. by giving up the writing of Satire.

Horace. As long as you do nothing of that sort, be it as you please.

Damasippus. Oh, my good sir, that you may not deceive yourself, let me tell you once for all, you too are mad. We may indeed say that every one is, who is not a philosopher, if there is any truth in what is always on the lips of Stertinius, from which I wrote down word for word these marvellous lessons, the day that he consoled me, and bade me grow the beard of wisdom, and go home from the Fabrician bridge, a sad man no longer. For after my business failed, I was meaning to wrap my head in my mantle and fling myself into the river; but he stood like a good genius by my side, and said:

'Mind you do nothing unworthy of yourself. The shame which tortures you so is a false one. In a world of madmen you are afraid of being thought mad. For I will ask first, what is madness? If it proves to be something peculiar to you I will not say another word to prevent your dying like a man.

Chrysippus' Stoic flock holds that any one is a madman, who under the evil influence of folly, or indeed any ignorance of the truth, does not see where he is going. This definition covers whole peoples, mighty kings, every one in fact save the wise man only.

Now let me show you why all who have dubbed you "madman" are quite as crazy as you. When men miss the path in a forest and go astray in every direction, all miss it equally, though one is led wrong on the right side of the road and one on the left. So for yourself, believe that if you are mad it is only in such

a sense that the man who is laughing at you drags
a tail also[1].

One kind of folly is that of the man who fears
where there is nothing to fear—cries out that fire, that
rocks or rivers are in his way on an open plain.
Another kind, crooked at a different angle from this
but not a whit more wise, is his who rushes blindfold
through fire and water; though a fond mother, an
honoured sister, father, wife, and all his kith and kin,
shout at him "take care: there is a broad ditch in your
way, a precipice!" he will not listen any more than
tipsy Fufius in the story, when he over-acted the
sleeping Ilione, though not one Catienus[2] but twelve
hundred of them shouted at him "Mother, I call thee!"
The madness of the world at large, I shall show you,
belongs to this latter mode of missing the path.

Damasippus (say you?) is mad in buying old statues:
the man who lends Damasippus money to buy them
is of sound mind.   Indeed?   If I should say to you[3]

---

[1] A proverbial expression for being a fool without knowing it.
It is said to have been an amusement of Roman *gamins* to tie
a sheep's tail to the back of an innocent passer-by.

[2] Catienus is the actor, in a play of Pacuvius, of the part of the
shade of Deiphilus, Ilione's son. It appears and calls on the sleeping Ilione; but the actor of her part on this occasion could not
be woke, though the audience entered into the fun and shouted
with Catienus ' *Mater, te appello.*'

[3] The argument takes the form of a dilemma. Either the
man who lends Damasippus money does not expect to be repaid
or he does. In the first case surely Damasippus shows no madness in taking money on such terms. In the second the lender
must be trying to secure the repayment by notes of hand
('Nerius' seems to be either the lender himself or, more likely,

"Take this money—I never expect you to repay it,"
shall you be a madman if you take it? or would it
be a greater sign of insanity to refuse the special bounty
of Mercury? "Give note of hand for ten thousand
from Nerius." That is not enough—add bonds such as
Cicuta draws, a master in legal knots—add a hundred,
a thousand links of iron! yet the hardened debtor will
escape your bonds, like Proteus. When you try to
arrest him he will laugh at you from behind strange
masks, he will turn into a wild boar, and then into
a bird, and then into a stone or, if he likes, a tree.
If it proves the madman to lose a fortune and the sane
man to keep it, believe me, it is the brain of Perellius [1]
that is the more addled of the two if he lends you
money which you can never repay.

Now I bid my class arrange their gowns neatly and
listen. Every one of you who is pale from a bad attack
of ambition [2] or avarice [2], or in a fever with extravagance [2]
or gloomy superstition [2], or some other mental malady,
come nearer to me and hear the oracle each in his turn,
as I explain to you that all are mad.

Much the largest dose of hellebore [3] must be ad-

a banker or moneylender through whom the business is done)
and legal knots. But he may as well try to bind Proteus. So
that in any case the lender is more mad than the borrower.

[1] Perellius—the name stands here for the lender. It was
probably the name, either in literature or in real life, of some
notoriously sharp moneylender.

[2] This list of vices gives the framework of the rest of
Stertinius' lecture: each is taken in turn.

[3] A specific in the ancient pharmacopoeia for brain disease.
Anticyra in Phocis was a place from which much was procured.

ministered to the *avaricious*. I am not sure that it
is not for them that Reason intends the whole store of
Anticyra. Staberius bound his heirs to engrave on his
tomb the amount of the money he left : if they failed
to do so, they were under obligation to give a show
of a hundred pairs of gladiators and a funeral feast such
as would satisfy Arrius, to distribute of corn a whole
African harvest. "Whether I am right or wrong in
so ordering"—that was his tone—"don't come the
uncle [1] over me." What, I imagine, Staberius looked
forward to is this. "What do you mean was in his
mind," you ask, "when he bade his heirs carve on stone
the amount of his estate ?" So long as he was alive
he had thought poverty the worst of moral vices, and
spent all his pains in avoiding it. For every farthing
less that he proved to have died worth he would seem
to himself the worse man. Riches, you know, are the
beautiful things : everything else, worth, repute, honour,
things divine and things human, bow down to them.
Any one who has gathered a pile of them will be
famous, gallant, just. "And wise too ?" Certainly—
and a king and anything else he could wish. Wealth
proved the worth by which it must have been won, and
would be to him, he hoped, a security for fame.

What Aristippus the Greek did is at first sight very
different. When he was crossing the Libyan desert
he bade his slaves throw away a load of gold because
it delayed their march. Which of the two is the
madder ? An instance carries us no further which
settles one quarrel only by opening another. If a man

[1] See note on Ode 3. 12.

were to buy citherns and then only make a pile of them, without the slightest interest in the cithern or in any one of the Muses,—if a man who was not a shoemaker did the same with shoemakers' knives and lasts,—a man who hated sea voyages with sails,—every one would call them crazy and mad, and deservedly so. What is the difference between them and the man who stores money and gold plate, though, after he has stored them, he does not know how to use them, and treats them as though they were sacred from his touch?

If a man were to arm himself with a big stick and lie at length, keeping perpetual guard over a great heap of threshed corn, and yet never venture to touch a grain of it though he was hungry and though he was the owner of it all, but were to feed himself rather, like a miser, on bitter herbs : if again with a thousand jars—that is nothing—with three hundred thousand—of old Chian and Falernian in his cellars, he were to drink mere vinegar—nay, if he were to lie on straw at the age of eighty save one, though he had rugs and coverlets rotting and moth-eaten in his wardrobe—few would think him mad ; no doubt, because the larger part of the world really tosses in the same fever. What are you keeping it for so carefully, you god-forsaken old man? that a son or even a freedman heir may drink it all out? or for fear you should come yourself to want? Why, how small a sum will be each day's deduction from your capital, if you begin the practice of using rather better oil for your salads and for your untidy hair? If you say that anything is good enough for you, why then

do you perjure yourself, filch, plunder right and left?
Can you be sane?

If you were to take to throwing stones at passers-by,
or at your own slaves who are your chattels, you would
be hooted as a madman by every boy and girl in the
street.   When you hang your wife and poison your
mother [1], no doubt, your head is untouched!   Of course,
as you say, you are not doing this at Argos, nor killing
a mother with a sword, as did poor mad Orestes [2].   You
do not suppose he went mad after he had killed a parent.
No, he had been driven out of his mind by the wicked
Furies before he warmed his sword point in his mother's
throat.   Nay, from the moment that Orestes was held
to be of unsound mind he did nothing whatever that
you can find fault with.   He did not venture to attack
Pylades with the sword, or his sister Electra.   He
contents himself with using bad language, calling one
a Fury, and the other by some other name which his
melancholy suggested.

Opimius [3], a poor man though with cellars full of
silver and gold, who would drink from an earthen

---

[1] The purpose of the imagined crimes is, of course, to get
money.

[2] The argument is not very clear, but this seems to be best
taken as ironical defence of the crime. 'No doubt, as you say,
Rome is not Argos. Such crimes are the fashion here and the
methods are more artistic.' The following sentences only
emphasize and justify the epithet 'mad' as applied to Orestes.
'Yes, mad he was—his act was purely an act of madness—and
so is yours.'

[3] Opimius, though a familiar Roman name, is chosen here for
its etymology, as we might say 'Mr. Moneybags, a pauper, &c.'

nipperkin wine of Veii on holidays, and on working days
wine that had gone flat, was once lying in a fit of
drowsiness so profound that his heir was already
running in delight and triumph round his cupboards
and handling his keys. But his physician, a man of
resource as well as a good friend, brings him round in
this way. He bids them set a table near him and
empty some bags of coin upon it, and begin several of
them at once to count it. This is the way he wakes
him up, and then to finish the business he says, " If you
don't take care of what belongs to you, your hungry
heir will be off with it." "While I am alive?" "If
you want to live, then rouse yourself; attend to me."
"What do you wish of me?" "Your veins are half-
filled, and your system is on the point of collapsing
unless you give it some extraordinary support. There
is not a moment to lose. Come now, take this little
cup of rice gruel." "Rice!—What did it cost?" "Oh,
very little." "How much, I say?" "Threepence."
"Good heavens! sir, what matters it in what way
I come to my end—by disease, or by robbery and
plunder?"

"Who then is sane?" The man who is not foolish.
"What of the avaricious?" He is both foolish and
mad. "Well, if a man is not avaricious, is he then
and there sane?" Certainly not. "Why, Sir Stoic?"
I will tell you. "This patient" suppose Craterus [1] to
have said "has nothing wrong with his stomach." He

[1] The name of a physician named in Cicero's letters, and so
standing for an eminent doctor.

is well then, and may leave his bed? "No," he will say, "for lungs, or else kidneys, are suffering from acute disease." A man is not a perjurer nor a miser. Let him slay a porker as a thank-offering to the kind Lares. But he is ambitious and reckless. Put him on board for Anticyra: for what is the real difference between flinging all you have into a gulf and making no use of what you have troubled yourself to get?

The story goes that Servius Oppidius, a rich man as property was counted in old days, divided two farms at Canusium [1] between his two sons, and when he was dying called his boys to his bedside and said: "Ever since, when you were children, I saw you, Aulus, carrying your knucklebones and nuts [2] in a loose bosom-fold, making presents of them freely, and staking them in play—you, Tiberius, counting them over and hiding them in corners morosely, I have feared much that you might suffer from two different kinds of madness—that one of you should grow up like Nomentanus and the other like Cicuta. I adjure you both, therefore, by our household gods, the one not to reduce, the other not to increase what your father thinks enough, and what is Nature's limit for you. Further, lest you feel the itch of ambition, I shall make you both bind yourselves by this oath, that if either allows himself to be aedile or praetor, he be outlawed and accursed. You would waste

---

[1] We are in Horace's native country in Apulia, so that, as with Ofellus in the preceding Satire, there is a basis of fact in the story.   [2] A Roman child's playthings.

your wealth on vetches and beans and lupines[1] that you might walk with an air in the Circus and have a statue of bronze, though stripped of the lands and the money that your father left you, O you madman; and all that you may be greeted with the applause which greets Agrippa, like the fox with his cunning trying to imitate the natural gifts of the lion."

[2] You forbid us to think of burying Ajax. Son of Atreus, why do you so?

"I am king."

And I am a commoner: so I ask no more.

"And my command is a reasonable one, and if any one doubts my justice, I give him free leave to say his mind."

Mightiest of kings! may the gods grant you to take Troy and bring your ships safe home afterwards! Do you really mean that I shall be allowed to ask questions and answer again?

"Pray, ask."

Why does Ajax, the hero second only to Achilles, who has won glory so often by saving the Greeks, lie rotting, that Priam's people and Priam himself may rejoice at the thought that he is unburied, through whom so many of their young sons came not to the burial-place of their fathers?

---

[1] Apparently to be scrambled for by the populace—a form of bribery.

[2] An imaginary dialogue between Agamemnon and a speaker who represents the views of Stertinius. The point is that political ambition leads to crimes. Ajax slew the sheep, taking them for men—' Agamemnon sacrifices his daughter as if she was a lamb. Which was most the act of a madman?'

"He went mad and slew a thousand sheep, crying that he was slaying the great Ulysses, and Menelaus and me."

For yourself now, when in Aulis you set a sweet daughter at the altar instead of a calf, and sprinkled salt meal on her head, O cruel man, were you quite in your senses?

"What can you mean?"

Why, what did the crime of Ajax, the madman as you call him, come to, when he slew the sheep with the sword? He used no violence towards wife or child. He cursed the sons of Atreus plentifully, it is true; but he lifted no hand against Teucer or even Ulysses.

"Nay, it was with full purpose that, to release my fleet from its durance on the wrong side of the water, I appeased the gods with blood."

Aye, and blood of your own, madman.

"Of my own, yes; but no madman."

The man whose mind is the confused scene of insurgent ideas, some true, some wicked, will be judged to be of disordered brain, and it will matter nothing whether he go wrong from folly or from rage. Ajax has lost his wits when he slays the harmless lambs. When, as you say, "with full purpose" you commit a crime for the sake of empty honours, are you sound in mind? Is your heart free from flaw, when it is swelling with ambition? If one were in the habit of dressing up a pet lamb and carrying it in a litter, of furnishing it with millinery, with attendants, with gold ornaments, of calling it Rufa or Posilla, and arranging a marriage for it, the praetor by sentence of court would take from him control of his property, and he would be put under the charge of his sane relations. Well, if a man treats a daughter as a dumb lamb, and vows her to the altar, is he of sound intellect? Do not say so!

So then where there is folly which makes a man go wrong, there in its fullest sense is madness. The man who is criminal will be also out of his senses. One who is attracted by fame, as glittering as glass and as brittle, is as one that has in his ears the thunders of Bellona, whose joy is in deeds of blood.

Next, come, arraign with me *extravagance*, and with it Nomentanus: for Reason will prove that spendthrifts too are fools, and if fools, madmen.

A man of this stamp the moment he had received his patrimony of a thousand talents issued a notice in praetor-like style that fisherman, fruitseller, fowler, perfumer, and all the god-forsaken gang of the Tuscan street, cooks and buffoons, every purveyor in Velabrum or in market, should come to his house next morning. Need I say, they came in crowds—one is the spokesman. "Whatever I and each of these gentlemen have of our own, believe me, sir, is at your service—command it to-day or command it to-morrow." Hear the youth's generous answer: "You sleep in hunting-boots in the snow of Lucania that I may have a wild boar for supper. You sweep the winter seas for fish. I am a lazy fellow quite unworthy to possess all this fortune. Take it and divide it. Here is a million for you—the same for you —thrice as much for you."

The son of Aesopus [1] for the pleasure of swallowing a clear million at a draught, took a splendid pearl from Metella's ear and melted it in vinegar. How was he more sane than if he had flung the very same thing into a running river or a sewer? The sons of Arrius, a well-matched pair of brothers, twins in worthlessness, trifling, and perverted desires, used to breakfast on nightingales bought up at great cost. To which category are they to go? Shall they have mark of chalk as sane men, or of charcoal?

If a bearded man were to amuse himself with building toy-houses, harnessing mice to a toy-cart, playing odd and even, riding a long stick, it must be madness that is turning his head. If Reason shall convince you that the lover's ways are even more childish than those, that it makes no difference whether you play at building castles on the sand as you did when you were three years old, or whimper in distress for love of a mistress, I put it to you, will you do what Polemon [2] in the story did when he was converted, lay aside the trappings of your disease, stockings, elbow-pillow, muffler [3], as he, arrested (we are told), as he was returning from a revel, by the voice of his master who was still fasting, pulled off the chaplets from his neck? When you hold out

[1] Aesopus is the famous tragic actor of Cicero's time. The story is told by Pliny together with the similar story of Cleopatra.

[2] The story is a common one. Polemon heard Xenocrates lecturing as he passed his school, entered, was converted by what he heard, took to philosophy, and succeeded the lecturer.

[3] Additions to ordinary dress which only the effeminate and luxurious would wear.

† W. T. H.

apples to a sulky child he refuses them. "Take them,
darling." He says "No." If you did not offer them
he would cry for them. What is the difference when
the lover, who has had the door shut on him, deliberates
whether he is to go or not to the place whither, when
he was not invited, he was meaning to return, and hangs
about the doors which he hates: "She[1] invites me
herself: shall I not go to her? or shall my thought
be rather to have done with these pains? She shut
the door on me. Shall I go again? No—not if she
went on her knees to me." Hark to the slave, the wiser
man far of the two: "My master, a thing in which
moderation and reason have no part cannot be handled
according to reason and moderation. Love involves
necessarily these troubles—quarrelling, and then again
peacemaking. These phases shift much like the weather,
and rise and fall by blind chance. If one tries to make
them in his own case obey rule, he will not undo the
tangle any more than if he set himself to be mad by
rule of reason and moderation." Why, when you pick
the pips from your Picenian apples[2] and are delighted
when by good luck you have hit the ceiling with one,
are you master of yourself? Suppose now bloodshed
added to folly—the sword used to stir the fire[3]. The
other day, for instance, when Marius murdered Hellas
and flung himself from a rock, was he mad? Or will

[1] In these lines Horace is recalling almost verbally a scene from
one of Terence's plays, the 'Eunuchus,' act 1, sc. 1.

[2] The pips were shot from between thumb and finger, and if
they hit the ceiling it was an omen that love was returned.

[3] A proverb.

you acquit him of disordered mind and find him guilty
of crime—giving things, as men so often do, names
that are first cousins to one another?

There was a freedman who in his old age, though
he had not been drinking, used to wash his hands and
run from shrine to shrine of the Lares, and pray, "Save
me—me only—it is such a small boon—me only—from
death. To gods, surely, there is no difficulty." He
was sound in both ears and eyes—his mind a master who
wished to sell him would not have warranted unless he
wished for a lawsuit. Him and others like him (i. e.
the *superstitious*) Chrysippus will assign to the house of
Menenius [1]. "Jupiter, who givest and takest away the
great pains of life," cries the mother of a boy who has
been keeping his bed for five months, "if my boy gets
well from his quartan ague, on the morning of thy fast-
day [2] he shall stand naked in the Tiber." So, if chance
or the doctor shall have rescued the boy from the edge
of the precipice, his mother in her madness will kill
him by planting him on the cold bank and bringing
back his fever. What in her case is the malady
that has shaken her reason? Fear of the gods.'

This was how Stertinius, eighth of the sages, armed
his friend, that I might never again be called names
without having an answer to make. Any one who shall

[1] The context shows that this means lunatics, but the origin of
the phrase is unknown.

[2] i. e. Thursday. The division of time by weeks, and the
naming of the days after the sun, moon, and five planets, was coming
into vogue in Horace's time. The 'fast' is a Jewish practice,
one of the two fastings in the week mentioned in St. Luke xviii. 12.

speak of me as a madman shall hear a word for every one of his, and shall be taught to look into the wallet on his own back, of which he knows so little.

Horace. Sir Stoic—as you answer me, may you sell everything at greater profits than before your bankruptcy!—in what special folly (since there are more kinds than one) do you think my madness shows itself? For to myself I seem sane.

Damasippus. Do you suppose that when Agave[1] is carrying in her hands the head of her unhappy son which she has cut off, she seems even then to herself to be mad?

Horace. I am ready to confess to folly—let me pay that tribute to truth—and madness into the bargain. Expound to me only this: what do you think my special mental disease?

Damasippus. Let me tell you. First, you build. This means, you ape full-grown people though you are a dwarf[2], two foot high and all in proportion. Yet you are the man to laugh at the spirit and gait of poor Turbo the gladiator as too big for his body. How are you less laughable than he? Is it right that whatever Maecenas does you should do too, so different as you are and such a poor match for him?

In the absence of their mother some little frogs had been trampled under the foot of a calf. One having

---

[1] The mother of Pentheus, whom in her Bacchic frenzy she tore to pieces.

[2] A figure, but in playful allusion to the fact that he was really man of small stature. See the end of Epist. I. 20.

escaped relates to its mother how a huge beast had crushed its brothers to death.

How large, she asks, had it been ? so large ?—puffing herself out.

'Half as big again.'

As much bigger as this ?

As she puffed herself up more and more, 'if you puff till you burst' he says, 'you will not be as large.' The fable hits you off very neatly. Now throw in your poetry—in other words, throw oil on the furnace. If any one ever wrote poetry who was sane, then you are sane in writing it. I do not speak of your awful rages—

Horace. Stop there.

Damasippus. Your style of living, too grand for your estate—

Horace. Keep to your own business, Damasippus.

Damasippus. A thousand frenzies of foolish passion—

Horace. O master, be merciful to your humble imitator in madness!

IV   *Unde et quo Catius?*

Catius : or The art of dining.

Among the supreme pleasures of his country life Horace reckoned (see Sat. 2. 7) his escape from the vapid talk of a town supper-party. In this talk-as-it-should-not-be he gave a high place to talk about the cookery, and he devotes two Satires (this and the last Satire of this Book) to ridiculing persons who set up as connoisseurs in the art of gastronomy. The humour of the Satire lies perhaps in part in the selection of the interlocutor who (if we can trust the Scholiasts) is the Catius of Cicero's letters (ad Fam. 15, 16), an Epicurean writer—in any case, in the affectation of Lucretius's philosophical phraseology, and the suggestion which comes out in the last words, but which has been prepared for throughout, that we are hearing the teaching not only of the art of dining but of the art of living.

The precepts are miscellaneous, a mixture probably of platitudes and paradoxes. It is to be noticed that they follow the order of a Roman supper, 'from the eggs to the apples' (see p. 166).

Horace. WHENCE, and whither away, Catius?
Catius. I have no time. I am in a hurry to set in order my notes of some new teaching such as will drive from the field Pythagoras and the [1] accused of Anytus and the learned Plato.

Horace. It is a crime, I confess, to have interrupted you at such a bad moment. I pray you, generously pardon me. If anything has slipped from you now you will recover it soon; for your memory is a marvel, whether of nature or of art.

Catius. Aye, that was what I was thinking of— how to keep it every word: for indeed they were nice points and handled throughout in nice style.

Horace. Reveal [2] to me the man's name, and also whether he is a Roman or a stranger.

Catius. The teaching itself I will utter [2] as I remember it—the teacher's name must be a secret.

Eggs of oblong shape remember to serve, as of

[1] Socrates.

[2] The words are chosen as though it was an oracle which was asked of and uttered.

better flavour and whiter than round ones: the white is firmer, and the yolk within belongs to the cock bird.

Kales grown on the dry lands are sweeter than from gardens near the city: nothing is more washy than the produce of your much-watered ground.

If a guest has surprised you in the evening, you will know what to do that the fowl disappoint not his taste by its toughness. Mix Falernian with the water and plunge the fowl alive into the kettle. This will make it tender.

Mushrooms grown in the open meadow are the best —others are untrustworthy.

He will pass healthy summers who shall finish his early meal with mulberries which he has gathered from the tree before the sun is hot.

Aufidius used to mix his honey with rough Falernian —a mistake; for when the veins are empty you should let nothing pass into them but what is soft: soft should be the draught with which you begin the meal.

If the habit is costive the mussel and other shellfish will be a cheap remedy, with groundling sorrel; but do not forget white wine of Cos.

The succulent shellfish are fuller at the new moon. But it is not all waters that yield the best kinds. The giant mussel of the Lucrine is better than the purple-fish of Baiae. Circeii is the home of oysters, Misenum of urchins. Soft Tarentum prides itself on its broad scallops.

But no one must lightly set up as professor of the art of dining unless he has first mastered the subtle theory of flavours. Nor is it enough to sweep fish indiscriminately from an expensive stall without knowing which are best boiled, and which, if broiled, will tempt a guest to eat till he is tired before he sinks back on his elbow [1].

A man who would not have flavourless meat must see to it that the wild boar which makes his round dish bend double is an Umbrian fed on acorns from the holm-oak. One from Laurentum is inferior. He has been fattened on reeds and rushes.

The roes that the vineyard rears are not eatable at all seasons. The wise man will take care to choose the fore-legs of the doe-hare, always in young. The natural condition and age for different kinds of fish and birds are points of study never cleared up by any taste before mine.

There are some whose genius is exhausted in inventing new kinds of pastry: but it is by no means enough to spend all one's trouble on a single department—just as if a man cared only to see that his wines were good, giving no thought to the quality of the oil with which he souses his fish.

Massic wine you may put out of doors in fine weather and the night air will refine anything that is coarse in it and its heady fumes will pass off. On the other hand, to strain it through linen spoils it and ruins the natural flavour. Surrentine the connoisseur mixes with some lees of Falernian, and clears it perfectly with a pigeon's egg, for the yolk sinks to the bottom and carries with it all foreign matter.

---

[1] Or 'tempt the jaded guest to raise himself again on his elbow.'

To the flagging drinker you will give fresh zest by fried prawns and African snails.   Lettuce the stomach rejects, when it is hot after drinking wine.   It desires to be freshened by the sharp sting rather of dried ham, rather of sausage.   Nay, it would prefer any of the savoury dishes that are brought steaming from the coarse cookshops.

It is worth while to spend much study on the nature of the two kinds of sauce [1].   There is the simple kind which consists of sweet olive oil.   This you should mix with some rich wine and with pickled roe of the kind of which a Byzantine jar [2] has reeked.   When this has been mixed with chopped herbs and boiled, sprinkled with saffron from Corycus and let stand, you will add besides some of the best oil from a Venafran press.

Apples from Tibur yield in flavour to those of Picenum, though in look they have the advantage.

Of grapes the Venuculan is best for the preserving jar : that of Alba is safer for smoke-drying.   This last the inquirer learns that I set the example of serving at dessert, as I set the example of putting wine-lees with caviare, and of setting to each guest white pepper sifted with black salt in clean little salt-cellars.   It is a gross fault to spend three thousand at the fish-market and then to squeeze the sprawling fish into a dish all too small for it.   Again, it turns the stomach, if a waiting boy have handled the drinking cup with hands greasy from gobbling stolen morsels ; or if the mixing bowl be

[1] Or ' of the compound sauce.'
[2] Byzantium was the centre of the tunny fishery.

an antique, but never cleaned. How much is the cost of a cheap broom, napkins, sawdust? Yet the offence of not supplying them is great. To see you sweeping your tesselated pavement with dirty palm-broom and putting covers that want washing over Tyrian stuffs! You forget that in proportion as the care and expense which these things involve is less, so any complaint about them is more just than about things which cannot be found save at a rich man's table.

Horace. O learned Catius, by your friendship and by the gods I beg you, be sure to take me with you to hear the lecturer, however far you have to go. For however accurate the memory with which you relate them you cannot give me the same pleasure at secondhand. Then there is the look and manner of the man. You think little of seeing him, happy fellow, because you have had that good fortune: but to me it is a matter of no small anxiety to be able to approach the distant well-spring, and drink deep of the teaching of a happy life.

V   *Hoc quoque, Tiresia*

Tiresias : or Legacy-hunting.

An attack, more satirical than is usual with Horace, in the sense of Satire as Juvenal understood it, on the base arts by which men made up to wealthy persons without natural heirs. It is lightened by being thrown into the form of a burlesque continuation of the dialogue between Ulysses and the shade of Tiresias in Odyssey 11. The starting-point is the words of Tiresias (v. 114, Butcher and Lang's translation): ' Late shalt thou return in evil plight with the loss of all thy company, on board the ship of

strangers, and thou shalt find sorrows in thy house, even
proud men that devour thy living.'
The art of legacy-hunting has never been wholly unknown,
but its prevalence belongs (as does the bitterness of tone
with which 'heirs' are spoken of in Horace's writings)
to the time when a disinclination to marriage and its
responsibilities was a marked feature of social life.

Ulysses. THIS one question answer me, Tiresias,
besides what you have told me. By
what arts and methods can I recover my lost substance?
Why do you laugh?

Tiresias. Have we come to this, that a man of craft
such as yours is not satisfied to be brought back to
Ithaca, and to look on his home-gods?

Ulysses. O teller of truth to all, you see that as you
prophesied I am returning to my home stripped bare of
all things; and there neither storeroom nor flock has
been left unrifled by the suitors. And yet, without substance, blood and valour are more valueless than seaweed.

Tiresias. Since, to put things plainly, poverty is what
you dread, let me tell you how you can grow rich. If
a fieldfare or any other dainty be given you for your
own eating, let it wing its way to the place where there
is the splendour of a large fortune with an aged owner.
Your sweetest apples and any special pride of your trim
farm, before the Lares one worthy of more reverence
than the Lares, the rich man, must taste. He may be
a perjured man, a man without birth, one stained with
a brother's blood, a runaway slave, yet if he ask you to
walk abroad with him, do not refuse to give him the
wall side.

Ulysses. I to give the wall to some scum of a Dama[1]!
That was not my way at Troy. I held my own against
my betters.

Tiresias. Then you will be a poor man.

Ulysses. Well, I shall bid my heart be brave[2] and
endure this. I have borne even greater things in my
time. But do you go on, prophet, and tell me how
I am to pile up wealth and heaps of money.

Tiresias. I have told you, and repeat it. Fish
cunningly in all waters for legacies from old men. If
one or two are clever enough to bite off the bait and
escape your snares, do not for that abate your hope, or
for the disappointment drop your profession. If by-and-
by a case large or small is before the court, choose the
suitor who is rich and without children; though he be an
impudent villain who is wantonly forcing a lawsuit on a
better man than himself, take his side: laugh to scorn
the citizen who has the advantage both in repute and in
case, if he has a son alive or a wife capable of bearing
one. Say 'Quintus,' we will suppose, or 'Publius,'
—sensitive ears are tickled by the praenomen—'your
virtues have made me your friend. I understand the
law with its ambiguities. I can defend a case. I will
let any one pluck out my eyes sooner than that he
should set you at nought, or rob you of a nutshell: this
care belongs to me to see that you are not cheated or made

---

[1] i. e. a slave.

[2] In reference to the words of Ulysses in Odyss. 20. 18 (Butcher
and Lang): 'Endure my heart; yea, a baser thing thou once
didst bear.'

fun of.' Bid him go home and nurse himself; act yourself as his representative; persist and persevere, whether

> 'the red Dog-star's heat
> Split the dumb statues,'

or (after a full supper of rich tripe) Furius [1], like Jove,

> 'bespit the wintry Alps with hoary snow.'

'Do you not see,' some one will say, nudging his next
neighbour, 'how untiring he is, how keen to serve his
friends?' More tunnies will swim within reach, and
your fishpond will fill. Then again, for fear you should
show your hand too plainly by making up to a bachelor,
look for a case where on a fine property a sickly son
is being reared as heir: there by constant attention
feel your way gently to what you desire, that if the
boy lives you may be the second legatee, and if some
accident have sent him to another world you may fill
his vacant place. This hazard seldom disappoints. If
a man hand you his will to read, be sure to refuse, and
push the wax tablets from you: yet do it so that
by a side glance you may catch the purport of the
second line of the first tablet [2]. Run your eye rapidly
along it to see whether you are sole heir or one of many.
Not once only the commissioner [3] who has gone into the
melting-pot and come out a clerk will cheat the raven

---

[1] For these quotations from Furius Bibaculus see note on p. 201.

[2] The first line contained the name of the testator, the second those of the legatees.

[3] Lit. 'one of five,' possibly the five who superintended the night police.

that opens its mouth, and a Nasica the will-hunter will make sport for a Coranus.

Ulysses. Are you gone mad? or are you purposely making fun of me with your dark oracle?

Tiresias. O son of Laertes, whatever I say will be or will not be; for mighty Apollo gives me the gift of prophecy.

Ulysses. I dare say: but tell me, if you please, the purport of the story you speak of.

Tiresias. What time a young hero, the terror of the Parthians, whose blood comes down from great Aeneas, shall be winning fame by land and sea, the tall daughter of Nasica, who never pays in full if he can help it, shall give her hand to the bold Coranus. Then and not before the new son-in-law shall do this: he shall give to his father-in-law some tablets and pray him to read them. After many refusals Nasica at length shall take them and read them to himself, and shall find that nothing is left to him and his but to weep. I have one more hint: if there chance to be a crafty woman or a freedman looking after a dotard, strike a partnership with them. Praise them that they may praise you behind your back: this too is a help. But much the best way is at once to take by storm the principal himself. If he is an idiot who writes bad verses, praise them. . . .

I will tell you something that happened while I was an old man. A determined old woman at Thebes was carried out to her burial, according to her will, in this way: her corpse was oiled all over, and her heir carried it on his bare shoulders. She wished to see (you understand) whether when she was dead she could slip through his fingers. I suppose when she was alive he had pressed her too hard. Begin with caution; let zeal be neither lacking, nor yet unmeasured and excessive. One who talks too much will offend the testy and morose. You should not go to the other extreme and be silent. Be the Davus of the comic stage: stand with bent head, for all the world as if you were shy. Make your first approaches by civility. Warn him, if the wind has freshened, to be careful and cover his precious head. Shoulder a way for him out of a crowd. Hold your ear at his service when he wants to chatter. Is he eager in season and out of season for praise? Press him with it till he lifts his hands to heaven and cries 'hold!' The more you see the bladder rise, ply the more the bellows of flattery.

When he shall have released you from your long servitude and anxiety, and, with the assurance that you are not dreaming, you shall have heard the words, 'One-fourth I give and bequeath to Ulysses.' 'Is my old companion Dama really no more? where can I find another so worthy and so true?'—let fall such utterances now and then, and if you can possibly manage a few tears, shed them at the news: you can hide your face if it betrays your joy. If the tomb is left to your discretion, build it handsomely: let the neighbourhood praise the brilliance of the funeral. If by chance any of your co-heirs is older than you and has a nasty cough, assure him that if he would like to buy an estate or a town-house which belongs to your share you would gladly let him have it for a nominal price.

But Proserpine summons me, and I must obey. Long life and health to you!

VI　　　　　*Hoc erat in votis*

The Mountain stronghold: or Country and Town.

The Satire will be compared especially with Sat. 1. 6, as completing the picture there given of Horace's mode of spending a day in Rome, and with Epist. 1. 14 and the beginning of 16 for the description of his country life and of the Sabine farm in which much of it was spent.

THIS used to be among my prayers—a portion of land not so very large, but which should contain a garden, and near the homestead a spring of ever-flowing water, and a bit of forest to complete it. The gods have done more amply and generously. I ask for nothing more, O son of Maia, than that thou make these gifts indeed my own. If I neither have made my estate larger by any evil practice, nor mean to make it smaller by fault or failing; if I make no such foolish prayers as these: 'Oh, if I could throw in that adjoining corner that spoils the shape of my little farm! Oh, if some chance might direct me to a jar of silver, like the hireling who found a treasure, and bought and ploughed as its owner the field in which he found it, a rich man by grace of his friend Hercules!'—if what I have pleases and contents me—then this is the boon I ask of thee: make my cattle fat, and all else that their master has except his wit, and be ever as of yore my chiefest guardian!

So now, when I have got me safely from the town to my mountain stronghold, what before it should I sooner glorify in my Satires with my Muse that goes afoot? Here no affectation of state vexes me to death; no leaden sirocco in the deadly autumn weather which makes the fortune of hateful Libitina.

O Father of the morning, or Janus if so thou wouldst rather be called, from whom men take the beginning of all the tasks and toils of life,—so the gods will,—be thou the source of my song! At Rome thou hurriest me to give bail for a friend: 'Come quick, that none be before you in answering the call.' Go I must, whether the north wind be sweeping the earth, or winter with narrower arc contract the snowy day. When I have uttered, as bidden, 'aloud and distinctly[1],' what may be to my own harm one day, I have to struggle in the crowd and do damage to those who are not quick enough for me. 'What do you want, you madman? what are you about?' repeats an unreasonable man with angry imprecations, 'are you, sir, to thrust and push any one that is in your way in your hurry to get back to an engagement that you remember with Maecenas?' Aye, there[2] is the pleasure, the sweetening of the cup—I will say the truth. But as soon as one reaches the gloomy Esquiline, a hailstorm is dancing over head and ears, in front and

---

[1] Apparently from the formula of the clerk of the court calling on a witness.

[2] i.e. in the relation to Maecenas.

on flank, a hundred questions of other people's business:
'Roscius begs you will give him your presence to-morrow
before eight o'clock at the *puteal*:' 'The Civil Servants beg you, Quintus, not to forget to come down again
to-day to the Forum on some fresh and serious business
which concerns you and them [1]:' 'Pray get Maecenas
to put his seal to this little document.' If you say 'I
will do my best,' 'You can, if you will' he urges.

It is now seven, or more nearly eight years since
Maecenas began to count me among his acquaintance, to
the extent at least of offering me sometimes a seat in a
carriage on a journey, and trusting to my ears chitchat
such as this, 'What o'clock is it?' 'Do you think
Gallina the Thracian is a good match for Syrus?'
'The morning frosts have a sting now if you are not
careful,'—and other things as safely stored in a leaky
ear. All through this time our friend has been daily
and hourly more and more the mark for envy. He had
shared Maecenas's seat at the games: he had played
with him in the Campus—'Fortune's own son' they
all cry. Some rumour is sending a shiver through the
town from the Forum to each place where men meet;
every one that runs against me asks my opinion: 'Oh,
my good sir, you must know—you live so near the gods:
have you heard anything about the Dacians?' Nothing
whatever. 'How you like, and always will like laughing at us!' May all the gods confound me, if I have
heard a word! 'Well, about the lands which Caesar

---

[1] Horace had himself held a place in the 'Civil Service' as a
scriba in the Quaestor's office.

has promised the soldiers—does he mean to give them
in the three-cornered island or on Italian soil?' When
I swear that I know nothing, they marvel at me as a man,
surely, in a thousand for unusual and profound reticence.
In such occupations, to one's misery, one wastes the
day, sighing all the time, O country home, when shall
I look on you again! when shall I be allowed, between
my library of classics and sleep and hours of idleness,
to drink the sweet draughts that make us forget the
troubles of life! Oh when shall I sit down to my
beans, Pythagoras' kinsmen [1], and with them the dish of
garden stuff that wants no rich sauce beyond the fat
bacon! O nights and suppers of gods! at which I and
my friends with me feast ourselves before my own
home-gods, and leave plenty of the food for my saucy
home-born slaves. The guests mix the cups which they
drink each after his several liking, for they are free from
crack-brained rules. One has a strong head and chooses
the fiery draught. Another prefers a more moderate
tipple. And so the talk that comes naturally is not
of smart houses in country or town which do not belong
to us, nor of the merits of Lepos as a dancer; but we
debate matters which come nearer home to us, and on
which it is a misfortune to be ignorant—whether riches

---

[1] See note on Epp. I. 12. It seems a complicated joke on
three points in the philosophy of Pythagoras: (1) his doctrine of
the transmigration of souls; (2) his vegetarianism; (3) a proverbial
saying traced to him, 'Abstain from beans.' Horace suggests
that the ground of the precept must have been the fear that in
eating a bean you might without knowing it eat a kinsman.

or virtue is the key of happiness, whether the attraction to friendship is interest or right, what is the nature of the good and what is the chief good. From time to time our neighbour Cervius in his easy way tells some nursery fable that hits the point. For instance, if any one praises the wealth of Arellius without knowing its anxieties, he begins thus: 'Once upon a time, the story goes, a country mouse received as a guest in his poor hole a town mouse, an old friend whom he had entertained before. He lived roughly and had the soul of thrift; but he could unbend on occasions of hospitality. Need I say more? He grudged not his precious store either of round pease or of long oats, he even brought in his mouth a dried raisin and nibbled morsels of bacon, so eager was he by variety of fare to coax the dainty stomach of his guest, who in his lordly way just put his teeth first to one thing and then to another. Stretched on his sofa of fresh straw, the master of the house is making his own meal on spelt and tare, leaving the delicacies to his friend; when the townsman, getting impatient, cries to him: "What pleasure can you find, my friend, in living such a hard life on this wooded bank? Let me persuade you to prefer company and the town to these wild woods. Take my advice and start with me. Since all that is on earth is mortal, and there is no escape from death for great or small, draw the true conclusion, my dear sir, and live whilst you may in the enjoyment of what is pleasant; live, and remember how short the time is!" These words greatly impressed the countryman. He was out of

doors in a trice. And so they make the best of their
way to the town, in haste to creep safely within its walls
under cover of night. Night was already at its zenith
when they halted at a wealthy house, where scarlet
coverlets were glowing on ivory couches, and a pile of
dishes was standing in baskets, the remains of a great
supper of that evening. Then the townsman assumes
the host, and having made his friend stretch himself on
a purple coverlet, hurries about like a waiter with his
tunic tucked up, and serves course upon course without
pause, and plays to the life the part of a home-bred
slave, for he licks every dish before he hands it. The
other, lying at his ease, is congratulating himself on his
changed lot, and in happy case is playing the contented
guest; when suddenly a noise of slamming doors made
both leap from the sofas. Terror-stricken they scurry
from end to end of the banqueting hall, their panic
increasing momently as the house rang with the barking
of Molossian dogs. Then is the countryman's turn:
"This is no place for me," quoth he, "and so fare
you well: my wood and my hole safe from sur-
prises, and my humble vetch-pods, will satisfy my
needs."'

VII   *Iamdudum ausculto*

Davus : or Freedom and slavery.

*A companion Satire to the third of this Book. It deals
with another Stoic 'paradox,' namely, that 'every one but
the wise man is a slave.' Horace dramatizes the theme
by putting it into the mouth of his own slave Davus,*

*who avails himself of the licensed freedom of the Satur-
nalia (which were supposed to recall the equality
of men in the golden age) to speak his mind as to his
master's failings. On the one side we notice the good-
humoured ironical way in which he turns the edge of
his Satire upon himself. We are not to take his quasi-
confession too literally here any more than elsewhere. On
the other it must be allowed that (perhaps with the usual
Roman lack of real dramatic instinct) he makes no
attempt in the bulk of the Satire to make Davus speak in
character. The style is the declamatory style of a Stoic
lecturer, as in the case of Ofellus in Sat. 2 and Stertinius in Sat. 3.*

Davus. I HAVE been listening a long time and
wishing to say a few words in reply, but
as a slave I hesitate.

Horace. Is that Davus?

Davus. Aye, Davus, a chattel with some affection
for his master, and passably honest, though not quite
too good to live.

Horace. Come, take full benefit of December's
franchise—so our fathers have ruled it for us. Say
your say.

Davus. A part of the world finds its pleasure
consistently in vice and keeps steady to its purpose.
Another and a larger part wavers, at one moment
setting its hand to what is right, at another giving way
to evil. Priscus, who attracted attention on many days
by wearing three rings, sometimes by wearing none,
was so variable that he never wore the same stripe [1]

---

[1] He dressed now as a Senator with the broad stripe down the
front of the tunic, now as a knight with the narrow one.

two hours running. From a grand house he would plunge suddenly into quarters from which a freedman of any self-respect would be ashamed to be seen emerging. Now he followed the life of a rake at Rome, now that of a philosopher at Athens. Vertumnus [1] with all his thousand faces had frowned on his birth. Trencherman Volanerius on the other hand, when the well-deserved gout had crippled his own fingers, hired a journeyman to pick up the dice for him and put them in the box. Just as he was the more persistent in his course of vice, so he was the less to be pitied, and higher in the scale than one who suffers from having the rope now strained too tight, now hanging loose.

Horace. Shall you be the whole day before you tell me what all this stale stuff is about, you gallows-bird?

Davus. About yourself, is my answer.

Horace. In what way, you villain?

Davus. You praise old-world fortunes and old-world manners; and yet if some god offered to take you back to those times you would flatly refuse; either because there is no real feeling behind that loud talk, or because you are a weak-kneed champion of the right, and, in spite of vain desires to lift your foot from the mire, stick fast in it. At Rome you are all for the country: in the country you extol to the stars the distant town. There is fickleness for you! If you happen to have no invitation to sup out, you praise your peaceful meal of herbs, and call yourself a lucky man, and hug yourself that you have not to go abroad to drink

[1] The god of change.

your wine—just as though when you went out anywhere
you had to be dragged in chains !　　Let Maecenas have
sent you an invitation to his table about the time of
lamp-lighting : ' Will no one make haste and bring the
oil ?　Is any one attending to me ? ' you bluster and shout,
and off you go.　　Mulvius and his brother trenchermen
go their ways too, with a prayer not meant to be repeated
to you : ' Yes,' he would say, ' I confess that I am a poor
creature, that must follow where my belly bids me.
I open my nostrils at a savoury smell.　I am weak,
lazy, if you like you may add a glutton.　Well, sir,
and are you, though you are as bad and perhaps worse,
to go out of your way to write Satires on us as though
you were our better, and wrap up your own failing in
decorous words ? '　What if you betray yourself as more
silly even than me, a slave who cost five hundred
drachms ?　Nay, do not try to frighten me by your looks.
Keep a check on hand and temper while I reveal to you
the lesson which Crispinus'[1] doorkeeper taught me. . . .

Are you, in my eyes, lord and master, you who bow
your neck to so many and such imperious calls of
circumstance and of men—you whom the praetor's rod[2]
laid on your head three times or four times over cannot
free from slavish fear ?　Ask another question not
less interesting—I do not care whether one who does
the bidding of a slave should be called, as the custom of
your world calls him, a ' deputy ' or a ' fellow slave '—

---

[1] Crispinus (see end of Sat. 1. 1) is a Stoic lecturer.　Davus
professes to have picked up his philosophy from the lecturer's
doorkeeper.　　　　　　[2] The form of manumission of a slave.

In either case what am I in your eyes? The truth is, you who domineer over me are the miserable slave of some one else, and are moved like a wooden puppet by strings in the hands of another.

Who then is free? The wise man alone, who is a stern master to himself, whom neither poverty nor death nor bonds affright, who has the courage to say 'no' again and again to desires, to despise the objects of ambition, who is a whole in himself, smoothed and rounded, with the surface on which nothing from outside can find lodgement, against whom, if she assail him, Fortune is crippled.

Can you recognize as your own any one of these traits? A woman asks four talents of you, bullies you, shuts her door in your face, drenches you with cold water, and then—invites you to come to her house again. Snatch your neck from the dishonouring yoke: 'I am a free man, a free man' say. You cannot do it; for there is a master, and no gentle one, driving your soul, goading you sharply if you are weary, and tugging at your mouth if you jib.

Again, when you are entranced by a picture of Pausias, how is your shortcoming less than mine when I stop to admire rough drawings in red ochre or charcoal of the encounters of Fulvius and Rutuba or Pacideianus with their straining haunches as if they were heroes really fighting, striking, and parrying by movement of their weapons? Davus is a 'worthless dawdler,' but you are a 'fine and accomplished critic of ancient art.' If I feel the attraction of a smoking cake I am a good-

for-nothing. Do your own prodigious virtue and
intelligence say 'no' to a dainty supper? Why is it
more harmful to me to obey a gluttonous appetite than
it is to you? You say that I pay the penalty with my
back. But how do you escape punishment more than I,
when you set your heart on dainty dishes which cannot
be had without their price? The truth is that rich fare,
indulged in without limit, turns bitter in the mouth; and
the feet that have been made fools of refuse at last to
support the bloated body. Is it a deep offence in a boy
after a day's work to barter a *strigil*[1] of his master's
for a bunch of grapes, and has the man nothing of the
slave about him who breaks up an estate to gratify his
gluttony? Say besides that at the same time you cannot
bear your own company for an hour together, you cannot
employ leisure wisely, you would give yourself the slip,
a runaway and a vagrant, seeking now with wine, now
with sleep, to cheat care. In vain: fast as you run,
black Care is at your side or at your heels.

Horace. Who will find me a stone?

Davus. What do you want it for?

Horace. Are my arrows all gone?

Davus. Why, if the man isn't raving he is composing verses[2]!

Horace. If you don't take yourself off with all speed,
you will be sent as a ninth hand to my Sabine farm.

---

[1] Used at the bath.

[2] Davus is supposed to notice both the word 'arrows' as
though Horace were thinking in tragic style, and also the suggestion of metrical form.

VIII   *Ut Nasidieni*

Nasidienus Rufus : or An upstart's supper-party.

The motive of this Satire is in part the same as that of the fourth of this Book, the talk about eating *which Horace found so odious : but a new and dramatic turn is given to the subject by putting this talk into the mouth of a vulgar personage (the name of Nasidienus Rufus is no doubt a disguised one) who invites Maecenas to supper, asks three leading literary men to meet him, and then entertains them with disquisitions on cookery which at last tire their patience so much as to drive them from table.*

It is interesting to notice, when we seem to be coming into close contact with Maecenas, that beyond the fact of his presence we hear nothing of him.   Fundanius, who describes to Horace the scene of the supper, is the Comic Poet praised in Sat. i. 10.   Four of those pests of a Roman entertainment, the ' scurrae,' the hangers-on of the tables of the great, are present ; two brought according to custom as uninvited guests by Maecenas, and two supporting the host.   Nasidienus puts one of the latter into his own place next the chief guest.   The party is arranged on three couches.

	Maecenas	Vibidius	Servilius Balatro	
Nomentanus				Varius
Nasidienus				Viscus
Porcius				Fundanius

Horace. WELL, how did you like the supper with our lucky friend Nasidienus? When I came to ask you to sup with me yesterday I was told that you were at an early entertainment there.

Fundanius. Vastly. I never in my life enjoyed myself more.

Horace. Tell me, if you do not mind, what was the first dish to appease your ravenous appetites?

Fundanius. First came a wild boar. It was a Lucanian, and was caught, so the father of the feast told us, when the south wind was blowing softly. The table was garnished with salads and all things that whet the appetite, skirwort, fish-pickle, lees of Coan. When these were removed, a bustling page wiped well the maple-wood table with a purple napkin, while another gathered up the scraps and anything that could offend the guests. Then, like an Attic maiden bearing the sacred emblems of Ceres, came in procession a dusky Indian with Caecuban wine, a Greek with Chian that had not been brined [1]. Then the host: 'If Alban, Maecenas, or Falernian is more to your taste than what is served, there are both.'

Horace. Ah for the sorrows of wealth! But I am anxious to know, Fundanius, what was the company with which you shared your enjoyments?

Fundanius. I was at the top: next to me Viscus of Thurii, and below him, if I remember rightly, Varius.

[1] It seems to have been the custom with certain wines to add a little salt water.

On the middle couch Maecenas and the two 'shadows[1]'
whom he had brought with him, Vibidius and Servilius
Balatro.   On the host's couch, Nomentanus[2] above
him, and below him Porcius[2], who made us laugh
by swallowing his cheesecakes whole at a mouthful.
Nomentanus was so placed for the purpose of pointing
out with his forefinger anything that might escape
[Maecenas'] notice: for the rest of us, the un-
distinguished crowd, sup at hazard on birds, shellfish,
fish, whose look was no key to their unfamiliar taste;
as I, for instance, very soon found out when I was
handed the inside of a plaice and a turbot, a dish I had
never before tasted.   After this he explained to me that
honey-apples have red cheeks if they are gathered under
a waning moon.   What difference this makes, you must
ask himself.   Then Vibidius whispers to Balatro, 'we
shall die unavenged if we do not drink him out of house
and home'; and asks for larger cups.   At this the host's
face changed and grew pale: for he dreaded nothing so
much as hard drinkers, either because their tongues are
too free, or because hot wines dull the fine edge of the
palate.   Vibidius and Balatro tilt whole wine-jars into
the Allifan ware[3].   All followed suit, save the guests
on the host's couch, who took care to spare the flagons.

Then is brought in a lamprey at all its length on a

[1] *Umbrae*, 'shadows,' the name given to uninvited guests
brought in the train of a great man.

[2] Two fictitious names, one the stock name in Satire for
a spendthrift, the other implying greedy ways.

[3] Allifae was a town in the valley of the Vulturnus, where,
according to the Scholiast, cups were made of special size.

dish, with shrimps swimming in sauce round it. On this the host: 'It was caught' says he 'before spawning. The flesh is less good if it is taken later. The ingredients of the sauce are these: oil from Venafrum of the first pressing, pickled roe of the Spanish fish [1], wine five years old, but of home growth, stirred in while it is simmering,—when it has cooled Chian suits better than anything else,—white pepper, and plenty of vinegar made from the fermenting of the grape of Methymna [2]. It is a recipe of my own invention to add while it is simmering green rockets and sharp-tasted elecampane; Curtillus bids add sea-urchins that have not touched fresh water; for what the shellfish from the sea yields of itself is something better than any prepared pickle.'

Just at this juncture the awning above us fell heavily upon the dish, bringing down with it a cloud of black dust worse than what the north wind raises on the plain of Campania. We feared that something greater was coming; but recover ourselves when we find that there was no danger. Rufus [i.e. Nasidienus] laid his head on the table and wept as if his son had been cut off in his prime. I know not what would have been the end, if Nomentanus had not restored his friend by a philosopher's reflections: 'Ah Fortune, what divine power is more cruel towards us than thou! How thou delightest ever to make sport of human affairs!' Varius could scarcely control his laughter by use of his napkin.

[1] Said to be the mackerel.
[2] In Lesbos.

Balatro, who has a sneer for everything, says, 'Such are the conditions of life; and this is why fame will never give full response to your efforts. To think that in order that I may be entertained sumptuously you should be racked with every kind of anxiety, lest the bread be over-baked, lest the sauce be ill-seasoned, that every waiting boy be girt and trimmed according to rule! And then think of such accidents as these—if the awning fall as it did just now, if a clownish boy slip and break a dish! But as with a commander, so with a host—it is rough weather that discovers the genius, fair weather puts it out of sight.' Nasidienus replies, 'Heaven answer all your prayers, for a kind and courteous guest as you are!' and he calls for his slippers[1]. Then on each of the couches you might notice a buzz of whispering, one into another's ear. I know of no show that I would rather have seen.

Horace. Pray, tell me, what was your next amusement?

Fundanius. While Vibidius is asking the waiters whether the flagon had been broken also, and while we are laughing at pretended jests, Balatro giving us our cue, back you come, Nasidienus, with altered countenance, as one that means to let art mend fortune. Presently there enter waiters bearing on a huge platter a crane dismembered and sprinkled plentifully with salt and meal, and the liver of a white goose fattened on figs, and hares' wings separated, as much nicer so than if you eat them with the back. Then we had the sight of

_____
[1] i. e. to leave the table.   Guests lay with their feet bare.

blackbirds served with the breast burnt, and pigeons the hind part taken off——nice things enough, if the host would not explain at length the philosophy and natural history of each of them. But we fled from him and had our revenge by tasting absolutely nothing, as though it had all been poisoned by Canidia's breath worse than that of Afric's serpents.

EPISTLES

Book I

I   *Prima dicte mihi*
                        To Maecenas.

A dedication of the new Book to Maecenas. It is an
apology (1) for his abandonment of lyric poetry, (2) for
the tone and subjects which will characterize the Epistles.

YOU were the theme of my earliest Muse, Maecenas, and must be of my latest; but what you
are asking is to shut on me again the door of the
training school, though I have already sufficiently
passed the test and received my wooden sword[1]. My
years are not what they were, nor is my inclination.
Veianius hangs up his arms at the door of the temple
of Hercules and then hides himself out of sight in the
country. He does not desire to have again and again
to appeal to the people[2] from the edge of the lists.
There is a voice that whispers ever in my ear, and my
ear is purged to listen, ' Be wise in time and turn your
horse out to grass when he shows signs of age, lest he
end in a ludicrous breakdown with straining flanks.'
So now I am laying aside verses among other playthings.
My thoughts and my questions are of what is right,
what is becoming. My whole soul is in these things.
I am storing and ordering what one day I may bring
out for use. If you ask who is my chief, in what home

---

[1] The gladiator's wooden sword, which was used for practice,
and given him on retirement as a token of discharge.

[2] i.e. for discharge.

I find shelter, I am not bound over to swear allegiance to any master: where the wind carries me, I put into port and make myself at home. At one moment I become the man of action and plunge in the troubled waters of civil life, the unbending champion and hench-man of strict Virtue. At another I slip back, when no one is looking, to the rules of Aristippus and would try to suit life to myself, not myself to life. As the day seems long to those whose labour belongs to another, as the year crawls[1] to minors burdened by a mother's irksome tutelage, so slow-flowing and thankless to me are the spaces of time which defer my hope and pur-pose of setting vigorously to that work which, if performed, profits equally the poor and the rich, if neglected, will injure by-and-by equally the young and the old. Meanwhile, for my own self I am fain to find guidance and solace in such child's-teachings as these. You may not be able to make your eyesight reach as far as Lynceus[2]; you would not on that account think scorn of putting salve to your eyes if they were sore. Because you do not hope for the fame of Glycon, the champion athlete, you would not refuse to take exercise enough to keep at bay the gout. You may advance a certain way, if you may not get further.

Is avarice, with its miserable desires, the fever of your soul? There are words and sounds of power by which you may assuage the pain and quit yourself in

---

[1] Shakespeare's 'Time travels in divers paces with divers persons.'

[2] The keenest-sighted of the Argonauts.

large part of the disorder [1].   Have you the dropsy of
ambition?   There are fixed forms of atonement :
read the book piously thrice through, and they will
have power to make you yourself again.   The envious,
the angry, the lazy, the sot, the rake—none is so wild
that he cannot become tame, if only he lend a patient
ear to treatment.   To flee vice is the beginning of
virtue, and the beginning of wisdom is to have got rid
of folly.   You see with what vast effort and risk of
life you strive to avoid what you think to be the greatest
of evils, a small income or the disgrace of defeat at the
polls [2].   You are indefatigable in sailing as a trader to
the utmost Indies, for from poverty you would fly
through sea, through rocks, through fire.   To save
yourself from trouble over the things which you foolishly
admire and wish for, are you not willing to learn and listen
and trust one wiser than yourself?   What hack prizefighter at village shows and town gathering-places would
think scorn of a garland at Olympia if he had the hope,
if he had the offer, of the palm's delight without the
dust?   Well, as gold is worth more than silver, so
is virtue than gold [3].

   ' O fellow citizens, fellow citizens, money is the

---

[1] The teachings of philosophy are likened to the spells with
which the leech of antiquity eked out his medical art.

[2] The two follow the order of the two vices named above,
avarice and ambition.

[3] The explanation of the parable of the prizefighter.   ' You
who spend such infinite pains to make money may have the much
greater prize of virtue for nothing.'   With this is contrasted the
parrot-cry of the business world, ' O fellow citizens,' &c.

first thing to seek : virtue after money !' this is the lore which the Janus-arches[1] teach from end to end : this is the repetition-lesson which the young have on their lips—yes, and the old too, like schoolboys 'with satchel and tablets slung on left arm[2].'

You have wit, you have character, a tongue at once and truth. Yes, but six or seven thousands are wanting to the four hundred[3] : so you will be one of the crowd. Yet schoolboys in their game say 'Do right the thing and you'll be king[4].' Be this your wall of brass, to have no guilty secrets, no wrong-doing that makes you turn pale. Tell me, pray, which is wiser, the law of Roscius[5], or the schoolboys' burden which offers the title of king to those who 'do the thing right'— the burden so often on the lips of true men like a Curius and a Camillus? Does he advise you better who bids you make 'money, money by right means if you can, if not, by any means money,' and all in order that you may have a seat further forward at the doleful plays of Pupius ; or he who in time of need exhorts you—yes, and helps you to fit yourself—with free soul and erect to defy the tyrant Fortune ?

[1] The chief place of business.

[2] Repeated from Sat. i. 6 (p. 188), 'like the schoolboys I described tripping to school at Venusia.'

[3] The property qualification for the equestrian order.

[4] A jingle used by schoolboys in some old game, and afterwards employed as a proverb. The nature of the game, and the exact bearing of the words, are not recorded.

[5] The law which gave special seats at the theatre to all whose property reached the knight's standard. See Epod. 4.

But if the populace of Rome should by chance ask why I am not glad to take my share in its opinions as I take my share in its colonnades, why I neither follow nor avoid what itself loves or hates, I shall answer as the wary fox in the fable answered the sick lion: 'Because I am frightened at seeing that all the footprints point towards your den and none the other way.' Yes, you are a wild beast—and a many-headed one. For *what* am I to follow, or *whom?* Half the world is greedy to take public contracts. Then there are some who, with tit-bits and presents of fruit, angle for miserly widows[1], and catch old men to stock their preserves. Many have a fortune which grows in the dark[2] by usury. But let us grant that some are attracted by some objects and tastes, some by others; can the same persons persist in a single purpose for an hour together? 'There is no bay on earth that out-shines lovely Baiae!' If so the rich man has said, lake and sea smart for the fancy of the eager owner. But by to-morrow, if his caprice shall have given the signal, you will be carrying off your tools, my men, to Teanum. If he has the bed of the genius[3] in his hall; 'nothing is better' he says, 'nothing happier than a bachelor's life.' If he has not; then he swears that the married alone know what bliss is. With what knot shall I hold fast this Proteus of changeableness? And what of the poor man?

---

[1] Cf. Sat. 2. 5.

[2] Horace's phrase for 'unearned increment.'

[3] A bed set in the *atrium*, which was the sign that the owner of the house was a married man.

You may well smile : he changes his garret, his bed, his bath, his barber.   He hires a boat, and is as sick in it as the rich man who sails in his three-banked yacht.   If I have come in your way with my hair trimmed by a barber who cuts unsteadily, you laugh at me.   If under a trim tunic there chance to show a worn vest, or if my gown sits unevenly and awry, you laugh at me.   What when my judgement is at issue with itself, spurns what it sought, and asks again for what it let slip, sways to and fro like a tide and is a succession of incongruities, pulls down, builds up, changes square to round ?   Do you think it only a fashionable form of madness, and neither laugh at it nor pronounce me to need either a doctor or a guardian appointed by the Court, though you are my protector, though you are cross if a nail is cut awkwardly, though your friend depends on you and looks in everything to you ?

[1] The sum of it all is, the wise man ranks only second to Jove.   He is rich, free, honoured, beautiful, king (in fine) of kings—above all, he is sound, except when the phlegm troubles him.

II   *Troiani belli scriptorem*
                              To Lollius.

Some thoughts on life and morals, such as in the last
   Epistle he represents himself as storing.   They are
   brought out now for the benefit of a young friend.

---

[1] The conclusion is ironical. ' You see that I am falling into the very tone of platitude and paradox which I am always laughing at in the Stoic lecturers.'

Homer's poems offer the text, but when Horace has got
to his sermon he does not go back to them.

WHILE you have been practising declamation [1]
at Rome, Lollius Maximus, I have been
reading again at Praeneste the story-teller of the war
of Troy; who shows us what is fair, what is foul, what
is profitable, what not, more plainly and better than
a Chrysippus or a Crantor.

Why I have come thus to believe, let me explain,
if you are not too busy to listen. The story, which
tells how on account of the amour of Paris Greece and
the barbarian world met in a stubborn war, is made up
of the heats of foolish kings and peoples. Antenor
advises to cut off at the root the cause of the war.
What says Paris? That to enjoy his kingdom in
peace and his life in happiness—no power shall compel
him. Nestor would fain compose the quarrel between
the sons of Peleus and of Atreus. Love is the fire
that kindles one, anger the other, each with a common
fury. For every folly of their princes the Greeks feel
the scourge. Faction, craft, wickedness, and the lust
and anger from which it springs—these are the sources of
wrong-doing within the walls of Troy and without them.

Again, of the power of virtue and of wisdom he
has given us a profitable example in Ulysses, the
[2] 'far-seeing tamer of Troy who looked on the cities and
manners of many men, and whilst making good for
himself and his comrades their homeward journey over

---

[1] In a school of rhetoric.
[2] A free translation of the first lines of the Odyssey.

the broad sea, endured many hardships, but could never be drowned in the waves of adversity.' You know the tale of the Sirens' songs and the cups of Circe, which if he had drunk foolishly and greedily, as his comrades did, he had been the shamed and witless victim of the harlot mistress, and had been turned into a dog in uncleanness or a sow that loves the mire. We are the ciphers, fit for nothing but to eat our share of earth's fruits, the worthless suitors of Penelope and young courtiers of Alcinous, more busy than enough in keeping their skin sleek, whose standard of honour it was to sleep till midday and to beguile care to forgetfulness to the sound of the cithern.

To cut men's throats, robbers rise in the night. To save yourself alive, can you not wake? But as surely as, if you will not take exercise in health, you will have to do it when you have the dropsy; so surely if you will not ask for a book and a candle before daybreak, if you will not set your mind steadily on honourable studies and pursuits, you will lie awake on the rack of envy or passion.

Why are you in such a hurry to take out of your eye what hurts it, while, if something is eating into your very soul, you put off till next year the time for attending to it? He who has begun his task has half done it. Have the courage to be wise. Begin! He who keeps putting off the moment of reform is like the countryman waiting for the river to run by. But the river slides and rolls, and will slide and roll on to all time. You are busy, you say, making money, finding a wife to be a fruitful mother of children; or you have forest land in process of being tamed by the plough-share. Well, when a man has enough, he should wish for no more. It is not town house or land, it is not a pile of brass or of gold, that ever freed their owner's sick body from fever or sick mind from care. The possessor must be in sound health if he thinks to enjoy the property he has got together. To one who still desires or fears, a town house and estate give as much pleasure as pictures to one who has sore eyes, or warm wraps to the gouty, or the cithern to ears aching from need of the syringe. Unless the vessel is clean, every-thing you pour into it turns sour.

Think scorn of pleasures. It is a bad bargain to buy pleasure at cost of pain. The covetous is a beggar always. Try to find a definite limit to your wishing. The envious man grows lean because his neighbour thrives. The tyrants of Sicily never invented a torture worse than envy.

He who will not control his anger will presently wish that undone which irritation and the feelings of the moment have made him do in his hurry to satisfy his vengeful hatred. Anger is a short madness. Rule your passion. Unless it obeys, it governs. Bridle it—chain it down, I pray you. While the horse is teachable and his neck is tender, the trainer breaks him in to go as the rider directs. The hound who does service in the forest began his hunting by barking at the stuffed stag's hide in the yard. Now while you are a boy with clean heart drink in my words, now let

yourself be guided by your betters. The crock will
long keep the fragrance with which it was once steeped
in early days. If, however, you loiter behind or push
vigorously before, I neither wait for the laggard nor
hurry to keep up with those that stride ahead.

III   *Iuli Flore*

To Julius Florus.

*Julius Florus, a young literary friend, is travelling on
the staff of Tiberius (Tiberius Claudius Nero, the son
of Livia, and so stepson of Augustus, and the future
Emperor Tiberius), who had been sent on a mission to
the East in the year* B.C. 20 *to place Tigranes on the
throne of Armenia.*

*Another letter to him may be seen in Epist. 2. 2, which
like this one assumes common literary interests between
the correspondents, and holds up to Florus 'divine
philosophy' as a better medicine of the soul than either
literature or the ambitions of practical life.*

I AM longing to know, Julius Florus, how far
Claudius, the stepson of Augustus, has got in his
campaign. Are you still lingering in Thrace by the
Hebrus, bound in its snowy fetters, or by the strait that
runs between the neighbouring towers[1], or on the rich
plains and hills of Asia? What tasks has his lettered
suite in hand? This is what interests me equally.
Who claims the office of writing the exploits of
Augustus? Who means to spread through long ages
the story how he made war and peace? What of
Titius, soon to be on all lips in Rome, who has not

[1] The Hellespont.

blenched at drinking from the fountain-head of Pindar,
daring to despise the pools and streams which all use—
how fares he? How often does he think of me? Is
he studying under the Muse's high guidance to fit the
measures of Thebes to a Latin lyre? Or is he
storming and laying on the colour thick as a tragic
writer? Tell me, what is Celsus about? He was
warned, and he needs constant warning, to seek wealth
that he can call his own, and to shrink from fingering
any writings to which Apollo of the Palatine has given
a home: lest, if by chance one day the flock of birds
come to reclaim their own plumage, the poor little
jackdaw, stripped of his stolen colours, set the world
laughing at him. And for yourself—what are you
venturing? Over what thyme-bed are you hovering
on your nimble wing? Yours is no small gift; nor
is it a plot that to your shame is untilled and bramble-
grown. Whether you are sharpening your tongue for
the courts, or furnishing yourself to give advice on
points of civil law, or building delightful verse, you
will win the first prize of the conqueror's ivy. But
if you had the heart to leave behind your useless
anodynes [1] for trouble, you would climb where heavenly
philosophy would lead you. This is the task, this
is the study at which we should all be busy, the little
and the great, if we would make our life of value to

---

[1] Literally 'applications' (as poultices), meant to be hot, but
'which have no heat in them.' What the special anodynes were
which Florus tried we cannot tell, whether wealth, ambition,
luxury, &c.

our country and to ourselves. This too, when you
write, you must tell me, whether you care for Munatius
as much as you should. Or does your broken friendship, like a wound ill-stitched, close to no purpose and
tear open again? Do you suffer still, in the fierceness
of untamed necks, be it from hot blood or from
inexperience of life? Wheresoever you are, you have
no business to break the tie of brotherhood. A votive
heifer is being fattened for the return of you both.

IV　　　　　　　　　　　*Albi, nostrorum*

To Albius Tibullus.

*Tibullus is the poet, and Horace seems to be suggesting to
him the same virtue which he hints in the Ode (1. 33)
addressed to him, viz. contentment.*

ALBIUS, generous judge of my 'Talks[1],' what
shall I tell myself that you are about just now
in your country near Pedum? Writing something to
beat the little poems of Cassius of Parma? Or strolling
in quiet thought through the health-giving forest with
your heart on all that is worthy of a wise man and
a good? You never were body without soul. The gods
gave you beauty, gave you wealth, and the art of enjoyment. What further could even a fond nurse ask for
a dear foster-child, if already he has the power to think
wisely and to utter his thoughts—if favour, fame, and
health belong to him abundantly, and 'a seemly household and a purse well lined[2]'? In a world of hope and

---

[1] *Sermones*, Horace's own name for his Satires.
[2] Conington.

care, of fears and angry passions, hold for yourself the
belief that each day that dawns is your last : the hour
to which you do not look forward will be a pleasant
surprise. If you ask of myself, you will find me,
whenever you want something to laugh at, in good case,
fat and sleek, a true hog of Epicurus' herd.

V   *Si potes Archiacis*

To Torquatus.

*An invitation to a modest entertainment on the night before
Caesar's birthday.*

IF you can lie down to table on couches of Archias'
making, and do not mind supping from a modest
dish on a mess of vegetables, I shall look for you here,
Torquatus, at sunset. Your wine will be what was
bottled in Taurus' second year [1] between Minturnae in
the marshes and Petrinum by Sinuessa. If you have anything better, you must bid it be brought, or else put up
with my ordering. The hearth has been brightened
this long while and the furniture made tidy for your
eyes. Let be, as idle things, the hopes and rivalries of
wealth and Moschus' cause [2]. To-morrow is the holiday
of Caesar's birthday, and gives excuse for lengthened
sleep. Without paying for it we shall be able to make
a long summer night of friendly talk. What is fortune
to me, if I may not enjoy it ? The man who for regard
of his heir spares and stints himself more than he need

---

[1] T. Statilius Taurus was consul for the second time in B.C. 26,
so the wine will be four or five years old.

[2] Some cause in which Torquatus was engaged. We hear in
Od. 4. 7 of his eloquence.

is next door to a madman. I shall set you the example of drinking and scattering flowers, and shall not mind even if you think me a madcap. What changes are not wrought by good drinking! It unlocks secrets, bids hopes be certainties, thrusts the coward into the fray, takes their load from anxious hearts, teaches new accomplishments. The life-giving winecup, whom has it not made eloquent, whom has it not made free even in the pinch of poverty! That there be no mean coverlet or soiled napkin to cause grimace, that cup and platter be polished till you see your very self in them, that there be none to repeat out of doors what is said between trusty friends, that the company be chosen and seated to match well—these are the things which I charge myself to see to; a task that fits me, and a task of love. I shall ask Butra to meet you and Septicius, and, unless a better supper and preferable company detain him, Sabinus. There is room besides for several 'shadows[1]' of your bringing; but the goat and her savours are close at hand when a party is too crowded. Do you write how large a company you like to meet; and then shirk your business; and, while your client waits in the front hall, give him the slip by the back door.

VI   *Nil admirari*

To Numicius.

A philosophical essay, for the benefit of his friend, on the duty of choosing deliberately an ideal or chief good, and then pursuing it with thoroughness. The first suggested

[1] See on Sat. 2. 8, p. 257.

is the apathy, or freedom from disturbing emotions,
recommended by the Epicureans. The length at which
this is set out seems to imply that for the moment at any
rate it catches Horace's fancy. After that, he takes the
more usual division of ideals, and goes through them in
succession—virtue, money, ambition, different forms of
pleasure. As he passes to the ideals which he holds to be
unworthy, the exhortations to their pursuit become ironical.

*N*OUGHT *to admire*[1] is perhaps the one and
only thing, Numicius, that can make a man
happy and keep him so. There are those who can
gaze with no tinge of awe at the sight of yonder sun
and stars and seasons passing in their appointed revolution. What think you of what earth gives, or the sea
which makes rich the Arabs and Indians at the world's
end; what of public games, of applause and presents of
the people's favour; in what fashion do you hold that
these things should be regarded, with what feelings and
countenance?

So with their opposites, he who fears them 'admires'
them in nearly the same way as the man who desires
them: in either case there is the disturbing flutter of
the heart. The sight that was not expected amazes
both men alike. Whether his feeling be joy or pain,
desire or dread, what does it matter, if, whenever he has
seen aught better or worse than he expected, his eyes

---

[1] Pope's translation has familiarized us with the phrase, but it
hardly represents to the English reader the meaning of *admirari*,
which is intended to cover any mental perturbation caused by
external things, whether by way of wonder, awe, admiration,
desire, or fear. Perhaps 'to think much of,' if somewhat clumsy,
most nearly approaches the breadth of the phrase.

are riveted and heart and limbs alike are spellbound?
The wise man would deserve the name of madman, the
just of unjust, if they were to pursue even Virtue herself too far.

Go then [1], gaze in rapt ' admiration ' at silver plate, at
ancient marbles and bronzes, at works of art, at gems and
Tyrian dyes : rejoice that a thousand eyes are looking
at you as you speak : in busy industry be early in the
Forum and late in coming home, for fear Mutus reap a
larger harvest from the estate he got with his wife than
you from your business, and (thought of shame, seeing
his lineage is worse than yours !) he make you ' admire '
him rather than you make him ' admire ' you ! But
remember that, as time will bring forth to the sunshine
what is now under the earth, so it will bury out of
view what is now in the light : when you have been
the familiar sight to all eyes in Agrippa's colonnade
and on Appius' road, it still remains for you to go where
Numa and Ancus have gone home before you.

If lung or reins are attacked by some acute malady, look
about for some escape from the malady. So you would live
for the true end (who would not?) : then if *Virtue* only
can secure you this, be bold, let delights be, and to work!

Suppose, on the other hand, you think Virtue so many
words, and a sacred grove so many yards of timber [2] :
then take care to be first in every harbour, to miss no

---

[1] This, of course, is an ironical exhortation to do what, in the
face of what has been said, is ridiculous. The absurdity is
emphasized by recalling the transitoriness of all things human.

[2] i. e. if (in modern phrase) you are a ' materialist ' all round.

bargain at Cibyra or in Bithynia : round off a thousand
talents ; as many again ; and let the third thousand be
added, and what is wanted to make the heap four-
square.   Of course, you know, a wife and dower, credit
and friends, even birth and beauty, are all in the gift of
Queen Money : the goddess of persuasion and the
goddess of love both honour the well-moneyed man.
The king of the Cappadocians is rich in slaves, but
lacks money—mind you are not as he.   Lucullus (the
story goes) was asked once if he could lend a hundred
soldiers' cloaks for the stage.   'How can I possibly
lend so many ? ' he answers, 'but I will see and send
as many as I have.'   Presently he writes that he has
five thousand cloaks in his house ; the man may take
some or all.   That is a mean house where there is not
plenty that goes to waste, beyond the master's knowledge
and for the service of thieves.   So then if *substance*
be what alone can 'make you happy and keep you so,'
let this be the task that you are first to go back to, last
to leave off.

If *show and popularity* make the favourite of Fortune,
then let us buy a slave to tell us names, to nudge us on
the left side and make us put out the hand over the
weights [1] : ' this man has much influence in the Fabian
tribe—that in the Veline.   This man will give the rods
to whom he will, or ruthlessly snatch away the curule

[1] A phrase of uncertain meaning, possibly of shaking hands
with a tradesman across the counter.   The scholiasts, however,
say that *pondera* were the high stepping-stones by which people
crossed a street.

ivory.' 'Brother, Father'—do not forget the title—
according to their ages with ready courtesy make each
your kinsman.

If again 'living well' means *dining well*: then—the
day dawns : off let us go whither our appetite leads us.
Let us fish and hunt, but after the fashion of Gargilius
in the story. He used in the morning to send a train of
nets, hunting-spears, and slaves through the Forum when
it was fullest, that in sight of the same crowd one mule
out of the lot might bring home a wild boar which he
had bought at a shop. Let us go to the bath crammed
full of undigested food [1], with no thought of propriety,
qualified for the register of Caere [2], like the worthless crew
of Ulysses of Ithaca, who cared more for a forbidden
pleasure than for their return to their country.

If, as Mimnermus tells us, without *love and mirth* is
no pleasure, then spend your life in love and mirth.

Long life and health to you. If you know anything
better than all this, be frank and let me share it. If not,
live by these rules, as I try to do.

VII   *Quinque dies*

To Maecenas.
Patronage as it should and should not be.

The letter begins with Horace's excuses for breaking a
promise to return to Rome, but the main purpose (for
the letter is clearly written for public reading) is to give
a picture of patronage honourable to patron and poet, such
as that of Maecenas towards himself, and patronage as

---

[1] It was supposed to be a way of procuring a fresh appetite.

[2] A phrase equivalent to 'disfranchisement.'

it should not be, as illustrated in the story of Philippus
and Vulteius; of whom the former looked chiefly to his
own amusement, the latter allowed himself to be taken out
of his proper sphere and put in a false position.

FIVE days I promised you to be in the country, and
here I am breaking my promise and letting you miss
me all August. It is true. But if you would have me
alive and in sound and good health, the liberty which you
grant me when I am ill you will grant me, Maecenas, when
I am afraid of being ill, while the first figs and the heat
are furnishing the undertaker with his suite of black attendants, while every father and fond mother look pale with
fear for their boys, and assiduity of courtesies and petty
business of the Forum bring fevers in their train and
break the seals of wills. But as soon as winter begins
to fleck with snow the uplands of Alba your poet will
go down to the sea, take care of himself, and shut
himself up with his books. You, my dear friend, he
will revisit with the zephyrs, if you will allow him so
much, and with the first swallow.

In making me a rich man you have not acted as the
Calabrian host inviting a guest to eat his pears : 'Eat
some more, pray.' 'I have had enough.' 'But please take
away as many as you like.' 'No, thank you.' 'They
will be a welcome little present for your boys if you
will take them.' 'I am as much obliged by your
generosity as if you sent me away laden.' 'Well—as
you please—if you leave them, they go into the pig-tub
to-day.' The prodigal and fool gives what he despises
and hates : seed so sown has always produced, and will

always produce, a crop of ingratitude. The generous and wise professes to have his hand always open to the deserving, yet he does not forget the difference between real coins and counters. Deserving I shall try always to show myself, as becomes the merit of my benefactor. But if you wish me never to leave you, you must give me back the strength of lung, the black hair well down on the forehead, you must give back the charm of speech, give back the grace of laughter, and the lamentations, between our cups, over Cinara the saucy runaway.

Once on a time a half-starved little vixen [1] had crept through a narrow chink into a bin of corn, and when it had well fed was struggling in vain to get out again with its belly full. To it quoth a weasel hard by, 'If you wish to escape thence you must go back fasting to the narrow hole which you entered when fasting.' If this fable is addressed to me, I am ready to resign all I have. And do not think that I praise the sleep of the humble while my own belly is with fat capon lined. I have no mind to exchange my ease and freedom for the riches of the Arabs. You have often praised my modesty, and have been called my 'prince' and my 'father' to your face, and not a word more sparingly behind your back. Now see if I can cheerfully restore all you have given. 'Twas no bad saying of Telemachus, true child of enduring Ulysses, 'Horses [2] would be out of place in Ithaca, since it neither spreads into level courses nor is

[1] Vixens, outside Fable-land, do not eat corn, and Bentley, to save Horace's repute for natural history, wished to alter the text.

[2] A paraphrase of Homer's Odyssey 4. 601 foll.

lavish of much herbage.   Son of Atreus, I will leave your
gifts, which befit yourself better than me.'   Small things
beseem the small.   My pleasure now is not in queenly
Rome, but in leisurely Tibur or peaceful Tarentum.

As Philippus, vigorous and masterful and the famous
pleader, was returning home from his business about two
o'clock in the day, and complaining (for he was getting
on in years) that he began to feel the Carinae [1] incon-
veniently far from the Forum, he saw (so the story goes)
a man, who had just been clean-shaven, sitting in a barber's
empty booth and quietly cleaning his nails for himself
with a penknife.   'Demetrius' (this was the quick-witted
boy who waited his orders), 'go and ask and bring me word
where that man lives, who he is, what his estate, who his
father or his patron.'   He goes, and comes back with the
answer that his name is Vulteius Mena, an auctioneer,
of modest rank, of blameless repute, known at proper
seasons to be busy and to be idle, to gain and to spend,
finding his pleasure in his humble companions and a
home of his own, and when business is over, in the
games and the Circus.   'I should like to hear all you ·
tell me from his own lips.   Bid him come to supper.'
Mena, to tell the truth, could not believe his ears.   He
said nothing, but wondered what it could mean.   To
be brief, 'No, thank you,' he answered.   'Do you
mean the fellow refuses me?'   'He has the face to do
so.   He either thinks little of you, or he is afraid of
you.'   Next morning Philippus comes on Vulteius

[1] A fashionable quarter of Rome where Philippus would have
a house.

selling cheap wares to a humble crowd of men in their tunics [1], and hails him first. Vulteius makes his business, the bonds of one who works for hire, his excuse to Philippus for not having called on him in the morning, and finally for not having seen him first. 'Take it that I have pardoned you on condition that you sup with me to-day.' 'As you please.' 'You will come then after three o'clock. Meanwhile go and make your fortune as busily as you may.' So he came to supper, and after chattering on every topic, wise and foolish, is let go late to bed. When the fellow has been seen running often as a fish to the well-concealed hook, attending early levées like a client, and by this time a daily guest, he is invited to come as companion, when the Latin holidays [2] were fixed, to a country house not far from Rome. Mounted behind the ponies, he kept praising without stint or stay the soil, the air of the Sabine hills. Philippus marks and smiles, and, thinking only of his own ease and his own amusement from any quarter, offers him seven thousand sesterces as a present and seven thousand more as a loan, and so persuades him to buy a little farm. He buys it. Not to waste your time with too long a story, from a smart townsman he becomes a countryman, and has on his tongue nothing but furrows and vineyards, trains elms for the vines, kills himself over his busy work, and ages before his time with the desire of

---

[1] As we should say, 'in their shirt-sleeves.'

[2] A holiday in each year at a time to be fixed by the Consul for the year. The law-courts would be shut during it.

getting. But when he has lost his sheep by theft, his goats by sickness, when his crops have belied his hopes, his ox has been worked to death at the plough, enraged at his losses, he seizes a horse in the middle of the night and in wrath makes straight for the house of Philippus. As soon as Philippus sees him all rough and unshorn, 'You are too hard on yourself, I am sure, Vulteius,' he says, 'and too intent on your business.' 'By Pollux,' he answers, 'you would call me a miserable wretch, my patron, if you would give me my true name. But by your genius, by your right hand and household gods, I pray and beseech you, restore me to my former life.'

Who once has seen how much what he has let go excels what he has sought should go back in time and return to what he left. The true course is that each should measure himself with the foot-rule which belongs to him.

VIII   *Celso gaudere*

To Celsus Albinovanus.

The purpose of the Epistle is to be looked for in the hint of the last line. Horace prepares for it, after his manner, by the half-ironical confessions which lead to it : 'You may say worse things of me than anything I suggest of you. I don't listen to my friendly critics, so I cannot expect you to listen to me.'

The person addressed is probably the Celsus of Epist. 1. 3, another of the literary circle of Tiberius.

BEAR, my Muse, as I pray you, messages of greeting and good wishes to Celsus Albinovanus, the companion and secretary of Nero. If he shall ask after

my doings, tell him that in spite of many fair promises my
life is neither wisely ruled nor happy, not that hail has
bruised my vines and heat blighted my olives, nor that
I have herds sickening on some distant pasture; but
because with mind less sound than any part of my body,
I yet care not to listen to anything or learn anything
that can lighten its sickness, am affronted by my faithful
physicians, angry with my friends for their anxiety to
rescue me from my deadly lethargy; because I pursue
what hurts me, avoid what I fully believe would help
me; at Rome love Tibur, fickle as the wind, at Tibur
Rome[1]. Thereafter question him of his own health, his
estate, his life—how he is in favour with the prince and
his staff. If he says 'well,' first wish him joy; presently
remember to drop in his own ear this one word of advice,
' As you bear your fortune, Celsus, so we shall bear you.'

IX   *Septimius, Claudi*
              To Tiberius.

A letter of introduction addressed to the young prince.
The tact and grace of it have always been admired.
See the commendation and translation of it by Steele in the
' Spectator,' No. 493. Septimius is no doubt the friend
to whom Od. 2. 6 is addressed. Horace therefore knew
well whom he was commending.

SEPTIMIUS understands, I see, Claudius, as no one
else does, how much you make of me: for when he
asks, nay insists that I shall undertake to commend him
and introduce him (if you will believe it!) to you as

---

[1] It is worth noting that when Horace is writing for a different
purpose he says just the opposite of himself. Epist. 1. 14.

one worthy in mind and manners of the carefully chosen
circle of a Nero—thinking, no doubt, that my part is
that of a nearer friend,—he must see and know the
extent of my power a great deal better than I do myself.
I gave him plenty of good reasons for excusing me.
But I feared that he would think that I was making
myself out as less well off than I am, and on selfish
grounds denying powers which I really possess. So to
avoid an imputation of this graver fault I made up my
mind to take the privileges of a town-bred assurance.
So now, if you can see merit in the sacrifice of modesty
to the claims of friendship, enter my friend's name on
your list and believe all good of him.

X   *Urbis amatorem*

To Aristius Fuscus.

*Horace, in his country retreat, writes to Aristius Fuscus,
still in Rome, in praise of country as against town life.
This turns eventually into praise of moderation and contentment as against grandeur and the desire of wealth.
Compare the Epistle with Ode 1. 22, addressed to the
same person and with something of the same moral.*

OUR greeting to Fuscus, who loves the town as we
       love the country. In this one point, you see, we
differ much : but in all else nearly twin brothers with
brothers' hearts (when one says 'no,' the other says 'no'
too) we nod agreement like two old familiar doves. You
keep the nest; I am full of the streams and lichen-
touched rocks and woodland of the country which I
love. Ask no more. I live and feel a king as soon as
I have left behind what, amid favouring voices, you

extol to the sky. Like the priest's runaway slave, I have no stomach for cakes : bread is what I want, and prefer now to honeyed wafers.

If our business is to 'live agreeably to nature [1],' and we must begin by choosing a place to live in, do you know any place to be preferred for happiness to the country? Is there any place where you can keep warmer in winter, where a pleasanter air tempers the Dog-star's rage and the Lion's passage when he has been frenzied by the sun's keen edge? Is there where churlish Care breaks less the thread of sleep? Does the grass smell less sweet or shine less brightly than mosaic of Libyan marble? Is the water purer which in town streets struggles to break its leaden pipe than that which hurries murmuring down the sloping stream-bed? You see that among your many-coloured columns you take pains to grow green trees, and you praise a town house which has a distant country view. If you drive nature out with a pitchfork, she will soon find a way back and, before you know it, will burst triumphantly through your foolish caprices.

The man who lacks the skilled eye to compare wool dyed at Aquinum with true Tyrian purple will not receive surer damage, or one nearer the life, than one who shall not be able to distinguish the false from the true. Whom prosperity has charmed too much, adversity will shatter. If you shall admire anything, you will be loth to lay it down. Flee grandeur : under a humble roof you may live a far happier life than kings and kings' friends. A stag had the better of a horse in fighting, and used to

[1] A Stoic catchword.

drive him from the pasture they had shared, until, worsted in the long contest, the horse begged the help of a man, and let him put the bit between his teeth. But from the day when, appealing to force, he parted from his enemy a conqueror, he never got the rider off his back or the bit out of his mouth. So one who for fear of poverty loses liberty, which is more precious than gold and silver, will carry a master for his shameless greed, and will be a slave all his life, because he will never learn the lesson of contentment. Like the shoe in the fable, when a man's circumstances do not fit him, if they are too large for his foot they will trip him up, if too small they will gall it. You will live I know, Aristius, like a philosopher, well contented with your lot; and you will not let me off unscolded when I seem to be gathering more than I want and never taking a holiday. A store of money is to each man either a master or a slave : but by rights it should follow the rope when it turns on the windlass, not turn the windlass itself.

I am dictating this letter to you behind the crumbling shrine of Vacuna [1], happy in every point save that you are not with me.

---

[1] Identified probably with a temple of Victory which stood in the village now named Rocca Giovane, close to the site of Horace's country house. Such a temple we know, from an inscription found on the spot, to have been restored in Vespasian's reign. Vacuna is said to have been the Sabine name of the goddess. But Horace is playing on the name as derived from *vacare* and its cognates, as though the phrase gave the idea of 'in holiday land.'

XI   *Quid tibi visa Chios*

To Bullatius.

*Among the forms of restlessness foreign travelling is one
of which Horace more than once complains. Bullatius is
to be thought of as still in the East, perhaps as having
written a letter to which this is an answer, and in which,
after the way of travellers, he has expressed an alternation
of interest in what he saw and of weariness of travel.*

WHAT thought you of Chios, my Bullatius,
and of famous Lesbos? What of pretty Samos?
What of Sardis, the royal home of Croesus? What of
Smyrna and Colophon? Are they greater or less than
their fame? Do all alike pale before the Campus and
Tiber's stream? Or have you a hankering for one of
Attalus' cities? Or are you by this time so tired of
travelling by land and sea that you are prepared to
sing the praises even of Lebedus:—'You know what
Lebedus [1] is, a town more deserted than Gabii and
Fidenae: yet I could find it in my heart to live there, and,
forgetting my friends and forgotten by them, to gaze
from a safe distance ashore on Neptune's wild play'?
Yet as the traveller who is bound for Rome from Capua
will not wish, because now he is drenched with rain
and bespattered with mud, to spend a lifetime in the
wayside inn,—as the man who takes a hot bath when
he is chilled through does not praise it as a full security
for a life happy at all points,—so neither will you,
because boisterous Auster has tossed you on the sea, for

---

[1] A town of Ionia with a history, but which had been desolated
about 300 B.C.

that reason sell your ship on the other side of the
Aegean. To a sound man Rhodes and fair Mytilene
are what a travelling cloak is in summer, what light
drawers are when a snowy wind is blowing, what the
Tiber is in mid-winter, what a stove in the month of
August. So long as you may, so long as Fortune wears
a smiling face, stay in Rome: praise Samos and Chios
and Rhodes; but praise them at a distance. Whatever
happy hour God has given you take, my friend, with
grateful hand; and do not put off enjoyment from year to
year: so that, wherever your lot be cast, you may say
that you have lived as though life were worth living.
For, if what takes away care be reason and prudence,
not a place that commands a wide sea-view, they change
their sky, not their soul, who run across the sea.   We
work hard at doing nothing: we seek happiness in
yachts and four-horse coaches. What you seek is here
—is at Ulubrae [1]—if an even soul does not fail you.

XII   *Fructibus Agrippae*

To Iccius.

*The Epistle has the interest of bringing together two
friends of the poet whom we know in the Odes ; see Od.
1. 29 and 2.16. He writes partly to commend Grosphus,
who, as the Ode indicates, had property in Sicily, to Iccius,
who is in charge of Agrippa's Sicilian estates. Iccius
has apparently complained to Horace that he is managing
another person's property instead of possessing one of his
own. Horace rallies him gently, but his remonstrance*

---

[1] A little town near the Pomptine marshes, dull and probably
not very wholesome.

*ends in compliments on his simple life and philosophical
tastes. We remember that in the Ode he is spoken of as
having accumulated a philosophical library.*

IF you are enjoying as you should, Iccius, the fruits
which you gather of Agrippa's Sicilian estates, it
is not possible that Jove himself could give you greater
abundance. A truce to murmurings : for he is not poor
who has the full use of property. If all is well with
digestion, with lungs, with feet, the wealth of kings
will not be able to give you more. If it so be that,
denying yourself what all make free with, you live on
nettle salad ; so will you continue to live though this
moment a Pactolus-stream of fortune should drench you
with gold ; be it because money has no secret of changing
nature, or because you think everything else a trifle
in comparison with virtue. We marvel at the story how
Democritus [1] let his cattle eat bare his farm and standing
crops while his soul, far away from the body, was on its
swift travels ; and yet here are you, while the itch of
gain spreads from palm to palm, keeping as in old days
your great tastes and caring for high questions ; what
causes set bounds to the sea, what makes the year warm
or cold, whether stars wander through their courses of
their own motion or by law, what shrouds the moon's
disk in darkness, what brings it forth again, what are
the purpose and effects of nature's harmony in discord [2],

[1] The Eleatic philosopher, a standing instance in Cicero of
absorption in philosophical study.

[2] Phrases of the natural philosophy of Empedocles. For
Stertinius see Sat. 2. 3. He represents here the Stoic physics.

whether it be Empedocles that is doting, or the wit of Stertinius. But whether you have got to slaughtering fish or only leeks and onions[1], make a friend of Pompeius Grosphus, and if he asks anything of you, readily give it him: Grosphus will ask nothing but what is right and fair. Friends are always cheap in the market when good men have lack of something. But that you may not be ignorant how the world is going in Rome, the Cantabrian has fallen before the valour of Agrippa, the Armenian before that of Claudius Nero: Phraates, humbled to his knees, has submitted to Caesar's imperial rule: Golden Plenty from a full horn is pouring her fruits upon Italy.

XIII   *Ut proficiscentem*

To Vinius Asina.

Under the form of a letter supposed to be sent after the messenger who has just been dispatched to carry a copy of some poems (doubtless the three Books of Odes) to Augustus, Horace is making a playful apology to the Emperor for any untimeliness in the presentation. The play on the name of Asina which supplies so much of the imagery of the Epistle belongs to a form of wit which the Romans thought urbane. Who Vinius Asina was, and what his relations to Horace, is unknown.

AS I explained to you often and at length when you set out, Vinius, you will deliver my rolls with seal

---

[1] There is a play both (as in the 'nettle salad' above) on Iccius' vegetable diet, and (as in other places in Horace) on the supposed view of the Pythagoreans that souls in their transmigrations passed into animals and sometimes even vegetables.

unbroken to Augustus, if he be well, if he be in good spirits, if, finally, he shall ask for them ; lest in desire to help me you blunder and bring odium on my book by the officious service of excessive zeal.   If perchance the parcel of my writings prove too heavy and gall your shoulders, fling it away at once, rather than dash down in ill temper the pack-saddle when you reach your destination, and turn your family name of Asina into a jest, and become the talk of the town.   Over hillsides, streams, sloughs, you will put out your full strength. When once you have won your purpose, reached your goal, and laid down your burden, you will keep charge of it not so as to carry the parcel of parchments under your arm, as a rustic carries a lamb, as tipsy Pyrria[1] the hank of stolen wool, as the guest at a tribesmen's dinner his slippers and felt cap.   Push steadily onwards, and remember my earnest request that you will not tell all the world what a heavy load you found the poems which are to occupy the eyes and ears of Caesar. So go your way ; farewell ; beware of stumbling and breaking the brittle goods entrusted to you.

XIV   *Vilice silvarum*
To his bailiff.

The 'Vilicus' was the slave-bailiff who, with eight slaves under him, took charge of Horace's country house and home farm.   Under the form of a letter to him, contrasting their tastes, Horace sets forth his own love of country life and preaches against restlessness.

[1] A character, we are told, in a comedy.

BAILIFF of my woods and of the little farm which makes me myself again—which you despise, though it gives a home to five households and sends off to Varia [1] five worthy senators—let us try whether I am more strenuous in weeding the mind or you in weeding the land, and whether Horace or his property is in the better condition. For me, though I am kept in town awhile by Lamia's tender heart and his sorrow as he mourns his brother, grieves inconsolably for his lost brother, yet every impulse of my soul bears me to the place where you are, and loves to burst the barriers that close on its course. I call happy the man whose life is spent in the country, you the man whose life is spent in town. One who likes the lot of another of course mislikes his own. Each is a fool, unjustly laying the blame on the place, which does not deserve it: the true culprit is the mind, which never can run away from itself. When you were a common drudge, the country was the object of your secret prayers; now that you are bailiff you long for the town, its games and its baths. You know that I am consistent, and that it is with a heavy heart that I go away whenever the business which I hate draws me to Rome. Our ideals are not the same—there is the point of difference between us. What you hold to be desert and 'unharboured wilds' are hailed as lovely by one who feels with me; and he hates what you think beautiful.

---

[1] Now Vico Varo, the little town seven miles above Tivoli, where the Digentia (Licenza), the stream of Horace's valley, joins the Anio. 'Senators' is a playful exaggeration for the members of some communal council.

It is the arch and the savoury cookshop that send through you a thrill of longing for the town. I see it, and understand that 'that[1] nook at the world's end will grow pepper and spice as soon as it will grow grapes,' and that 'there is no tavern near that can supply you with wine, nor flute-player to whose music you can dance till the earth is tired,' and yet that 'you have to keep the fields busy which have been long since they felt the mattock, and to care for the ox after he is unyoked, and pull leaves to fill his belly, and when you would like a holiday the river finds you fresh work if there has been a rainfall, and it has to be taught by many a dam to spare the sunny meadow.'

Now come, hear what it is that prevents our singing the same tune. One whom fine-spun gowns became and shining curls, one whom you remember finding favour, though empty-handed, with greedy Cinara, whom you remember fond of drinking the clear Falernian before midday was past, now finds his pleasure in a simple meal and a sleep on the grass near the stream. Shame is not in having played, but in not knowing when to break off the play. In the place where you live, no one spoils the edge of my enjoyments with sidelong glances or poisons them with the tooth of secret hate. My neighbours smile to see me moving sods and stones. You would rather gnaw the tough rations of a city slave: that is the company into which your wishes bear you. The sharp-witted town slave envies you the free use of wood and flock and garden. The ox longs for the horse's

---

[1] These seem to be meant as echoes of the bailiff's grumbling.

trappings: the horse, when he is lazy, longs to be set ploughing. If they consult me, I shall advise each that he ply the trade he understands and be content.

XV   *Quae sit hiems Veliae*
                        To Vala.

Horace, ordered by his physician to discontinue his yearly visit to Baiae, is looking for a watering-place, and doubting between Salernum, (Salerno) and Velia, some fifty miles further down the coast. He writes to ask questions about them of Vala, who had a country house in the district. The last part of the Epistle is a humorous and ironical apology for the minuteness of his inquiries about the fare: 'You see I am like Maenius—a philosopher when I can't help it, but a "bon-vivant" when I can be.' Modern readers who have experience of the humours of a 'health-resort' will recognize the picture of the indignation felt at Baiae at the slighting of its sulphur baths.

WHAT the winter is at Velia, what the climate at Salernum, my Vala, what kind of folk live there and what the road is like—(for you must know Antonius Musa's fiat pronounces Baiae useless to me, and yet makes Baiae look on me as an enemy when I drench myself in cold water through the cold of mid-winter—'really that their myrtle-groves should be abandoned, and the sulphur baths despised, so famous for driving the most obstinate rheumatism from the muscles'—so the town groans, and hates the silly invalids who are bold enough to place head and stomach under the springs of Clusium or to visit Gabii or the cold uplands. My quarters have to be changed and

the horse driven past the well-known halting places.
'Where are you going? I am not for Cumae or Baiae,'
so the rider will say with an angry tug at the left rein—
the horse's ear, you know, is in his mouth, when the
bit is in it)—which place is best supplied with corn,
whether they drink rain-water from tanks or wells fed by
perennial springs—(the wines of that district I do not
stop to ask of: in my country home I can put up with
and submit to anything you like; but when I have come
to the seaside I want something generous and mellow,
which may drive away care, which may flow into my
veins and into my heart with rich hope, which may find
me speech, which may make me young again, and give
me favour in the eyes of the kind ladies of Lucania)—
which of the two neighbourhoods breeds more hares,
which wild boars, the waters of which sea give more
covert to fish and sea-urchins, that when I come home
from thence I may be in good case and fit for Phaeacia—
all these questions it is yours to answer, ours to give
you full credence.

Maenius—when, after using up like a man of spirit all
he inherited from mother and father, he set up as a city
wit, a trencherman at every table, with no crib to call
his own, a man who when he lacked a dinner knew no
difference between citizen and foeman, ruthless in inventing scandal of any kind and against any person, a very
whirlwind and whirlpool of desolation to the market—
used to spend whatever he gained upon his insatiable
appetite. This fellow, when he had got little or no spoil
from those who encouraged or who feared his villainy,

would make a supper large enough for three bears on plate
after plate of some cheap tripe or lamb's flesh. To such
a point had he changed his tone that (like Bestius in
his reformed days) he would say that men who spent
their substance on gluttony ought to have their bellies
scored with white-hot iron. At the same time, if he
ever took any larger booty, when he had reduced it to
smoke and ashes 'I do not wonder, by Hercules,'
he would say, ' at those who put their patrimony down
their throats, since there really is nothing better than a
fat fieldfare, nothing nobler than a broad sow's paunch.'

To tell truth, that is a picture of me. When means
fail me, I sing the praises of the safe and the humble,
and put a bold face on cheap fare : but at the same time if
anything better and more savoury falls to my lot, I say
that you, gentlemen, are the only philosophers, and
alone have the secret of a happy life, whose wealth has,
for all to see, solid foundation in well-appointed country
houses.

XVI   *Ne perconteris*

To Quinctius.

*Horace describes himself in Epist. 1. 1, as inclining now to
Epicurean now to Stoic views. In the last Epistle he
with some irony confessed to the former; in this one he is
a more serious preacher of the latter. He touches in the
course of it on many of the current Stoical doctrines and
with little or none of the banter with which he usually
treats them. The connexion between the description of
his country home and the rest of the Epistle is not made
quite clear. Perhaps that it is not is part of the easy
inconsequence of a letter. But there is, no doubt, an*

*unexpressed comparison between Horace's own life and
the life of reality and simplicity which he holds up to
Quinctius as the only happy one.*

TO forestall all your questions about my farm, my
good friend Quinctius, whether it finds its
master bread from its own corn, or makes him rich in
supply of olives or apples, or in meadow land, or in vine-
clothed elms, you shall have the character and lie of
the land described to you with an owner's garrulity.
Think of a mass of hills, unbroken were they not
divided by a well-timbered valley, so placed that the
sun when he comes to us looks on its right side, as
he leaves us in his flying car warms its left. The
tempering of the air you would praise. What if you
learned that the bushes grow generous store of cornels
and plums, that oak and holm-oak gladden the cattle
with abundant forage and their master with abundant
shade? You would say that it was the greenery of
Tarentum brought to your doors. A spring, too, fit to
give its name to a river—Hebrus, as he encompasses
Thrace, is not cooler or purer—flows with its medicine
for sick heads and sick stomachs. This is the hiding-
place, attractive to me, lovely even (if you trust my
judgement) in itself, which keeps me for you safe and
sound through September's season.

And now tell me of yourself—your life is all it should
be, if you are taking the trouble to be all that we call
you. We already have you on our lips, all we in Rome,
as a happy man. I am only afraid of your taking the
word of others rather than your own about yourself; or

thinking that any but the wise and good can be happy; or, if the world says often enough that you are in sound and good health, hiding a fever as the feast draws near, and pretending not to feel it, till the trembling falls on your hands already in the dish. It is a false shame which makes fools hide wounds instead of healing them. If one were to speak of wars fought by you on land and sea, and try to tickle your ears, when they could listen, with such words as these :

> Which is most,
> Thy people's health to thee, or thine to us,
> Long may He keep a secret still unguessed,
> Who guards both Rome and thee !

you would recognize that they came from a panegyric on Augustus [1]. When you allow yourself to be called 'a wise man without a flaw,' are you answering, pray tell me, to your own name ? 'Yes, I feel pleasure, of course, as you do, in being called a good man and wise.' The power that gave you this title to-day will take it away, if so it pleases, to-morrow ; just as if it shall have bestowed the rods on an unworthy claimant, it will with the same authority take them away again : 'Put it down, I have not given it you,' it says. I put it down and retire, hanging my head. If the same people were to cry after me 'Thief ! ', take away my good name, accuse me of having strangled my father, ought I to feel the sting of such false charges, and go red and white ? Who is

---

[1] They are actually lines, the Scholiasts tell us, from the 'Panegyric on Augustus' by the poet Varius.

pleased with baseless honour, or frightened by untrue
scandal, save the man who is still full of flaws and in
need of the doctor? Who is your ' good man '?
You answer ' one who observes the decrees of the
senate, statutes, and laws : one who is set as arbitrator
to decide quarrels many and grave : money is safe
when he is the security, a cause when he is the witness.'
Yet this very man all his household and all his neighbours see to be base within, beneath the fair-looking
skin of respectability.   If a slave were to say to
me ' I never stole or ran away ' : ' You have your
reward ' I should answer : ' you are not flogged.'   ' I
never committed murder.'   ' You shall not hang on a
cross for the crows to eat.'   ' I am a good and useful
servant.'   One of us Sabellians shakes his head and
says ' no, no ! '   For even the wolf learns caution and
fears the pitfall, the hawk the suspected snare, the pike
the covered hook : men who are really good hate vice
because they love virtue.   *You* will not commit wrong
because you dread punishment.   Give you the hope of
escaping detection, and you will put no difference between
what is sacred and what is not.   For when you filch
only one bushel of beans from a thousand, that makes
my loss less serious, not your offence.   Your ' good
man,' the paragon of the Forum and the law-court,
whenever he offers a porker or a bullock to the gods,
after saying aloud ' Father Janus,' and aloud ' Apollo,'
moves his lips as though he dreaded that any should
hear him : ' Fair Laverna [1], grant to me not to

[1] The goddess of thieves and impostors.

be found out : grant me to pass for just and con-
scientious : shroud in night my wrongdoing, in clouds my
fraud ! '

How the miser is better than a slave, or more free,
when he stoops for the brass coin nailed to the ground [1]
at a crossway, I do not see : for he who shall have
desires will have fears too ; and again he who shall
live in fear will never, in my judgement, be a free man.
One who is always in a hurry, always over head and
ears in the amassing of wealth, has lost his shield, has
run away from Virtue's post. Since you can sell your
captive [2], do not think of killing him : he will make a
useful slave : he is tough—let him feed your cattle or
guide your plough : send him to sea, and let him pass the
winter in mid-seas as a trader : let him make corn cheaper,
let him fetch and carry breadstuff and household goods.

The truly ' wise man and good ' will venture to say,
' Pentheus [3], lord of Thebes, what will you compel me to
bear and suffer that is unworthy of me ? ' ' I will take
away your goods.' ' You mean my cattle, my substance,
furniture, silver ? You may take them all.' ' I will
keep you in handcuffs and fetters and under stern
gaolers.' ' God himself at any moment that I shall

---

[1] Nailed, according to the Scholiast, by idle boys for the pleasure
of watching to see who would stop first and try to pick it up.

[2] This is addressed to the supposed captor of this runaway
from Virtue's army. Divested of the figure, ' such a man will
not make a philosopher, a "good man" : he is fit for the menial
and money-getting professions.'

[3] The remainder of the Epistle is an adaptation of a scene in the
Bacchantes of Euripides.

choose will set me free.' I imagine this is his meaning :
' I will die '— Death is the limit that ends everything.

XVII *Quamvis, Scaeva, satis*

To Scaeva.

*The subject of the Epistle, like that of the following one, is
the relations of patron and protégé. So far as regards
the attitude of the patron this was treated in Epist. 1. 7.
In these Epistles it is treated from the other side. We
do not know who Scaeva was nor what his connexion
with Horace. The Epistle has an air of irony and
of satire. Its natural effect is to suggest a class of
aspirants, irresolute at first and half ashamed of being
patronized, yet driven to it by greediness and the im-
portunity of relatives, and in danger when they enter on
it of turning out beggars and grumblers.*

ON the difficult question how one should live with
one's betters, although your own care for yourself and your knowledge suffice, Scaeva, yet listen to
the advice of a humble friend who needs still himself
much teaching. It is rather like a blind man offering
himself as a guide; yet blind though we be, look and
see whether we have anything to say which you may
care to make your own.

If your delight be to take your ease and sleep till the
sun is up, if the dust and the clatter of wheels and
tavern noises distress you, I shall advise you to go off
to Ferentinum : for joys are no monopoly of the rich ;
he has not had an unhappy life who from birth to death
has lived out of the world's knowledge. If, on the other
hand, you wish to be able to help your friends and to

treat yourself more generously, you will find your way
from your dry crust to the savoury dishes.

'If Aristippus could dine contentedly on garden-
stuff he would not care to live with princes,' said one.
'If my critic knew how to live with princes ' was the
answer, 'he would have a soul above garden-stuff.'
Tell me whose words and life of those two you approve ;
or let me tell you, as you are the younger, why
Aristippus' view is the better.   For this is the way, as
the story goes, that he parried the thrust of the snappish
Cynic : 'I play the parasite for my own pleasure, you
for the people's.   My plan is the better and more
honourable by far.   I render my services that I may
ride on horseback and be fed by my patron.   What
you ask is paltry, but you have to humble yourself to
the giver, though you say that you want from none.'
Aristippus was at home in every phase of condition
and circumstance, venturing to aim at a rise, ready
to be content with his present level.   On the other
hand, I shall marvel if he who wears the doubled
sackcloth of endurance proves to feel at home if his
mode of life is changed.   The first will not wait for a
purple mantle ; he will put on what comes and walk
through the most crowded streets, and will play not
ungracefully the one part or the other.   The second
will shun a cloak from the looms of Miletus with
more horror than a dog or snake [1], and will die of
cold if you do not give him back his sackcloth.   Give

[1] A proverbial expression. They were of ill omen to meet ;
see Od. 3. 27, p. 107.

it him, and let him live out his silly life. To levy war and drag foemen in triumph before the eyes of your fellow citizens is a lot that touches the throne of Jove and essays the life of heaven. To have found favour with leaders of mankind is not the meanest of glories. It is not every one that can get to Corinth. Who feared to fall did not climb at all. Be it so—what of him who has climbed where he would? Has he done as a man ought? But in this, if in anything, lies what we are aiming at. One dreads the burden as too heavy for a small soul and a small body. Another lifts it on his shoulders and carries it home. If manhood is not a name and no more, it is one who tries like a man that is taking the right road to glory and reward.

Who in their lord's presence say nothing of their need will get more than one who asks. There is a difference between taking modestly and trying to snatch. But this [1] was the fountain-head of the business. 'My sister has no dower, my poor mother is a beggar, and my farm is neither saleable nor able to keep us.' Who speaks so, calls aloud 'give us food.' A second chimes in with 'for me too.' So the gift will be divided and a quarter broken off for him. But if the raven could eat in quiet he would have a better meal and much less wrangling and envy.

The man who, when taken as a travelling-companion to Brundisium or lovely Surrentum, grumbles that the road is rough or the cold and rain disagreeable, or that his box has been broken open and its contents plundered, recalls

[1] i. e. getting more.

the familiar tricks of a mistress who weeps now for a
pet dog, now for an anklet she has had stolen, so that
presently her real losses and sorrows are not believed.
The man who has once been fooled does not care to
lift up a beggar with a broken leg in the streets, though
he shed ever so many tears, and swear by holy Osiris,
or say ' Believe me, I am not cheating you—cruel men,
lift up the lame.' ' You must look for a stranger' the
neighbours shout back at him till they are hoarse.

XVIII   *Si bene te novi*
To Lollius.

*The general subject is the same as that of the last Epistle, but
the tone is different. The person addressed is a man of birth
and self-respect, and the position contemplated is not that
of a mere parasite or protégé, but of some one attached to
a man in a public sphere, and likely to be entrusted with
important secrets. It recalls such a post as that which was
offered to Horace himself and refused by him—that of
private secretary to the Emperor. Lollius (a young man of
birth and promise, to whom Epist. 1. 2 was addressed)
may be supposed to have been offered such a relation to
some one high in the political world. Horace, with a certain degree of playful exaggeration, sets out for him the
difficulties which it involves, with a conclusion which
means either 'decline it, as I did a similar offer,' or at
least ' escape from it as soon as you can into a more
dignified, free, and simple life.'*

IF I know you well, my Lollius, frankest of men [1],
you will shrink from wearing the guise of the

---

[1] Horace's fear for him is evidently not that he will be too
subservient, but too independent for a post which demands
considerable self-suppression.

parasite when you have professed the friend. As the matron will differ in look as well as character from the mistress, so the loyal friend will stand quite clear of the faithless parasite. There is a vice the opposite of this vice—it may be, a greater one—namely rudeness, which marks the clown, and is awkward and disagreeable, which commends itself by a skin like a stubble-field, and discoloured teeth, in the desire to pass for simple frankness and for Virtue's self. True Virtue is the mean between vices, as far from one extreme as from the other. The one man, grovelling in the excess of servility, a jester of the lowest couch [1], so shivers at the nod of the man of wealth, so echoes his utterances, and gathers up his words as they fall, that you would think a schoolboy was repeating his lessons to an ill-tempered master, or a mime actor playing a second part. The other man quarrels often about goatswool [2], dons his armour to fight about trifles—' to think indeed that I am not believed soonest, or that I must be muzzled from saying outright what I really feel! A second life were a poor compensation.' What think you is the question at issue ? Whether Castor or Dolichos has most science, or whether the road of Minucius or of Appius is the best way to Brundisium !

A follower stripped bare by the extravagance of women or the chances of the gaming table, one whom vainglory clothes and perfumes beyond his means, who

---

[1] i.e. a henchman of the host; such as Nomentanus and Porcius in Sat. 2. 8 (p. 257).

[2] A proverbial expression for a subject not worth argument.

is possessed by an insatiable hunger and thirst for
money, by a shamefaced dread of poverty, his wealthy
friend, though by ten vices the more accomplished,
hates and shudders at; or if he does not hate him,
schools, and like a fond mother would have him wiser
than himself and his better in virtue; and says to him
(what is about the truth) 'My wealth— do not try to
rival me—allows of folly: your means are paltry.
A close-fitting gown beseems a companion of sound
sense : cease to match yourself against me.' Eutrapelus,
when he wished to injure some one, made him a present
of some costly clothes : 'for (said he) the proud and
happy man will at once with his smart tunics take to
him new plans and hopes, will lie in bed till daylight,
will postpone honest business to a mistress's whims,
will make the fortune of money-lenders; to end the
story, will become a gladiator or the hired driver of a
market gardener's nag.'

As you will never pry into his secrets, so if he trusts
you with one, you will keep it, even if put to the question
by wine or anger. Again, as you will neither praise your
own pursuits nor find fault with those of every one else, so
you will not be composing verses when he is wishing to
go hunting. This is the way that a gulf opened in the
friendship of the twin brothers Amphion and Zethus, till
the lyre was hushed on which the sterner frowned.
Amphion, we are given to believe, yielded to the temper
of a brother. Do you yield to the commands, so gently
laid, of a powerful friend; and when he takes out into
the country his train of mules laden with the nets of

Aetolia, and his dogs, rise and cast aside the moroseness of the unsocial Muse, that you may share the toil which earns the relish even as you share the supper—'tis the wonted pursuit of Rome's heroes, good for name as well as for life and limb—the more since you are in sound health and can beat even the hound in swiftness and the boar in strength. Add that there is none who handles more gracefully manly weapons : you know amid what shouting of the ring you maintain the fights of the Campus. Lastly, you saw hard service in the Cantabrian campaigns under the captain who is even now taking down the standards from Parthian temples and, if aught is still wanting, is adjudging it to the arms of Italy.

Once more, that you may not hang back and absent yourself when you are not likely to be excused, remember that, with all your care to do nothing that is not strictly in time and tune, you sometimes play the trifler on your father's estate: the warriors divide the pleasure-boats; you captain one side, and the fight of Actium is represented by your slaves in true foemen's style ; your rival is your brother, your pond is the Adriatic; till victory crowns with bays the one or the other combatant. One who believes that you feel with his interests will further and back with both thumbs [1] your own sport.

To pursue my lecture, if lecturing to you is not impertinent—look many times what you say, and of whom, and to whom you say it. Fly from a questioner ; he is sure to be a babbler also. Open ears never keep faithfully the secrets whispered to them ; and mean-

---

[1] A phrase from the usage of spectators in the amphitheatre.

while a word once let out of the cage cannot be whistled back. Never set your heart on a slave within the marble threshold of friendship's temple; lest the master make you happy for ever with a valueless present or miserable by a churlish refusal.

What sort of man you commend to him, look to it again and again, lest presently another's misdoings strike a pang of shame into yourself. We make mistakes, and sometimes introduce one who does not deserve it. If then you have been taken in, give up defending one who must bear the burden of faults that belong to him, in order that if charges assail one whom you know thoroughly, you may stand by him and protect him when he trusts your championship. For when Theon's tooth [1] is nibbling round him, you surely feel that the danger will come a little later to yourself. It is your own interest that is at stake when your next neighbour's wall is ablaze. Neglect a fire and it gathers strength.

Making up to a powerful friend seems a pleasant thing to those who have not tried : who has tried will dread it. For yourself, my friend, while your bark is on the sea, give all heed lest the breeze shift and turn your course back again. The gloomy hate the cheerful, the mirthful the gloomy, the hasty the man of calm, the indolent the man of action : drinkers, [who swill Falernian past midnight, hate] [2] the man who refuses the proffered winecup, however much you swear that it

---

[1] A proverbial expression, the sense of which is evident, but the origin unknown.

[2] A line of doubtful reading.

makes you feverish o' nights. Take the cloud from your brow: the rule of the world is that the shy is taken for deep, the silent for sour.

Through all this you will read the books, and cross-question the persons, that can tell you what is the way to pass through life smoothly—whether Desire, a beggar always, is to drive and harass you; whether the fear and hope of things useful only in the second degree; whether virtue is the prize of learning or the gift of nature; what lessens care, what makes you a friend to yourself, what gives unbroken calm—office, or the charms of gain, or a quiet journey in the untrodden paths of life. For me, as often as Digentia gives me new life, the icy stream of which Mandela drinks, that village all wrinkles from the cold—what do you suppose I feel? what think you, my friend, I pray for? Give me what I have, or even less; and therewith let me live to myself for what remains of life, if the gods will that anything remain. Let me have a generous supply of books and of food stored a year ahead; nor let me hang and tremble on the hope of the uncertain hour. Nay, it is enough to ask Jove, who gives them and takes them away, that he grant life and subsistence; a balanced mind I will find for myself.

XIX   *Prisco si credis*

To Maecenas.

Imitation, false and true.

Horace has been criticized as an imitator. His answer is to contrast slavish, inartistic, second-hand imitation, of which he has himself been the object, imitation of manners, garb, peculiarities, faults, with the free imitation of great models, which the greatest Greeks had themselves practised.

In the later part of the Epistle he defends himself more generally against detraction, tracing it to his unwillingness to adopt vulgar arts of self-advertisement.

YOU know, Maecenas, as well as I, that, if you trust old Cratinus, no poems can please long, nor live, which are written by water-drinkers. Ever since Liber enlisted poets, as half crazed, among his Satyrs and Fauns, the sweet Muses have usually had a scent of wine about them in the forenoon. Homer by his praises of wine is convicted as a wine-bibber. Even father Ennius never sprang forth to tell of arms but when he had well drunk. The Forum and the well-cover of Libo [1] I shall award to the sober, song I shall deny to the staid. From the moment that I issued this judgement, poets have never ceased to drink against one another by night and to reek of wine by day. What, if a man tried to imitate Cato by the fierceness of a grim look, by bare feet and the cut of a narrow gown, would he in this way restore to our eyes Cato's virtuous life? The countryman of Iarbas burst himself through emulating the tongue of Timagenes [2], in his

[1] It is doubtful whether this is named as near the law-courts or the place of business.

[2] Timagenes was a witty rhetorician of the day. 'The countryman of Iarbas' (lit. 'son of Iarbas') should mean 'Numidian' (Iarbas is the name of a Numidian king mentioned by Livy, and Virgil took the name for Dido's Numidian suitor); but the story here referred to is unknown.

zealous efforts to be held a wit and a man of eloquence.
Models lead us astray of which the faults are the things
easy to imitate. If it so chanced that I had a pale
skin, they would drink the bloodless cummin. O
imitators, you slavish herd! How often have your
false alarms stirred my wrath, how often my mirth!
I have planted free steps on unoccupied ground where
none was before me, not trodden in the footsteps of
other men. Who trusts himself will be king and
leader of the swarm. I was the first to hold up to
Latin eyes iambics of Paros[1], following the rhythms
and the spirit of Archilochus, not the matter, or the
language with which he hunted down Lycambes.

And lest you should be disposed to decorate me
with a humbler garland for fearing to change the measure
and poetic form, bethink you that Sappho, no weak
woman, tempers her Muse with the rhythm of Archilochus; Alcaeus tempers his; though he differs much
in matter and arrangement, nor chooses a father-in-law
to befoul with venomous verse, nor twists a halter for his
betrothed by libellous song. He is the model, not so
much as named by other tongue, whom I, the lyrist of
Latium, have made known abroad: my pride is in
bringing things untold before to be read by gentle eyes
and held in gentle hands.

Would you know why ungrateful readers praise and
love me at home, disparage me unkindly abroad! I am
not the man to hunt the suffrages of the windy crowd
at the cost of suppers and by the gift of worn raiment.

[1] The island from which Archilochus came.

I am not the man, after listening to writers of name
and giving them as good again, to stoop to canvass the
lecture-desks of schoolmasters[1]. 'Thence the tears,
you see[2].' If I have said 'I am ashamed to read
aloud writings unworthy of crowded theatres and to add
weight to trifles,' 'You are laughing at us' one answers,
'and keeping them for Jove's ears. Beautiful in your
own eyes, you believe that you, and you only, drop the
true honey of poetry.' Meet this with open sneer I
dare not; and lest I smart under his sharpened nail if
I close with him, 'The place you offer mislikes me' I
cry, and claim an adjournment of the sports: for sport
sometimes breeds eager and angry rivalry, anger fierce
enmities and war with its horrors.

XX   *Vertumnum Ianumque*

To his own book.

*An epilogue. Under the form of a playful deprecation of
publicity he anticipates the fame which his book is to
attain and the interest which the world will take in all
that relates to its author. To appreciate the real meaning the Epistle should be compared with the Odes which
have a similar purpose, 2. 20 and 3. 30.*

*The book is addressed as if it were a spoilt home-born
slave who is desiring to escape from his master's house
into the great world.*

YOU are looking wistfully, it seems, my book, at
Vertumnus and Janus[3], bent (save the mark !)

[1] The schoolmasters (*grammatici*) taught and criticized poetry,
and so could make or mar the fortune of a young poet.

[2] A quotation from Terence which had passed into a proverb.

[3] These stand for the booksellers' quarters in Rome.

on being set for sale, neatly smoothed with the pumice
of the brothers Sosii [1].   You hate the keys and seals
which the modest are so fond of; you grumble at being
shown to few, and praise publicity, though I did not
breed you thus.   Well—off to the town, whither you
are so anxious to go.   When you are once out of the
cage there will be no returning.   'Woe is me!   What
have I done?   What was it I wished?' you will say
when something has hurt you, and you are conscious
that you are being rolled up small, when he who has
fancied you has had enough and is tired.   But if he
who is forecasting your future has not lost his craft in
vexation at your folly, you will be well loved at Rome
till your prime is past : when you have begun to show the
thumb-marks of the vulgar, you will either be left in
silence to be the food of bookworms, or will run away
to Utica, or be sent in bonds to Ilerda [2].   Then the
monitor to whom you would not listen will only laugh
at you, like the man who in anger thrust his obstinate ass
against the rocks [3].   Who would take trouble to save one
who will not be saved ?   This also is in the future: second
childhood shall overtake you when you are set to give
reading lessons to schoolboys in the outskirts of the town.

When the cooler sun brings you a larger audience
you shall tell them of me ; how born of a freedman

[1] Booksellers of the time.   The pumice was used to smooth
the edges of the papyrus when rolled up tightly.

[2] Utica in Africa, Ilerda in Spain.   'You will be exported
for the provincial book-markets.'   But the figures, 'run away'
&c., are of a slave.

[3] One of many fables only known from an allusion in Horace.

sire and in a modest home I spread wings too wide
for my nest (so all that you take from my birth
you will add to my merit); how I found favour, both
in the field and at home, in the eyes of the first man of
Rome; of small stature, early grey, made by nature for
the sunshine, quick to be angry, but as quick to be
appeased. If by chance any one asks you of my age,
let him know that I completed my forty-fourth December
in the year when Lollius received Lepidus as a
colleague [1].

[1] i. e. in B.C. 21. 'December,' because Horace's birthday was
on Dec. 8.

BOOK II

I *Cum tot sustineas*

To Augustus.

Augustus had expressed a strong desire that Horace should address an Epistle to him, and with tact and judgement Horace selects as its subject a defence of the poetry of the Augustan age as against the school of critics who decried it in comparison with the poetry of the Republic, for which they professed an indiscriminate admiration. The main points of the Epistle are :

1. *That it is absurd to judge poetry by its age, not by its intrinsic merits. The arguments put into the opponent's mouth are intended to make his case ridiculous.*

2. *That the conditions under which Roman poetry had been developed, its rustic origin, the lack of generally diffused taste, and of the artistic temperament of which Greece gave such an example, had made it certain that perfection could only come late.*

3. *That Augustus' literary judgement was a true one—that in Virgil and Varius and (it is hinted, not said) in Horace he has patronized poets who have the true stamp of Classics and whose works will live, in a sense in which those of the earlier poets will not.*

WHILE you have on your shoulders alone the burden of so many and such weighty charges, guarding the Roman world in arms, furnishing it with fair manners and faultless laws, it would be a sin against the public weal if I were to waste your precious time, Caesar, with long talk. Romulus and father Liber, and Pollux with his twin Castor, who when their mighty tasks were done found place among the temples of Gods, so long as they were making fruitful the earth and civilizing

mankind, laying to rest fierce wars, assigning lands,
founding cities, made grievous complaint that the public
favour they had looked for did not answer to their
deserts.   He who crushed the dire Hydra and with
predestined toil subdued the monsters which story tells
of, found that Envy is a monster to be tamed by the
end and by nothing before it.   One who is a dead
weight on excellence below his own scorches by his
very brilliance, yet, when his light is quenched, he too
will be loved.   In your case, while you are still among
us we shower honours upon you betimes, and set up
altars to swear by in your name, and confess that
nought like you will arise hereafter or has arisen at any
time before.

But yet this same people of yours, wise and just as it is in
setting you, you only, before our own captains and those
of Greece, weighs other things on a wholly different
principle and method ; and has distaste and hatred for
all but what it sees to have vanished from earth and to
have had its day.   Such a partisan is it of antiquity that
the Tables which the Ten enacted to forbid wrongdoing,
treaties of right made by the kings with Gabii or the
stern old Sabines, the volumes of the Pontiffs, ancient
scrolls of poet-seers, it loves to speak of as though
they had come from the lips of the Muses on the Alban
hill.

If you argue that, because among Greek writings the
oldest are actually the best, Roman writers must be
weighed in the same balance, the conclusion needs no
words.   On that principle the olive has nothing hard

inside, or the nut has nothing hard outside [1]. We have come to fortune's zenith—we paint and play the cithern, and wrestle with more skill than the Greeks in their palaestra.

If you say that poetry is like wine which improves by keeping, then I must ask you to tell me what the year is that gives writings their claim to a higher price. A writer who died a hundred years ago, should he be reckoned among the perfect and ancient, or among the worthless and new? Name a limit, to bar future quarrels. 'He is old' you say, 'and excellent, who completes a hundred years.' What then of one who has been dead less than that by a single month or year— amongst which is he to be reckoned, the ancient poets, or those whom the present and all succeeding ages must hold in contempt? 'He certainly shall find place of honour among the ancients whose age is less by such a short space as a month or even a whole year.' I make the most of what you grant me; and like single hairs of the horse's tail, little by little I pull away one and then another, till, by the trick of the heap that slips from under him [2], I have landed on the ground my friend who goes back to dates, and measures merit by years, and admires nothing but what the Funeral Goddess has consecrated.

Ennius the 'wise,' the 'gallant,' the 'second Homer' (so these judges of literature name him), heeds little, I take

---

[1] i. e. you are forgetting that as all fruits are not made on one model, so national gifts are not all of one type.

[2] The reference is to the famous logical puzzle—'how many grains are necessary to make a heap? A thousand? nine hundred and ninety nine?' and so on till the heap is gone.

it, what has become of his big talk and dreams after
Pythagoras [1]. Is not even Naevius in all hands and
remembered as though he wrote yesterday? So sacred a
thing is any ancient poem. When the question is debated
which has the advantage of the other, Pacuvius is
awarded the fame of the 'learned,' Accius of the
'lofty' poet of the old school. The 'gown' of
Afranius, such is the cant phrase, 'was of the very cut
of Menander.' The 'quickness' of Plautus was 'after
the pattern of Epicharmus of Sicily': Caecilius takes
the prize for 'dignity,' Terence for 'art.' These are
they whom this mighty Rome of ours learns by heart,
these she crowds the packed theatres to gaze at, these
she holds as the full list of poets from the days of
Livius the writer to our own.

At times the world sees straight: there are occasions when it goes wrong. If it admires the ancient
poets and praises them in such a sense as to put nothing
before them, nothing on a level, it is in error. If it
holds that some of their utterances are out of date,
a large number harsh, if it confesses that many are
careless, it has some taste and takes my side and Jove
smiles on its judgement. I certainly make no assault
upon the poems of Livius, nor desire that what I

---

[1] Ennius is said to have dreamed that by a transmigration of
souls such as Pythagoras taught, the soul of Homer had become
again incarnate in him. Horace says he may let the dream go—
these good critics vouch for it that he *is* a second Homer. All
through the passage Horace is laughing at the cant phrases of
the critics of the day who cried up the ancients in order to lower
the more modern writers.

remember learning as a child under the rod of Orbilius
should be blotted out of existence : but that they should
be held faultless, models of beauty, and next door to
perfection, I marvel. The truth is that if in them a
chance phrase of grace lightens the darkness, if one verse
and another are a little more neatly turned than the rest,
they are unfairly made a specimen and set the value of
the poem.

I feel how unjust it is that anything should be
criticized not because its composition is thought coarse
or out of taste but because it is modern, and that men
should claim for ancient writings not indulgence but
honour and all the prizes. If I were to express
a doubt whether or not a play of Atta keeps its footing
over the saffron-essence and flowers[1], nearly every
father of a family would cry out that I must have lost
all shame if I ventured to criticize what ' grave ' Aesopus
and ' learned ' Roscius used to act. Either they think
nothing can be right but what has pleased themselves,
or else they think it shame to be led by their youngers,
and to confess in their old age that what they learned
before their beard grew is poor stuff.

The truth is, the man who praises Numa's Salian
hymn and professes to understand as no one else does
what he is just as much in the dark about as I am is
not backing and applauding the genius of men who are
dead and gone : he is really making war on our own
age : it is jealousy and hatred of ourselves and all that
belongs to us.

[1] i. e. the stage, which was sprinkled with these.

Now if novelty had been viewed as grudgingly by the
Greeks as it is by us, what in these times would be
ancient ? Where would be that variety which the world
now has to read and thumb each according to his taste ?
As soon as her wars were over Greece began to find
time for trifling [1], and, while fortune smiled, to slide down
the slope towards folly : she was all fire now for athletes
and their pursuits, now for horse-racing : she was in love
with workers either in marble or ivory or bronze : she
let her eyes and soul hang intent on the painter's panel :
she delighted now in flute-players, now in actors of
tragedy. Like a little girl at play in the nursery, what
she sought eagerly she soon tired of and let be. What
likes and dislikes are there that you cannot believe to
be easily changed ? This was what her happy times of
peace and prosperity brought.

At Rome for many generations it was men's pleasure,
as it was their unbroken habit, to be up betimes with
houses open, to deal law to clients, to open the cash-box
when suitable names were the security, to learn from
elders and teach youngers by what courses an estate
might be increased, light desires—so ruinous to the
pocket [2]—diminished. The fickle populace has changed
its taste, and nowadays is fevered with a universal
passion for writing. Boys and grave fathers alike sit

[1] Horace does not really think art and literature ' trifling ' or
' folly.' He is speaking as a Roman might, who undervalued
the Greek artistic temperament in comparison with the practical
and imperial gifts of Rome.

[2] Notice the ironical suggestion of the connexion in Roman
minds between morality and thrift.

at supper with their brows crowned with leaves and have an amanuensis to take down their poetry. Even I myself, who declare that I write no verses, turn out a greater liar than the Parthians, and am awake before sunrise, calling for pen and paper and portfolio. A man who knows nothing of a ship does not dare to handle one. No one ventures to prescribe southernwood for the sick unless he has learnt the use of drugs. Doctors undertake what belongs to doctors: carpenters handle carpenters' tools. Poetry we all write, those who have learnt and those who have not, without distinction.

It is a mistake, and even a mild form of madness: yet it has its virtues—how great they are, let us reckon. A poet's heart is not easily given to avarice. He loves verses; they are his one interest. Money losses, runaway slaves, fires—he laughs at them all. He does not lay plans to cheat his partner or the boy who is his ward. His fare is pulse and coarse bread. Though he be no hero in the field, he is of use to the commonwealth, if you grant this, that even small things help great ends. It is the poet that gives form to the child's utterance while it is still tender and lisping. He gives the ear a bias from the first against coarse ways of speaking. Presently he moulds the heart also with kindly teaching, correcting roughness and envy and anger. He tells the story of right deeds, with famous examples equips the dawning age, and gives solace to the helpless and sore of heart. Whence should the virgin band of girls and boys learn their prayers, if the Muse had not found them the poet? Their chorus asks for aid of deities and feels their presence, cries for water from heaven, and wins its wish by the prayer which the poet has taught, averts pestilence, drives far the perils that are to be feared, gains both peace and a year rich in fruits. It is song that makes favour both with the gods above and the good powers below.

The farmers of old days, with their stout hearts and simple wealth, when after harvesting their corn they were giving a holiday to body and to spirit too, which had endured hardness for the hope of the end, together with the partners of their toil, their lads and faithful wife, would worship Earth with a porker, Silvanus with milk, with flowers and wine the Genius who forgets not the shortness of life. The Fescennine licence, which owed its origin to this custom, flung to and fro rustic ribaldry in metrical dialogue; and the freedom, welcomed for old usage once in the year, was amiable in its play, till jest, turned earnest, became a vent for angry feelings, and began unrestrainedly to threaten one honest house after another. Men assailed with a tooth that drew blood felt the sting. Even those who were unhurt were concerned for a risk which touched all. It went so far that a law was enacted with a penalty to forbid libellous verses. So they changed their strain, brought back by fear of the cudgel to a civil tongue and to the aim of pleasing.

When Greece had been enslaved she made a slave of her rough conqueror, and introduced the arts into Latium, still rude. This was how that uncouth Saturnian measure ran its stream dry, and refinement drove out the offensive rankness. Yet for long ages there remained, and there still remain, traces of the farmyard. For time had run on ere the Roman brought his wit to bear on Greek writings; and, in the quiet that followed the Punic wars, began to ask whether Sophocles and Thespis and Aeschylus had anything to offer that was of use. Presently he made the essay whether he could worthily translate them, and satisfied himself, headstrong and eager as nature had made him; for he has something of the breath of tragedy and makes happy hits, but is foolishly ashamed and afraid of blotting out what he writes.

It is commonly thought that, because Comedy finds its subjects in common life, it involves less labour, but really the burden is greater as the allowance to be given is less. See how Plautus fills the part of thè young lover, of the strict father, of the plotting pander; how well in his parasites he reproduces the stage glutton of farce, with what a slipshod sock [1] he runs across the stage. He is always in a hurry to pocket the money: when that is done, he recks little whether his play fall or stand firm on its legs.

The writer who is brought to the stage by Glory in her windy car [2] is put out of heart by a dull spectator, filled with pride by an attentive one: so light, so small is what breaks down or builds again the soul which is greedy of praise. Farewell for me to the stage and

---

[1] The special shoe worn in comedy.

'If Jonson's learned sock be on.'—Milton.

[2] The comic poet who takes to the drama from desire for fame, and therefore thinks too much of the audience, as the other thought too little of it.

its concerns if the refusal of a palm-branch is to send me home pining, the granting of it in good flesh.

Another thing that often routs and terrifies even the venturesome poet, is that part of the audience, the stronger in numbers, though the weaker in merit and in rank, unlearned and stupid and ready to fight it out if the knights differ from them, in the middle of a play calls for either a bear or a boxing match. These are the things in which the rabble delights. But even with the knights all pleasure now has migrated from the ear to the empty delight of the restless eye. For four hours or more the curtain is kept down [1] whilst squadrons of horse and bodies of foot are seen flying: presently there passes the spectacle of unfortunate kings dragged with hands behind their backs: chariots of every shape and kind hurry along and ships; spoil of ivory is borne by, spoil of Corinthian brass. If he were on earth, Democritus would laugh at the sight, whether it were a half-panther-half-camel, or a white elephant, that made all faces turn one way. He would think the people a show to be studied more carefully even than the games, as giving him very much the more to look at. But for the poets—he would think them to be telling their tales to a deaf ass [2]. For what voices have been of force enough to overcome the din with which our theatres ring? You would suppose it was the Garganian forest roaring or the Tuscan sea: such the shouts with which the games

---

[1] The curtain was drawn up at the end of the performance, not let down as with us.

[2] A proverb for wasted labour.

are viewed, and the works of art and knick-knacks of foreign wealth with which the actor bedizens himself. As soon as he steps on the stage right hands clash with left. 'Has he said anything?' Not one word. 'What then pleases them so?' That woollen stuff whose Tarentine dye is such a good imitation of the violet.

And now that you may not by chance suppose that I am stinting praise when others handle well tasks which I refuse to attempt myself, let me say at once that it seems to me a feat like that of one who walks a tight rope, when the poet gives my heart anguish about nothing[1], awakes its passions, soothes it again, when like a magician he fills me with imagined terrors, and places me one moment at Thebes, another at Athens.

But come, you must include in your care those of us[2] who prefer to appeal to a reader rather than face the caprices of an unfeeling audience, if you mean to fill with volumes that gift[3], so worthy of him, which you dedicated to Apollo, and to spur poets to make with greater zeal for green Helicon.

We poets, it is true, (that I may apply the pruning-hook to my own vineyard) often do harm to our own cause—when we offer a book to you when you are anxious or tired; when we are injured if a friend has ventured to criticize a single verse; when uninvited we

---

[1] 'What's Hecuba to him or he to Hecuba?'

[2] i.e. other poets besides those of drama.

[3] The Palatine Library founded by Augustus in the temple of Apollo on the Palatine hill.

turn again to passages which we have already read;
when we lament that there is nothing to show for our
toil and for the poems spun of such delicate thread;
when we hope that the result will be that, so soon as
you have learnt that we compose verses, you will at
once send for us just as we wish, and bid us never
want, and press us to go on writing.

Yet it is worth while at some trouble to see what
keepers of the shrine are found for valour proved in the
field and at home; for it may not be entrusted to an
unworthy poet. The great king Alexander made a
favourite of the miserable Choerilus, who as the reward
of uncouth and ill-bred verses received philips [1] from
the king's own mint. But just as if you handle black
dyes they leave mark and stain, so writers too often
daub over bright deeds with ugly verses. That same
famous king who in his lavishness paid such a high
price for such ridiculous poems, issued an ordinance
that no one but Lysippus should mould the bronze to
copy the features of the brave Alexander. Yet if you
called that judgement, so fine in view of works of art,
to books and what the Muses have to give, you would
swear that he was born in the heavy air of Boeotia.

But Virgil and Varius, those true poets of your
choice, discredit neither your judgement of them nor the
many gifts which, to the great glory of the giver, they
have received from you. And features copied in bronze
do not show more clearly than the manners and souls
of heroes of renown in the poet's work.

[1] The name of a coin; as a 'louis' or 'napoleon.'

In my case too, I should not prefer my 'talks' that crawl along the ground to making great exploits my theme, and telling how lands lie, and streams, and forts on mountain ledges, and barbaric realms, and wars ended under thy auspices throughout the world, and doors shut on Janus, the guardian of peace, and Rome a terror to the Parthians while thou art prince—if only my power were as my desire.   But as thy greatness admits of no mean song, so my modesty dares not attempt a task which my strength refuses to bear.   But the folly of officious affection never shows itself more clearly than when the art with which it would win favour is that of verse. For men learn more quickly and remember more readily what they laugh at than what they approve and look up to.   I do not care for an attention which annoys me, and as I do not wish to have a waxen mask hung up for view anywhere which makes me uglier than I am, so I do not wish to be complimented in badly written verses, lest I be made to blush by the clumsy gift and find myself stretched out at length with my poet in a closed chest and carried off to the street where frankincense and perfumes are sold, and pepper and everything else that is wrapped in scribblers' sheets.

II   *Flore, bono claroque*

To Florus.

Horace's reasons for refusing to write more lyrics.

The theme is the same as that of Epist. I. I, *but it is handled more fully.   This means, no doubt, that there is a more serious purpose in view.*

Florus (see Epist. I. 3) *was one of the literary men of*
the new generation in the intimacy of the future Emperor
Tiberius (the 'Claudius' of that Epistle and 'Nero' of
this one).   Either as the mouthpiece of his own circle,
or more probably in the interests of the young prince,
he has been putting pressure on the poet to do what
a few years later, and with a similar purpose, he
actually did—to resume his lyric writing.   The reasons
given for his refusal are playful and ironical, and come
to little more than 'I am not in the mood,' but they
give opportunity for at least two interesting passages,
the satirical picture of 'mutual admiration' cliques in
Roman literary society, and the glowing description (in
which he seems to be pourtraying his friend, whether
recently dead or still alive, the poet Virgil) of the poet
who takes his art seriously.
The later part of the Epistle has also its personal purpose.
When it is read with the earlier Epistle to Florus, it
seems clear that Horace is pressing on his young friend
the prescriptions in which he has himself found health
of mind.

FAITHFUL friend to Nero good and great, my
Florus, suppose some one should be wishing to
sell you a slave bred on an estate at Tibur or Gabii,
and should deal thus with you: 'This lad is clear-
skinned and well-formed from head to foot; he shall
be yours to have and to hold for eight thousand
sesterces, money down, a home-bred slave, apt for
service at his master's beck, with a smattering of
Greek learning, fit for any employment—the clay is
still moist; you may mould it to any shape.   More-
over he will sing, not indeed as an artist, but so as
to give pleasure over your wine.   Many promises lessen

credit, when one who wishes to thrust off his wares praises them beyond truth. I am under no pressure; of modest means, but what I have is my own. None of the slave-dealers would make you such an offer. It is not every one who would easily get such an offer from me. He had a lazy fit once, and hid himself, as boys will, in fear no doubt of the lash that hangs on the staircase. Pay your money, unless you find a diffi-culty in the escapade of which I have duly warned you' : he would be on the right side of the law, I trow, in taking his price. The goods are damaged, but you bought them with your eyes open : the con-ditions of sale were told you. Do you yet pursue him with a frivolous and vexatious suit ?

I told you when you started that I was lazy — for such attentions, as a man without a hand — lest you should presently be angry and scold that your letters received no answer from me. What good did I do, if you yet assail me when the law is on my side ?

You complain of this besides, that I have broken my promise and send you none of the lyrics that you look for.

A soldier of Lucullus one night, when he was tired out and fast asleep, was robbed of all his hard-won earnings to the last *as*. It was after this that, while he was a very wolf in his fury, angry no less with himself than with the foe, his teeth keen set with hunger, he dislodged one of the king's [1] garrisons (so the story goes) from a position strongly fortified and rich in treasure. He gained glory by this exploit, and was decorated

---

[1] i. e. Mithridates.

with gifts of honour, and received besides ten thousand
sesterces in hard money.   It so chanced that a little
later the commander, when he was wishing to take some
fort, tried to urge our friend with words which could
have given inclination even to a coward: 'Go, my
good man, whither valour calls you.   Go—and fortune
go with you—to receive the rich reward of your deserts.
Why do you stand still?'   At this the man, who was
a shrewd fellow for all that he was a countryman, made
answer: 'Go—say you?   Aye, he will go, go whithersoever you wish, who has lost his purse.'

At Rome 'twas my good fortune to be bred, and
taught how much Achilles' wrath harmed the Greeks.
Kindly Athens added a little further accomplishment,
namely to give me the desire to learn the difference
between the straight and the crooked, and seek for
truth in the garden of Academus[1].   But the stress
of the time drove me from my pleasant place; and the
tide of politics bore me, a tyro in war, into arms that
were to be no match for the thews of Caesar Augustus.
From thence as soon as Philippi gave me my discharge,
humbled, with my wings clipped, and robbed of the
home and estate which I had inherited, poverty found
me courage and drove me to compose verses.   But now
that I have what forbids want, what dose of hemlock
will be sufficient to clear my brain, if I do not think it
better to sleep o' nights than to write verses?

[1] The point is that philosophy was his first love, poetry only
an episode in his life, and due to his want of money.   We are
not to take him too seriously.

Years as they pass plunder us of one thing after another. They have snatched from me mirth, love, banquets, play. They are on the way to wrench poetry from my grasp. What would you have me do?

Once more, people do not all admire and like the same things. Your pleasure is lyric poetry. My friend yonder delights in iambics[1], another in 'talks[2]' in Bion's satiric vein and with a spice of malignity. It seems to me like three guests at a banquet all at odds, asking, from their various taste, each for a different dish. What am I to give? What not? You refuse what the next desires. What you ask for, that, you see, is sour and distasteful to the two others.

Beyond all other reasons, do you think I can possibly write poetry at Rome amid all my cares and toils? One summons me to give security for him; another to leave all my duties and listen to his writings. One is ill in bed on Quirinus' Hill, another on the further side of the Aventine. Both must be visited. The distances, as you see, are nicely convenient. Perhaps you think the streets are clear and there is no difficulty in composing as I go. You meet a contractor hurrying in hot haste with his mules and porters: a huge machine is hoisting now a block of stone, now a beam. Funerals with their mourners are encountering wagons of solid timber. This way flies a mad dog: that way rushes

[1] Horace's name for his Epodes: see Epod. 14.

[2] i. e. the Satires. Bion is the philosopher and wit at Athens in the third cent. B.C., the traditional author of many pungent sayings.

a sow from the mire. In such circumstances try
whether you can quietly compose verses with music
in them. The whole choir of poets loves the woodland
and flies the town, in due imitation of their patron
Bacchus, whose joy is in sleep and the shade. Do
you wish me, amid this riot night and day, to sing
and tread the poet's narrow pathway? The gifted
soul who has chosen as his home the empty streets
of Athens, and given seven years to his studies, and
aged before his time over books and their cares, when
he issues to the world is usually more dumb than a
statue, and makes the town shake with laughter. Can
I possibly, with self-respect, here amid the surging sea
of life and tempests of the town, try to weave together
words which shall stir the music of the lyre?

A lawyer at Rome had in an orator such a good
brother that one heard from the lips of the other
nothing but compliments. The orator was to the other
a Gracchus—the lawyer to him a Mucius. Are we poet-
songsters at all less subject to that form of madness?
I write lyric poems, my friend elegiacs: 'a marvellous
work of art, from the graving tool of the nine Muses!'
See first with what pride, what importance, we look
round the temple [1] with its spaces ready for the poets
of Rome. Presently too, if you have leisure, follow
and listen at a little distance, and hear what each of
the two promises, and on what grounds he twines
for himself a garland. We submit to blows and be-
labour the foe, thwack for thwack, in the long-drawn

[1] i. e. the Palatine Library.

duel [1], like very Samnites, till evening's lights. Before we part, I have been dubbed by his vote an Alcaeus. What is he by mine? What, but a Callimachus! If he seems to claim more, then a Mimnermus he becomes, and grows to the height of the name he desires.

So long as I am writing and wooing on my knees the people's suffrages, I have to submit to much in order to pacify the sensitive race of poets. Now that my literary work is over and my sense recovered, let me close my open ears and allow them to read without fear of reply.

Those who write bad verses get laughed at; but yet they enjoy writing them and pay reverence to themselves, and if you should hold your tongue, take the lead in praising their own composition, be it what it may — happy people! But the man who shall desire to leave behind him a poem true to the laws of art, when he takes his tablets to write will take also the spirit of an honest censor [2]. Any words that he shall find lacking

[1] He describes the dishonest criticism which only ends in mutual compliments between two poets who read their compositions to one another. There seems to be a special reference to Propertius, who had called himself 'the Roman Callimachus,' and whom Horace accuses of belonging to such a mutual admiration clique: 'Perhaps he will call me an Alcaeus. If he does, I will fall in with his own style and call him a Callimachus, even a Mimnermus if he wishes it.'

[2] The function of the Censor which gives its imagery to this passage is that of revising the lists of the Senate and the Knights with the view of striking off unworthy members. These lines, by a happy transference of their application from the poet to the lexicographer, were taken by Dr. Johnson as the motto on the title-page of his Dictionary.

in dignity, or without proper weight, or that are held
unworthy of the rank, he will have heart of courage
to degrade from their position, however unwilling they
may be to retire, and bent still on haunting Vesta's
precincts.   Phrases of beauty that have been lost to
popular view he will kindly disinter and bring into the
light, phrases which, though they were on the lips of
a Cato and a Cethegus of old time, now lie uncouth
because out of fashion and disused because old.   He
will admit to the franchise new phrases which use has
fathered and given to the world.   In strength and
clearness, like a crystal stream, he will pour his wealth
along, and bless Latium with a richer tongue.   What
is too luxuriant he will prune: what is too rough he
will smooth with sober refinement: what wholly lacks
force he will away with.   He will look to you as
though at play, much though it will cost him[1], like the
dancer who can represent now a Satyr, now the
clownish Cyclops.

   I should prefer, no doubt, to be thought by others
a silly and dull writer, if only my faults might delight
myself, or at least be hidden from me, rather than to
have a philosopher's knowledge and his cynical smile.
There was once a man in high place at Argos who
used to fancy that he was listening to a wonderful
company of actors while he sat happily and clapped his
hands in an empty theatre — a man who would fulfil every

---

[1] Well paraphrased by Pope:
   'But ease of writing flows from art, not chance:
   As those move easiest who have learned to dance.'

other function of life without offence, a good neighbour,
you may be sure, an amiable host, kind to his wife, one
that could excuse his slaves and not fly into a frenzy
if the seal of a flask were broken, one that could avoid
a precipice or an open well in his pathway.   This man,
when by the resources and trouble of his friends he had
recovered, having expelled by doses of neat hellebore the
madness and the bile that caused it, and come again to
himself, cried 'By Pollux, my friends, you have killed me,
not saved me alive, in that you have torn a pleasure from
my grasp, and by force robbed me of a delightful illusion.'

The truth is, it is profitable indeed to turn philosopher,
if it means to lay aside trifling and give up play to
lads whom it beseems, no longer to hunt for words
that will go to the music of a Latin lyre, but to get
by heart the rhythms and melodies of a rightly ordered
life.   Wherefore I talk to myself in this way and, for
no one to hear, recall old sayings thus :—

If no quantity of water could quench your thirst, you
would tell the doctor.   Have you not the courage to
confess to any one that the more you get the more you
want ?   If a wound were not alleviated by some root
or herb that had been prescribed, you would desist from
treating yourself with the root or herb which did you
no good.   You had been told that if the gods gave
a man wealth, folly and its perversities left him : yet
seeing that you have grown no wiser since your purse
has been fuller, will you still listen to the same adviser ?
No doubt if wealth could really make you wise, if it
could make you less apt to desire or to fear, your blushes

should be if there lived on earth one more greedy of it than you.

If that is a man's own which he buys with balance and coin [1], there are cases also (so the lawyers tell us) where occupation gives ownership. The land from which your food comes is yours. The bailiff of Orbius, when he harrows the corn-land which is presently to supply you with grain, feels you to be his master. You give coin; you receive a bunch of grapes, chickens, eggs, a jar of wine: in that way, you see, you buy by instalments the land, even though perhaps, to buy it at once, it cost three hundred thousand sesterces or more. What matters it whether the money which finds your food was paid down just now or years ago? Again, the man who once purchased a farm at Aricia or Veii purchased the vegetables he sups on, though he thinks otherwise, purchased the logs with which he boils his kettle on a cold evening. Yet he calls it all his own to the spot where the line of poplars is set to prevent neighbours from quarrelling: as though anything were a man's own, which in a moment of flying time, now by request, now by purchase, now by force, now, if not before, by death, changes owners and becomes the property of another. Inasmuch then as to no one is given perpetual occupation—heir follows heir as wave follows wave—what is the profit of estates or storehouses, what of forests in Lucania added to forests in Calabria,

[1] In a formal act of sale a witness held a balance and the purchaser touched it with a brass coin, which he then handed to the vendor.

if death mows down great and small, and no gold will buy him off? Gems, marble, ivory, Tuscan seals, pictures, silver plate, raiment dipped in Gaetulian purple, there are those who have not these—one I know who cares not to have them.

Why of two brothers one cares to idle and play and use unguents more than to own the rich palm-groves of Herod; the other, wealthy and insatiable of wealth, from daybreak to the shadows of evening is busy taming with fire and steel his woodland estate, is known to the Genius[1], the companion who tempers the birth-star, the god of human nature, that is to die with each life, that changes in face with it, is black or white.

I shall use and take from my modest heap as much as need requires, nor shall I fear what an heir may think of me because he does not find more than I leave him. And yet, at the same time, I shall wish to remember how far the frank and gay differs from the spendthrift, how great the variance between the thrifty and the miserly. For difference there is whether you scatter your substance lavishly; or, while neither grudging any expense nor anxious to add to your store, are ready, like the schoolboy when the holidays come, to take and enjoy the short and pleasant moment. Far from me be the poverty that makes a squalid home! But if the ship carries me, it will carry me, and I shall be myself still,

---

[1] The 'Genius' is the idea of the man projected outside of himself. To say therefore that the Genius knows why he differs from another man is only to say that such differences are ultimate facts. Each man is what he is.

whether it be a large one or a small. Though we do not run with bellying sail before a favouring north wind, neither are we spending a lifetime with a south wind in our teeth; in strength, in wit, in looks, in virtue, in position, in estate, the last of the foremost, ever ahead of the hindmost.

You are no miser—excellent! Well, have all the other vices run away with that one? Is your bosom free from empty ambitions? Is it free from alarm and anger in face of death? Do you smile at dreams, the terrors of magic, marvels, witches, ghosts of the night, Thessalian portents? Do you count your birthdays with gratitude? Do you make allowance for your friends? Do you become softer and better as old age draws on? How does it relieve you to pluck out one thorn out of many? If you do not know how to live aright, make way for those who do. You have played enough, have eaten and drunk enough. It is time for you to leave the scene; lest, when you have drunk more than your fair share, you be laughed at and driven away by an age to which play is more becoming.

THE ART OF POETRY

Humano capiti

An Epistle addressed to Piso and his two sons.

'The Art of Poetry,' or 'A Book on the Art of Poetry,' are names given to the poem in the next generation, but it is unlikely that either of them was given to it by Horace. It is not an essay in verse, like 'L'Art poétique' of Boileau. It is a letter, with close relations of some kind to the actual circumstances of the persons addressed. It is these relations (uncertain, because we do not know the circumstances) which give to the Epistle (as to Epist. 1. 18) what in an essay we should feel to be a want of proportion and of completeness in the treatment of the subject. It is professedly addressed to a father and his two sons, friends of the poet and united in literary interests; but as the Epistle goes on, it becomes clear that one person is really in view, viz. the elder of the two sons, a young man who is contemplating some literary venture, probably a tragedy, possibly (see p. 347) on a Homeric subject, possibly also (see p. 351) involving an imitation of the Greek Satyric drama. But while the form and detail of topics are thus ruled by a special purpose, Horace has no doubt before him, as in all his writings, a larger audience, and is enforcing doctrines which he holds to be of value to Roman poetry generally. It will be noticed that the poem covers a good deal of common ground with the Epistle to Augustus (Epist. 2. 1). This has been interpreted both ways, but it seems most likely that the 'Art of Poetry' is the later of the two, and belongs to the last years of Horace's life.
It falls into three parts —

    1. Some general remarks on the essentials of poetry— on unity of conception, on diction, on types of poetry and their relation to feeling. (*pp.* 341–347.)

2. *Then follows a long passage in which the subject
seems to be narrowed, for some personal reason, to the
drama: plot, stage rules, the chorus and choral music,
the Satyric drama, metre.* (*pp.* 347–354.)

3. *A short sketch of the history of the drama as
invented in Greece and imitated at Rome, leads back to
a general consideration of the needs and duty of the poet,
the defects of the Roman temperament, the place for honest
criticism.* (*pp.* 354–*end.*)

IF a painter chose to set a human head on the neck
and shoulders of a horse, to gather limbs from every
animal and clothe them with feathers from every kind
of bird, and make what at the top was a beautiful woman
have ugly ending in a black fish's tail—when you were
admitted to view his picture, should you refrain from
laughing, my good friends?　Believe me, Pisos, a book
will be the very likeness of such a picture in which, like
a sick man's dreams, the images shall be impossible, in the
sense that no two parts correspond to any one whole.

Lack of unity 1. in con-

'Poets and painters,' you say, 'have always had an
equal licence in daring invention.'

We know it: this liberty we claim for ourselves
and give again to others; but it does not go to the
extent that savage should mate with tame, that serpents
should couple with birds, or lambs with tigers.

Often on a work of grave purpose and high promises
is tacked a purple patch or two to give an effect of
colour, when 'Dian's grove and altar,' and the water

2. in the poem.

'that round the fair fields lingers as it runs [1],'

---

[1] A quotation or a parody of such descriptive passages as
Horace condemns.

or the river Rhine, or the rainbow is being described. But at the moment, to tell truth, there is no place for them. Just so you very possibly can draw a cypress: but what is that, if the subject which you are paid to paint be a man swimming for his life from a shipwreck? It was a wine-jar that was to be moulded: as the wheel runs round why does it come out a pitcher? In a word, let your work be what you will, provided only it be uniform and a whole.

Whence comes it?   Most of us poets, O father and sons worthy of your father, are led into wrong by a vision of right[1]. It is when I am struggling to be brief that I become unintelligible. I am aiming at smoothness, and I fail of sinew and spirit. One promises the grand style, and is bombastic; another, over-safe and fearful of the storm, creeps along on the ground. So it is in seeking to give to a single subject a variety which is beyond nature that a man comes to paint a dolphin in a forest picture, a wild boar in a sea-piece. Effort to avoid a fault may lead astray, if it be not guided by art.

You will come across in the quarter of the Aemilian training school a worker in bronze of the lowest rank who will mould nails or imitate the soft curves of hair, but who is unhappy when his work is summed up, because he has no idea of representing a whole. I should no more take him for my model, if I were meaning to write a poem, than I should desire to be remarkable for black eyes and black hair while I had a crooked nose.

---

[1] This is the doctrine applied in Sat. I. 2 to morals and manners.

Choose a subject, ye who write, equal to your *The remedy.*
strength; and ponder long what your shoulders will
refuse, what they will be strong enough to bear. If
a man's subject be chosen effectively [1], neither ready
speech will fail him nor clearness of order.

Of order this will be the excellence and beauty, if
I am not mistaken, that, in a poem for which the world
is looking, one say at this moment what at this moment
needs saying; put off the mass of things and let them
be for the present; love this, despise that.

In the same way, if you are nice and careful in *Diction.*
combining your words [2], you may gain the finest effects
in language by the skilful setting which makes a well-
known word new. If so be there are abstruse things
which absolutely require new terms to make them clear,
it will be in your power to frame words which never
sounded in the ears of a cinctured Cethegus [3], and free
pardon will be granted if the licence be used modestly.
New words and words of yesterday's framing will find
acceptance if the source from which they flow be Greek,
and if the stream be turned on sparingly. Think you
that there is any licence which Romans will grant to
Caecilius and Plautus, and then refuse to Virgil and
Varius? Why should you grudge even such an one as
myself the right of adding, if I can, something to the

---

[1] Or 'to suit his powers.'

[2] *Order* is to be the key in the diction as in the conception of
the poem.

[3] The orator, see p. 335. The 'cincture' is a form of wearing
the tunic belonging to ancient times.

store, when the tongue of Cato and of Ennius has been permitted to enrich our mother-speech by giving to the world new names for things? Each generation has been allowed, and will be allowed still to issue words that bear the mint-mark of the day. As the forest changes its leaves with each year that runs swiftly by— those that came first drop off—so with words, the elder race dies out; like a young generation, the new ones bloom and thrive. Death claims us and all that belongs to us. Whether Neptune's sea taken into the bosom of the dry land gives fleets a shelter from the north winds— a work worthy of kings[1]—; or swamp, long a waste where boats could paddle, feeds neighbouring cities and feels the weight of the plough; or river has changed the course which damaged the corn-lands and learnt a better path; all the work of man's hands must perish. Think not then that the words he says can keep place and power undecayed. Many a term which has fallen from use shall have a second birth, and those shall fall that are now in high honour, if so Usage shall will it, in whose hands is the arbitrament, the right and rule of speech.

Types of poetry.

In what measure the feats of kings and captains and war's sad tale may be written, Homer showed us. To couplets of long and short was assigned in the first place

---

[1] This refers to the formation of the Portus Julius by joining the Lucrine and Avernian lakes, which is spoken of by Virgil in Georg. 2. 161 foll. The following lines must describe the draining of the Pomptine marshes and some rectification of the course of the Tiber.

the voice of complaint; afterwards also the sense of granted prayer [1] : but who it was who first gave to the world the modest elegy, scholars dispute, and the case is still before the courts.   The *iambus* was the fitting weapon which his rage found for Archilochus.   That foot both sock and lofty buskins borrowed, as fit for speech and reply and to be heard across a noisy audience, and by nature meant for men in action.   To lyric song the Muse assigned to tell of gods and children of gods, of the victor in boxing, the horse first in the race, and the troubles of young hearts and the lighthearted banquet.

The changing parts and tone of each kind of poetry *These to be* have had their limits set.   If from inability or ignorance *kept to.* I cannot keep to them, why am I hailed a poet?   Why through false shame do I prefer to remain ignorant rather than to learn?   A theme that belongs to Comedy will not be set forth in the verses of Tragedy.   So too the supper of Thyestes disdains to be told in strains of common life which suit well enough the comic sock. Each has had its becoming place allotted: let them keep to it.

But yet sometimes Comedy raises its tone and a *Yet some* Chremes in his wrath declaims his wrongs in mouthing *inter-* phrase; and in the same way Telephus and Peleus, so *change.* tragical generally [2], in their pain take to the language

---

[1] Horace is thinking of the use of the elegiac couplet as the metre of *inscriptions*, whether for memorials of the dead or for votive offerings.

[2] *Plerumque* may be taken also with the sentence, generalizing, ' a Telephus and a Peleus, in a tragedy, usually, &c.'

of prose when, in poverty and exile, one and the other throws aside his paint-pots[1] and his words a foot and a half long[2], if he cares that his sorrows should go home to the spectator's heart.

Feeling is the true basis.

It is not enough that poems have beauty of form : they must have charm, and draw the hearer's feelings which way they will. Men smile—such is human nature—on those who smile : on the same terms they wait on those that weep. If you wish to draw tears from me, you must first feel pain yourself : then, good Telephus or Peleus, your misfortunes will touch me. If the part put into your mouth be ill suited I shall yawn or I shall laugh. With a gloomy face go sad words, with an angry one words of bluster, jests with a playful face, saws of wisdom with a grave one : for Nature first makes us take in our souls the impress of external circumstance, makes us glad, or gives an impulse to anger, or bows us to the ground and tortures us under a load of grief; then, with the tongue for her interpreter, she makes known the emotions of the heart. If the speaker's language rings false to his circumstances, all Rome, front seats and back alike[3], will join the laugh against him. It will make grave difference whether a god be speaking or a demigod, a ripe old

---

[1] *Ampulla* is a painter's oil-flask, and is used for coloured language.

[2] Perhaps, as Sir Walter Scott translates it (in ' Woodstock '), ' seven-leagued.'

[3] Lit. ' horse and foot,' a proverbial phrase from the old Servian classification of the people, but also with reference to the special seats assigned in the theatre to the knights and men of equestrian *census.*

man or one in the flower and heat of youth, a wandering
trader or the tiller of a blooming farm, a Colchian or
an Assyrian, one bred at Thebes or at Argos.

Either follow tradition, or, if you invent, see that your *Characters.*
invention be in harmony with itself.   If so be that in *1. Traditional.*
your poem you are putting again before us the honour- *2. Invented.*
ing of Achilles, he must be spirited, hot-tempered,
ruthless, fiery, must disown law as never meant for
him, must claim the world as the prize of arms.   So
Medea must be defiant and untamed, Ino tearful, Ixion
forsworn, Io a wanderer, Orestes sad.

If you trust a new venture on the stage, and have the
boldness to frame a fresh character, see that it is kept
to the end such as it starts at the beginning and is
self-consistent.

It is a hard task to treat what is common in a way *Of taking*
of your own ; and you are doing more rightly in breaking *an Homeric*
the tale of Troy into acts than in giving the world *subject.*
a new story of your own telling.   You may acquire
private rights in common ground, provided you will
neither linger in the one hackneyed and easy round ; nor
trouble to render word for word with the faithfulness of
a translator ; nor by your mode of imitating take the ' leap
into the pit [1] ' out of which very shame, if not the law
of your work, will forbid you to stir hand or foot to
escape ; nor so begin as the old Cyclic writer :

' Of Priam's fate and glorious war I'll sing.'

What will this high promise give us that will not put to

---

[1] Reference to the fable of the fox and the goat.

shame such mouthing? Mountains will be in labour, the birth will be a single laughable little mouse. How much more wisely the poet who begins with no foolish effort:

> 'Of him, my Muse, who, when Troy's ramparts fell,
>   Saw many cities and men's manners, tell[1].'

His thought is not to give flame first and then smoke, but from smoke to let light break out. He means by-and-by to bring from his store things striking and marvellous, Antiphates and Scylla, the Cyclops and Charybdis. He does not begin a 'Return of Diomede' from the death of Meleager, nor the war of Troy from the twin eggs. He ever hastens to the issue, and hurries his hearers into the midst of the story, just as if they knew it before; and what he thinks his touch will never turn to gold[2], that he lets alone; and while he gives his imagination free play, he so mingles false with true, that the middle never strikes a different note from the beginning, nor the end from the middle.

A first condition of the Drama.

Listen now and let me tell you what I, and the world with me, expect. If you wish an applauding audience that will stay for the curtain and sit on till the flute-player gives the signal for applause, you must note the manners of each several age, and their fitting hue must be given to the tempers which change with the years.

Four ages of man.

A boy, from the minute when he can talk and set firm step upon the ground, loves to play with his young companions, grows passionate and cools again as lightly, and changes every hour. The beardless lad

[1] A rendering of the first lines of the Odyssey.   [2] Conington.

at last let go without a governor[1], finds his delight in
horses and dogs and the grass of the sunny Campus, pliant
as wax to those who would mould him to wrong, impatient of good advice, slow to all useful provision,
lavish of money, eager, with strong desires, and swift
to relinquish what a moment ago he loved best. The
heart of manhood has changed all its tastes and seeks
wealth and friendships, is the slave of ambition, is shy
of finding that it has done what soon it may be anxious
to change. Round the old man many discomforts are
gathering; whether that he is still seeking and stinting
himself—poor man—of what he has found, and fearing to
make any use of it; or that he does all he does without
courage or fire, dilatory in action, content to hope long,
slow to move, and greedy of the future, testy, a grumbler,
inclined to praise the way the world went when he
was boy, to play the critic and censor of the new
generation. The tide of years as it rises brings many
conveniences, as it ebbs carries many away. That you
may never give a youth the part that belongs to the
old nor a boy that of manhood, remember that our
attention will always be kept by traits that are attached
and fitted to the age.

Action is either performed on the stage, or its per- *Miscella-*
formance is narrated. What finds entrance through *neous rules*[2].
the ear stirs the mind less actively than what is
submitted to the eyes which we cannot doubt, and what

---

[1] *Custos* was the title of the slave-tutor who accompanied
a lad to his school, &c.

[2] These are all rules from Greek tragedy in its best time.

the spectator can vouch for to himself. Yet you will not bring forward on the stage what should be transacted behind the scenes; you will keep much from our eyes for the actor's eloquent tongue to narrate by-and-by in our presence: you will not let Medea slay her boys before the audience, or Atreus cook his horrid banquet of human flesh, or Procne be turned into a bird, Cadmus into a snake. Anything that you thus thrust upon my sight I discredit and revolt at.

A play which after representation would be called for and put again on the stage should be neither shorter than five acts nor lengthened beyond them.

Neither should a god intervene, unless a knot befalls worthy of his interference.

Nor should a fourth actor put himself forward to speak [1].

The Chorus. The Chorus has the part and duty of an actor and should discharge it manfully. Nor should it sing between the acts anything but what conduces to the purpose and fits its place exactly. It should take the side of the good, and give friendly counsels, and rule the angry, and cherish the law-abiding. It should praise the fare of a modest table, it should praise health-bringing justice and law and peace with her open gates. It should keep secrets, and pray and beseech the gods that fortune may return to the sad and desert the proud.

Music. The flute in old times not, as now, ringed with brass and become the rival of the trumpet, but of thin sound and simple with its few stops, was yet of use to

---

[1] The Greek tragedians did not allow more than three (speaking) actors to be on the stage at once.

support the Chorus by accompaniment, and sufficient to
fill with its sound the theatre not too closely packed :
for the people, itself small in number, met there in
audiences that could still be counted, men of honest lives,
of religion and modesty.   When they had begun after
conquest to enlarge their borders and compass their cities
with wider circuit of walls, and gratify the Genius
with wine in the daytime, without reproach if it was
on holidays, then there came greater licence to the
music both in time and tune.   What taste could you
expect of men untaught, out for a holiday, country-
men mixed up with townsmen, churl with gently born ?
So to his primitive art the pipe-player added movement
and wanton gesture, and as he wandered about the stage
trailed a long robe.   So too to the staid lyre new notes
were added ; and headlong tropes made the diction
strange ; and the purport of the utterance, with its wise
saws and prophetic tone, was the very echo of Delphi
and its oracle [1].

The poet who competed with a tragedy for the cheap *The Satyric*
prize of a goat [2] presently also brought naked on the *drama—*
stage his woodland Satyrs, and in that rough guise,
without sacrificing his dignity, essayed his jests, with

---

[1] A not unjust description of the actual style of the Chorus in
Greek plays, its sententiousness and dithyrambic abruptness of
metaphor; but Horace is perhaps playful in connecting it with
the more florid music.

[2] Horace is following the current derivation of *tragoedia* (goat-
song). His purpose is to connect the Satyric drama closely with
tragedy. It must preserve therefore a certain dignity. It is
not comedy.

the excuse that the attention of the spectator fresh from sacrifice, well drunk and in lawless mood, had to be *its general* kept by the attraction of pleasant novelty. But it will *tone ;* be fitting while you make your Satyrs attractive by their fun and sharp sayings, while you change from grave to gay, to see that any god or hero who shall be brought on the stage, having just been seen of all eyes in regal gold and purple, does not fall in the level of his talk to some dingy tavern ; or again, in avoiding the ground, clutch at clouds and emptiness. It misbeseems Tragedy to pour a flood of bantering verse ; and like a matron called to dance on a public holiday, when she mingles with Satyrs and their sport, it will be with *its diction ;* some reserve. For my part, Pisos, when I write Satyric drama I shall not be content with the plain nouns and verbs of common life ; nor so make it my endeavour to differ from the tone of tragedy, that none should know whether it be Davus t[']at is speaking and brazen Pythias who has just cheated Simo out of a talent, or Silenus, the guardian and attendant of his divine charge. *its plot ;* My aim shall be a poem so moulded of common materials that all the world may hope as much for itself, may toil hard, and yet toil in vain if it attempts as much : such is the potency of order and arrangement, with such dignity may things of common life be clothed. *its chorus.* If I am to be critic, the Fauns whom you bring to us from the forest must beware of philandering in too tender verses ; or again of rattling out obscene and vulgar jests, as though they had been born at the crossways or were wellnigh natives of the Forum. For those who own a horse [1], those who are free-born, and men of substance, are disgusted, and do not look with kindly eyes or bestow a crown on everything which the purchasers of bean and chestnut meal approve.

A long syllable following a short one is called an *iambus*, a quick foot, which explains how it came to give iambic verses the added name of 'trimeters,' because, though there were six beats, it was one and the same foot from first to last [2]. It is only the other day that, in order that it might fall on the ears with a more leisurely and weighty movement, it received to share its inheritance the staid *spondee*; for it was yielding and tolerant, though not so far as in its complaisance to surrender the second or the fourth place. But in what the world calls Accius' 'noble' trimeters the *iambus* is a rare sight; and for the verses which Ennius sent so heavily weighted on the stage, it whelms them with the dishonouring charge either of too hasty and careless workmanship or of ignorance of the art. It is not every critic that has an ear for ill-modulated verses, and an unworthy toleration has been extended to Roman verse-writers. Shall I, on this account stray beyond bounds and write lawlessly? Or shall I feel that every eye will see my slips, and so keep safely and cautiously within the hope of tolerance? After all I

Metre.

---

[1] i. e. who are knights.

[2] i. e. the *iambus* was such a short foot that the verse which contained six was called not a 'hexameter' but a 'trimeter.' The point is that Roman poets forgot the essential character of the iambic metre.

have saved myself from blame, I have not earned praise.
For yourselves, do ye thumb well by night and day
Greek models. 'Your forefathers' one answers 'praised
both the measures and the wit of Plautus.' Too
tolerant in both points, not to say stupid, was their
admiration, if indeed you and I know how to distinguish
vulgarity from wit, and have skill enough in fingers and
ear to perceive lawful rhythm.

*History of
the Drama.
1. Greek.*

Thespis, we are told, discovered the Tragic Muse,
a kind of poetry unknown before, and carried his plays in
wagons to be sung and acted by men with their faces
smeared with wine-lees [1]. After him Aeschylus, the
inventor of the mask and the decorous robe, made
a floor of short planks for a stage and taught the actors
to lift their voices and raise themselves on the buskin.
Next in succession to them came the Old Comedy; nor
lacked it great glory. But the freedom overshot itself
and became vice and violence which deserved to be
restrained by law. To a law it submitted, and the chorus
became dishonourably mute when it was robbed of its
right to injure.

2. Roman.

Poets of our own have left no style untried, nor has
the glory they have earned been least when they have
ventured to leave the footsteps of the Greeks and sing
of native subjects, whether they have put on the stage
Roman tragedies or Roman comedies. Nor would
Latium now be more mistress of the world in valour
and renown of arms than by her tongue, were it not that

---

[1] Horace seems here to be confusing the origins of Tragedy
and Comedy.

every one of her poets stumbles at the labour of the *Poetry a*
smoothing file. Do you, O sons of Pompilius' blood [1], *laborious art.*
condemn any poem which many a day and many an
erasure have not disciplined ten times over and smoothed
rigorously to the close-cut nail [2].

Because Democritus holds the native gift to be
something happier than poor rules of art and warns off
from Helicon all poets who are sane, half the world
take no care to shorten their nails or their beard, affect
solitude, avoid the baths—for so, surely, they will win
the rewards and name of poets, if they shall never have
let Licinus the barber lay hands on a head too crazy
for three Anticyras [3] to cure.   Alack for my clumsiness,
who purge me of my bile as the spring season comes on !
But for that, there is not another that would write better
verses. Well, it is hardly worth it. So I will play
the part of a whetstone which can make steel sharp,
though it has no power itself of cutting.   Though
I write nothing of my own I will teach the office and
the duty, whence the wealth of matter is gained, what
nurtures and forms the poet, what becomes him and
what not, what is the result of right doing and of
wrong.

[1] The Calpurnian house to which the Pisones belonged traced
its origin to a mythical Calpus, son of King Numa. Horace
appeals to them as the ' blue blood ' of Rome to help in lifting
the national literature.

[2] The image is from a sculptor testing with his nail the
smoothness of his work.

[3] For Anticyra see note on p. 220.

Need of moral philosophy.

Of writing well the source and fountain-head is wise thinking. Matter Socratic pages will be able to set before you : and when the matter is first found, the words will not be slow to follow. He who has learnt what he owes to his country and what to his friends, with what affection a parent, with what a brother and a guest should be loved, what is the duty of a conscript father, what of a judge, what the functions of one sent as a captain to the war, he, you may be sure, knows how to give his fitting part to each character. My advice to one who is to pass as a trained artist will be to take as his model real life and manners, and from thence to draw the language that will seem like that of real life. Sometimes, if adorned with commonplaces and supplied well with character, a plot without beauty or solid value or artistic skill takes the people more and holds their attention better than verses, as they will say, 'devoid of substance, mere tuneful trifles.'

Greek and Roman temperament.

It was the Greeks who had at the Muse's hand the native gift, the Greeks who had the utterance of finished grace ; for their sole greediness was for glory. Romans learn in their schoolboy days to divide the *as* by long sums into a hundred parts. 'Let Albinus' son answer : if an *uncia* be taken from five *unciae* what remains ? You used to be able to tell me.' 'A third.' 'Good, you will be able to take care of your property. Now put an *uncia* on the other side— what does it make ?' 'A half.' Nay, when once this copper rust, this slave's care of petty gain has given its dye to the soul, do we hope that poems can be

created worth smearing with cedar-oil and laying up
in polished cypress?

The aim of the poet is either to benefit, or to amuse, *Double aim*
or to make his words at once please and give lessons of *of the poet.*
life.   When you wish to instruct, be brief; that men's
minds may take in quickly what you say, learn its lesson,
and retain it faithfully.   Every word that is unnecessary
only pours over the side of the brimming mind.   Fictions
intended to please must keep as near as may be to real
life.   The plot must not ask our credence for anything
that it chooses : it must not draw a live boy from the belly
of a Lamia who has just dined on him.   The centuries of
the elders hunt off the stage what lacks profit.   The
proud Ramnes [1] will have nothing to say to dry poems.
He has gained every vote who has mingled profit with
pleasure by delighting the reader at once and instructing
him.   This is the book that makes the fortune of the
Sosii [2], that crosses the seas, and gives a long life of
fame to its author.

Yet there are faults which we can gladly pardon. *Perfection*
The string will not always sound the note which hand *not looked*
and will intend, but when you listen for a flat often *for.*
gives to your ear a sharp; nor will the bow always hit
what it threatens to hit.   But where a poem has many
shining beauties I am not the man to be offended by
a few spots which carelessness has let fall on it or
human weakness has failed to guard against.   What is
the truth?   Just as a copying clerk if he always makes
the same mistake, though he has been warned, is without

---

[1] i. e. young aristocrats.   [2] Booksellers. See p. 314.

excuse; as the harp-player is laughed at who always plays the same false note; so the poet who is always halting is to me a second Choerilus[1], in whom something good now and then causes a smile of surprise. But if Homer, usually good, nods for a moment, I think it shame; and yet it may well be that over a work of great length one should grow drowsy now and then.

As with the painter's work, so with the poet's: one piece will take you more if you stand close to it, another at a greater distance. This loves a dark corner, that will desire to be seen in a strong light, for it fears not the critic's keenest taste. This pleased but once; that will be asked for ten times and always please.

But second-rate poetry intolerable.

O elder of my young friends, though you have your father's voice to mould you to right judgement besides your own native wit, take home to yourself this saying and remember it, that there is a limit to the matters in which the moderate and the bearable are rightly tolerated. A second-rate lawyer or pleader has not the excellence of Messalla's eloquence or the legal knowledge of Aulus Cascellius, yet he has his value. To poets to be second-rate is a privilege which neither men nor gods nor bookstalls ever allowed. As at a pleasant banquet music out of tune, or a coarse unguent, or Sardinian honey with the poppy-seeds[2], offend us because we could have got through the supper without these things; so a poem, the purpose of which is to please the taste, if it fails at

---

[1] See p. 327.

[2] Roasted poppy-seeds and honey was a dish at dessert. Sardinian honey had a bad name.

all of the highest point, drops to the lowest. The man who cannot play the games leaves alone the implements of the Campus, and if he has never learnt the use of ball or hoop or quoit does not play with them, lest the dense ring of spectators laugh long and loud at him. Yet the man who cannot write verses writes them still. Why may he not? A freeman, the son of a freeman, nay more, one rated at the full property of a knight, and with not a fault or flaw about him!

You will say nothing, do nothing, unless Minerva pleases[1]. That is your decision, your first principle. Yet if ever by-and-by you shall compose something, let it have a patient hearing from some Maecius[2] as your critic and from your father and me; and then put the parchments in the cupboard, and let them be kept quiet till the ninth year. What you have not published you will be able to destroy. The word once uncaged never comes home again.

When men were yet savage, Orpheus, the sacred, *Value and* the mouthpiece of the gods, awed them from bloodshed *dignity of* and the foulness of their living; whence the legend *poetry.* said that he tamed tigers and ravening lions. So Amphion is said, because he was the builder of the walls of Thebes, to have moved stones by the sound of his shell, and to have led them whither he would by the spell of his entreaty. This was what men meant by 'wisdom' in old days—to separate the rights of one

[1] A proverb = 'against the grain.' 'You will consult your taste and capacity.'

[2] See note on p. 201.

from the rights of all, divine things from common, to
forbid lawless love and prescribe rules of wedded life,
to build cities and grave laws on wooden tables. 'Twas
so that poets and their song won the honour and the
name of divine.   Homer, whose fame is next to theirs,
and Tyrtaeus by their verses made manly hearts beat
high for battles of Mars.   In song oracles were given,
and men were guided in the ways of life; the favour of
kings was courted in strains learnt of the Muses, and
amusement was found to crown the close of long toil.
So little need the Muse skilled in the lyre or the singer
Apollo cause you a blush.

Is the poet born or made?

It is an old question whether a praiseworthy poem
be the creation of Nature or of Art.   For my part
I do not see what study can do without a rich vein of
native gift, nor what the native gift can do without
culture : so much does each ask of the other and
swear eternal alliance with it.   He whose ambition
is to reach the wished-for goal of the racecourse has
borne much and done much in his boyhood, has sweated
and shivered, has denied himself love and wine.   The
pipe-player who is chosen to play the Pythian piece [1]
has learnt his lesson some time ago under the fear of
a master.   In these days it is thought enough to say
'My poems are admirable.   Plague take the hindmost.
I am ashamed to be left behind in the race and to
confess that in good sooth I do not know an art which
I have never learnt.'

Venal criticism.

As the crier who gathers a crowd to his auction, so

[1] At the Pythian games.

a poet can bid flatterers flock where gain is to be had,
if he has wealth in land, wealth in moneys out at interest.   But if there be one who can serve a dainty dinner
as it should be served, and go bail for a poor friend of
small credit, or snatch one from the dread meshes of
the law, I shall wonder indeed if he prove to know the
difference—happy fellow !—between a false flatterer
and a true friend.   For yourself, if you have given or
are meaning to give a present to any one, do not introduce
him in the fullness of his joy to some verses of your own
composition.   For he will cry out ' Beautiful ! good !
well done ! '   He will grow pale at this passage : he will
even squeeze a dewy tear from his eyes for friendship's
sake : he will dance, will beat time on the ground.   As
the hired mourners at a funeral say and do almost more
than those who feel the grief in their hearts, so the man
who is laughing in his sleeve shows more emotion than
the true admirer.   Kings, it is said, when they are
anxious to know through and through whether a man
is worthy of their friendship, ply him hard with their
cups and put him on the rack of wine.   If you compose
poetry, you will never be taken in by the purpose that
hides itself deep in the fox [1].

If you ever read anything in old days to Quintilius [2] *Honest*
he would say ' Correct, if you please, this line and *criticism.*

[1] Perhaps a reference to the fable of the Fox and the Raven.
The Fox was the interested critic who praised the Raven's voice
and so persuaded him to drop the piece of meat.

[2] The Quintilius of Od. I. 24, the friend of Virgil, and one
whose characteristics were ' stainless faith, own sister to justice,
and naked truth.'

this.' If you said you could not do any better, you had tried many times with no good result, he would say 'Scratch it out then; the work has been badly turned; send it back to the fire and the anvil.' If you still preferred defending your mistakes to correcting them, he did not waste another word, but left you to admire without a rival yourself and your own work. The honest and sensible critic, if verses are dull will point it out; if they are harsh in rhythm, will find fault with them; if they are rough in style, will make an ugly cross with black ink opposite to them; he will apply the knife to redundant ornament; will bid you clear up ambiguities; will mark what should be changed: in fine he will be your Aristarchus[1]. He will not say 'Why should I quarrel with my friend about trifles?' These trifles will bring the friend into serious mischief, if he is

The self-willed poet. fooled and given this ill-starred reception. Like a leper or a man with jaundice[2], or one frenzied or lunatic, the rapt poet is the terror of all sensible people: they fly at his approach. Children tease him and rashly run after him. Away he goes, head in air, spouting his verses, and if, like the birdcatcher with his eyes on the thrushes[3], he falls into a well or a ditch, he may call as loud as he will 'Help, fellow citizens!': no one will take the trouble to lift him out again. If any one is inclined to

---

[1] The great Alexandrian critic who put a cross (*obelus*) against suspected verses in Homer.

[2] So commentators identify the *morbus regius* of the text. Did Horace think it an infectious malady?

[3] Perhaps from some fable.

lend him a hand or let down a rope to him, I shall say to them 'How do you know but that he threw himself in on purpose and does not wish to be rescued?' I shall tell them the end of the Sicilian poet: ' Empedocles in his desire to be thought immortal threw himself one cold day into the fires of Aetna. Poets should have the right and the power if they choose to destroy themselves. To save a man against his will is as bad as to murder him. And this is not the first time he has done it. If you pull him out now he will not then and there become like other people, or lay aside his passion for a notorious death. Besides, none of us knows how he came to be always writing verses. It may be he has defiled the graves of his ancestors, or set foot on some accursed ground and incurred un-cleanness: at the best he is mad; and, like a bear if he has broken his cage-bars, he sets unlearned and learned alike scampering away from fear of his reading his poetry to them. If he catches one, he hugs him close and reads and reads till he kills him; for he will not let him go, any more than a leech will let go the skin before it is gorged with blood.'

FIRST EDITION 1903
Reprinted lithographically in Great Britain
by LOWE & BRYDONE, PRINTERS, LTD., LONDON
from sheets of the first edition
1930, 1953

HORACE
FOR ENGLISH READERS